RAINBOW CONNECTIONS: VOLUME ONE

MEETING THE PEOPLE WHO BROUGHT JIM HENSON'S VISION TO LIFE

JONATHAN MELVILLE

FOUNTAINBRIDGE PRESS

First published in 2025 by Fountainbridge Press

Cover by Ben Morris / benmorrisillustration.com

ISBN: 978-0-9933215-4-2
eBook ISBN: 978-0-9933215-5-9

ALSO BY
JONATHAN MELVILLE

Seeking Perfection: The Unofficial Guide to Tremors

A Kind of Magic: Making the Original Highlander

Local Hero: Making a Scottish Classic

Hamish Macbeth: The Making of a BBCtv Classic

UPDATES

Sign up to my newsletter at jonathanmelville.substack.com

Contact me direct via linktr.ee/jonathanmelville

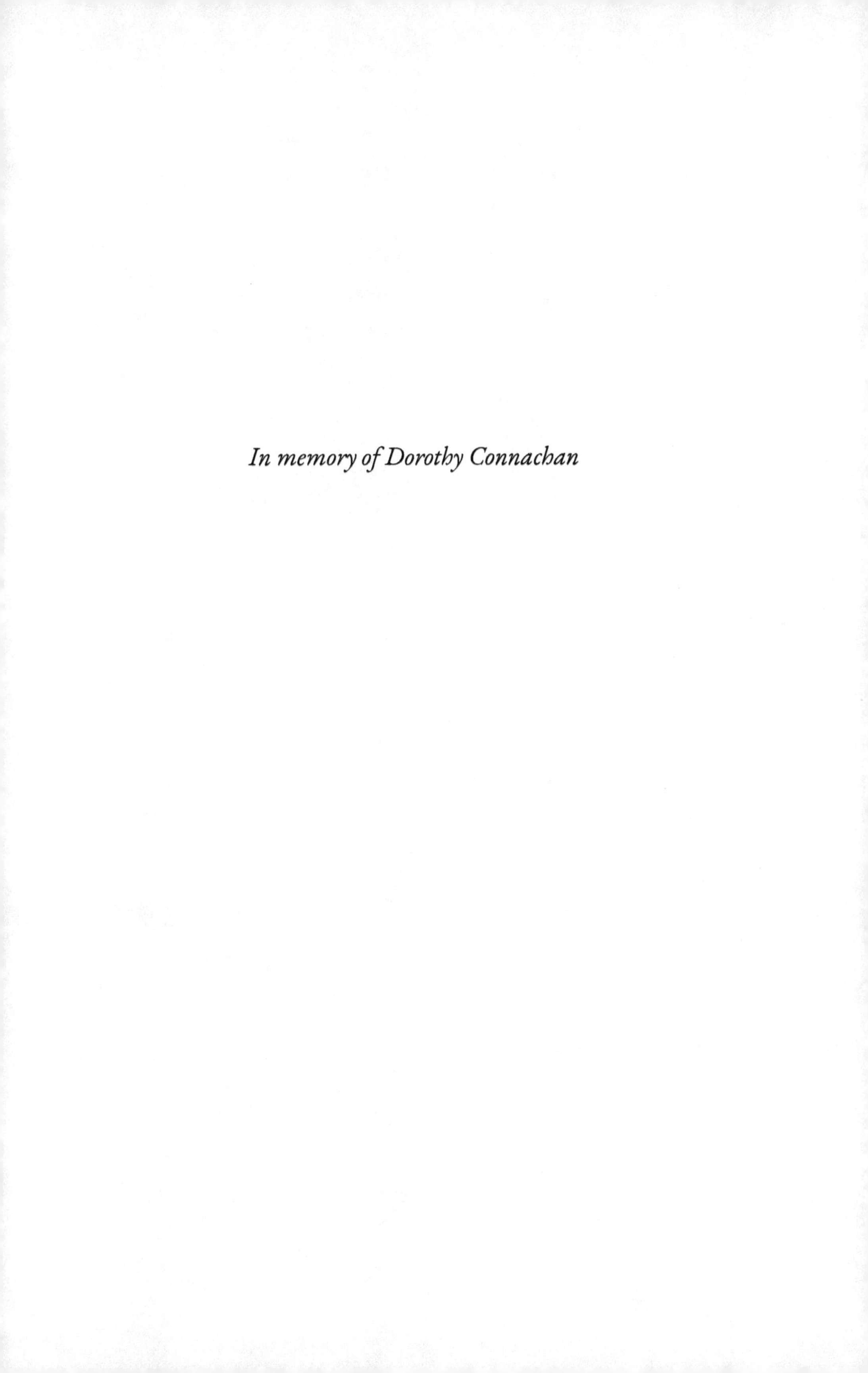

In memory of Dorothy Connachan

CONTENTS

INTRODUCTION

The Muppets have always been part of my life. *The Muppet Show* debuted on ITV in September 1976, when I was just five weeks old, potentially making me one of its youngest original viewers, assuming I was in the room at the time. Introduced by *The Glasgow Herald* as a "High-speed puppet programme, a spin-off from educational show *Sesame Street*", the series became a constant presence throughout my childhood: loud, colourful and completely unique.

The characters each had distinct personalities, the audience seemed to love their work (though Statler and Waldorf weren't too happy about it all), and *Pigs in Space* was, well, in space, therefore brilliant. Some jokes went over my head, but it was half an hour of insanity that made everyone laugh.

I also watched *Sesame Street*, *Muppet Babies* and the UK version of *Fraggle Rock*, while the last great Henson series from my childhood was *The Storyteller*, visually stunning, combining mystery and magic like few other series had done. Whether the messages of understanding, friendship and talking vegetables had a major impact on my psyche is difficult to tell, though if I ever see a cauliflower I still have to make sure it's not about to launch into song with that tomato next to it.

All of which is to say that I consider myself a fan of both the Muppets and Jim Henson, regularly reading books and blog posts, watching documentaries and listening to podcasts to glean new information about how those TV shows and films came to be. But while Jim was always the Muppet figurehead, his face almost as familiar as Kermit's or Piggy's at the height of their popularity, he was backed by teams of creatives who helped bring his vision to life. I wondered if there was more that could be done to add to our knowledge of what it was like either working with Jim or being part of the wider "Henson Universe".

It was after reading a volume of Didier Ghez's fascinating *Walt's People* series of books, featuring hundreds of interview transcripts with people who knew Walt Disney, that I realised something similar might work for Jim Henson.

I reached out to performers, writers, directors and other craftspeople who either worked with Jim Henson or who joined the team after his death in 1990, absorbing the "Jim seed"—as writer Jocelyn Stevenson calls it—from those who had worked directly with him.

From Austin Pendleton successfully advocating for his character's development in *The Muppet Movie* to Bill Barretta's creation of beloved characters like Pepe the King Prawn, these conversations reveal the collaborative spirit that defined Henson productions. We learn how Bruce McNally reluctantly transformed from freelancer to head of the Muppets' art department, while David Gumpel's chance meeting with Jane Henson led to modernising their production techniques.

The interviews capture groundbreaking moments, like Fran Brill becoming *Sesame Street*'s first female puppeteer, and unexpected career turns such as mime performers Gord Robertson and Rob Mills finding their calling on *Fraggle Rock*. Directors Jeremy Swan and Steve Barron share insights into the technical challenges of puppet production and bringing darker fairy tales to life in *The Storyteller*, while John Stephenson details the early days of the Creature Shop.

From Larry Mirkin and Louise Gold's lasting contributions to the Muppet family, to John Stevenson inspiring the character of Beaker, these conversations paint a picture of a creative environment where innovation thrived. The collection also captures important moments in Muppet history through Mark Eades' account of the unrealised Disney-Henson collaboration, and the international scope of *Fraggle Rock* through Jocelyn Stevenson and Victor Pemberton's pivotal roles. There's also a short chapter from late director Tony Charmoli's autobiography, offering a glimpse behind the scenes of a much-loved Muppet special.

The interviews can be read in any order, but if you're just beginning your journey into the world of the Muppets and beyond, you might want to start with the next chapter, Navigating the Henson Universe.

WHAT THIS BOOK ISN'T

This book isn't a critical analysis of Jim Henson's work or career. You won't find detailed deconstructions of his creative process, explorations of business strategies or scholarly examinations of his artistic influences, though the interviewees touch on some of this.

As the editor and interviewer, my role has been to provide context and continuity to the conversations, but the heart of this book lies in the voices of the interviewees themselves. Their stories may occasionally overlap or even contradict one another, but such is the nature of memory and personal experience. Throughout all these memories runs a common thread: Jim's remarkable ability to recognise talent, foster creativity and create an environment where artists could do their best work while having fun in the process. We get a glimpse of how he changed entertainment while changing the lives of those who worked with him.

For everyone who grew up watching these shows, and for those discovering them for the first time, these interviews offer invaluable insight into the craft, creativity and genuine warmth that made Jim Henson's work so special.

A 2025 article on the *Tough Pigs* website[*] highlighted a sobering milestone. If we treat the debut of *Sam and Friends* in 1955 as the birth of the Muppets, then 24th May 2025 marked the day when the Muppets had existed without Jim Henson—since his death in 1990—for exactly as long as they had with him: nearly 35 years each. From that point forward, the post-Jim era would be longer than the Jim era itself. A poignant reminder, and perhaps one more reason to preserve these interviews in print.

This also means that 2025 marks the 70th anniversary of the Muppets, something that's being celebrated on social media by both official and fan accounts, hopefully ensuring that a new generation of soon-to-be-fans will stumble across the antics of Kermit and friends.

Finally, it's worth me drawing attention to the words "Volume One" emblazoned on this book's cover. I already have more interviews lined up for a potential Volume Two, so please keep an eye out for future books wherever you bought (or borrowed) this one.

You can sign up for my newsletter via jonathanmelville.substack.com/ where I'll have some other Jim Henson-related exclusives.

Jonathan Melville, Edinburgh, May 2025

---

[*] https://www.toughpigs.com/12792-days-later/

NAVIGATING THE HENSON UNIVERSE
A READER'S GUIDE

I F Y O U ' V E   C H O S E N to read this book, you're probably either a longtime fan of Jim Henson's work or someone curious about the productions associated with his name.

The wonderful thing about the Henson universe is how interconnected everything is. A performer who worked on *The Muppet Show* in the late 1970s might go on to work on *Fraggle Rock* in the 1980s or help bring creatures to life for *Labyrinth* a few years later. The interviews in this book reflect that rich creative history. People pop up in different chapters, projects weave in and out of conversations and stories intersect in unexpected ways.

For dedicated fans, these recurring names and references will feel like catching up with old friends. But if you're newer to this world, all these Daves and Jerrys (and some Stephenson/Stevensons in this volume) might start to blur together. That's why this chapter exists. Think of it as your compact guide to the worlds of Jim Henson, an overview of some names and projects you'll encounter time and again. This overview doesn't mention everything or everyone, but hopefully it sets the scene.

THE EARLY YEARS

Born in Greenville, Mississippi in 1936, Jim Maury Henson spent his childhood fascinated by television, art and performance. He got his first break in television working as a puppeteer on a local Saturday morning children's show. This early experience sparked what would become a lifelong mission to push the boundaries of puppetry and television.

The Muppet story properly begins in 1955 with *Sam and Friends* (1955–61), a series of five-minute shows created by Jim and his future wife Jane Nebel for WRC-TV in Washington, D.C. while both were students at the University of Maryland. This pioneering series introduced a proto-Kermit (made from Jim's mother's old coat and ping-pong balls for eyes) and established the basic principles of television puppetry that would define the Henson style. Rather than using a traditional puppet stage, they performed directly for the camera, a revolutionary approach at the time.

Throughout the 1960s, the Muppets became popular fixtures on variety shows and in commercials, with Jim and his team creating memorable ads for everything from coffee to meatballs. Rowlf the Dog became the first Muppet to appear regularly on network television as a cast member of *The Jimmy Dean Show* (1963–75). Experimental pieces like the Oscar-nominated *Time Piece* (1965) showcased Jim's interest in pushing beyond puppetry into other forms of creative expression. This period also saw the creation of several TV specials including *Hey Cinderella!* (1969) and *The Great Santa Claus Switch* (1970).

THE CORE TEAM

Jim and Jane assembled an extraordinary creative family that would shape entertainment for decades:

- **Frank Oz:** Joined in 1963, aged 19, going on to become Jim's primary creative partner until transitioning away from puppetry in 2001 to focus on directing. His characters included Miss Piggy, Fozzie Bear, Animal and Bert from *Sesame Street*. The Henson-Oz partnership created many of the most memorable Muppet moments.
- **Jerry Juhl:** Starting as a performer, he became head writer and the literary voice of the Muppets until his passing in 2005, developing their distinctive humour and emotional depth while maintaining their warmth and whimsy.
- **Jerry Nelson:** The performer who continued bringing characters like Count von Count, Robin the Frog and Floyd Pepper to life until shortly before his death in 2012.
- **Dave Goelz:** Beginning as a builder, he became the performer behind Gonzo, Dr Bunsen Honeydew and Boober Fraggle, bringing technical expertise and deep character insights to his roles. He remains active with the Muppets today.
- **Richard Hunt:** The energetic performer behind Scooter, Statler, Junior Gorg and many others, he epitomised the playful spirit of the Muppets until his death in 1992 at the age of just 40.

Jim Henson's sudden death on 16th May 1990 at just 53 sent shockwaves through the entertainment industry. What began as seemingly routine flu-like symptoms rapidly developed and he died from organ failure resulting from streptococcal toxic shock syndrome, a severe bacterial infection. The speed and unexpected nature of his illness made the loss even more devastating for his family, colleagues and fans. Those who knew him noted that Jim had been reluctant to seek medical treatment, believing he could push through what he thought was just a bad cold.

This tragic loss came just as he was preparing to sell his company to Disney and embark on new creative ventures. However, his vision continued through the dedication of these performers and countless others who had learned from him. His death marked not just the end of an era, but the beginning of a complex transition period for the company and characters he'd created.

OTHER IMPORTANT FIGURES YOU'LL ENCOUNTER...

Throughout these interviews, you'll hear stories about many key creators who helped shape the Henson universe, including:

- **Jane Henson (née Nebel):** Jim's wife and essential creative partner in the Muppets' formation and early years. After meeting as students at the University of Maryland, she co-created and performed on *Sam and Friends* alongside Jim. They married in 1959 and had five children: Lisa, Cheryl, Brian, John and Heather. Though she stepped back from full-time puppeteering in 1961 to raise their family, Jane remained involved in the company. After Jim's death, despite having separated in 1986, she established The Jim Henson Legacy to preserve his work and served on the boards of the Jim Henson Foundation and the American Center for Children's Television until her passing in 2013.
- **Lisa Henson:** Jim's eldest daughter, who serves as CEO of The Jim Henson Company, overseeing the day-to-day operations and business strategy. With a background in film production and studio leadership, she guides the company's overall direction while developing new content and partnerships.
- **Brian Henson:** Jim's son, who directed several Muppet films including *The Muppet Christmas Carol* and

Muppet Treasure Island. He serves as Chairman of the Board of The Jim Henson Company, focusing on the creative and technical innovation side of the business, particularly through the Creature Shop that he helped develop.

- **Cheryl Henson:** Jim's second daughter, who has been President of The Jim Henson Foundation since 1992. She also served as a Vice President at The Jim Henson Company during the 1990s, working with *Sesame Street* during a crucial transition period. Cheryl remains an advocate for the art of puppetry both through the Foundation and her involvement with puppeteers and organisations around the world.

- **Heather Henson:** Jim's youngest daughter, puppet artist and board member of The Jim Henson Company, The Jim Henson Legacy and the Jim Henson Foundation.

- **John Henson:** Jim's youngest son, a puppeteer and performer best known for his work as Sweetums in later Muppet productions. He remained actively involved with the company for many years and continued to honour his father's creative spirit until his death in 2014, aged 48.

- **Don Sahlin:** The original puppet designer who created many of the signature Muppet looks and developed crucial building techniques.

- **David Lazer:** An executive producer who joined in 1965 and helped shape *The Muppet Show*, supervised numerous films and played a crucial role in keeping the company going after Jim's death. He was especially skilled at helping guest stars adapt to working with puppets. David died in May 2025, aged 89.

- **Martin G. Baker:** A prolific producer who started as floor manager on *The Muppet Show* and went on to

oversee countless Henson productions from *Fraggle Rock* through to *The Muppets* (2011). His long tenure helped maintain continuity across decades of productions.
- **Duncan Kenworthy:** Producer who helped develop international productions like *Fraggle Rock*.

These people might not always have been the ones performing the characters, but their behind-the-scenes work was essential to creating the magic that appeared on screen. Many of them worked across multiple productions over decades, helping maintain the high standards and unique creative spirit that Jim Henson established.

THE ART OF MUPPET PERFORMANCE

Something that sets the Muppets apart from other fictional characters is the unique nature of their performance. When you see Kermit on screen, you're not just seeing an animated character or an actor in a costume. You're witnessing a complete performance by a skilled artist who brings the character to life in real time.

Muppet performers don't simply "voice" their characters, they physically manipulate the puppet while simultaneously creating the character's voice, personality and emotional reactions. When Jim Henson performed Kermit, his right hand controlled Kermit's head and mouth, while his left hand operated the arms using rods. All while maintaining the character's distinctive voice, timing each word perfectly with the mouth movements and creating every nuance of Kermit's facial expressions through subtle manipulations of the puppet's fabric features. This physical connection gives the characters a tangible reality that few other fictional creations possess.

The transition of characters between performers (as when Matt Vogel took over Kermit after Jim Henson and Steve Whitmire) isn't just about matching a voice, but about capturing the full essence of how the puppet moves, reacts and exists in space. This continuity allows the Muppets to maintain their unique identities decade after decade, while still evolving and growing as characters.

THE CREATURE SHOP

The Jim Henson Creature Shop, established in London in the early 1980s, represented a huge step forward in puppet technology. While the Muppets were primarily hand puppets, the Creature Shop developed sophisticated animatronic characters that could perform complex movements through a combination of manual controls and radio-operated mechanisms.

The Shop's innovations made possible the fantastical beings of *The Dark Crystal*, the elaborate characters of *Labyrinth* and even the eponymous heroes of *Teenage Mutant Ninja Turtles*. Their work bridged the gap between traditional puppetry and modern visual effects, influencing countless films and TV shows. Today, the Creature Shop continues creating cutting-edge characters and effects for various productions.

THE JIM HENSON COMPANY

What we think of as "the Henson Company" has existed under several names throughout its history. Officially founded as Muppets, Inc. in 1958 by Jim and Jane Henson, it began primarily producing commercials and industrial films. As the business grew, it became Henson Associates, Inc. (known informally as "HA!") in the 1970s, then Jim Henson Productions in 1987.

Today, as The Jim Henson Company, it operates independently of both Disney's Muppet operations and Sesame Workshop. The company remains firmly in family hands, led by Jim and Jane's children: Brian, Lisa, Cheryl and Heather.

The company's renowned Creature Shop continues to create innovative characters and effects for both Henson productions and outside clients. Since 2000, the company has been headquartered at the historic Charlie Chaplin Studios in Hollywood, though in 2024 the lot was sold to musician John Mayer and producer McG for $40 million, announcing plans to consolidate their operations with the Creature Shop in Burbank.

While many people use "the Muppets" as a catch-all term for Henson creations, it's now actually a trademark owned by Disney, though Sesame Workshop maintains a licence to use the term for their characters.

RELATED HENSON ORGANISATIONS

In addition to the main production company, the Henson family established two other organisations to preserve different aspects of Jim's legacy:

- **The Jim Henson Foundation:** Established by Jim in 1982 and now headed by Cheryl Henson, this non-profit organisation provides grants to support American puppet artists and advance the art of puppetry. It runs the biennial International Puppet Festival and funds innovative work in puppet theatre.
- **The Jim Henson Legacy:** Created by Jane Henson in 1992, this organisation specifically focuses on preserving and perpetuating Jim's artistic contribution. It works to make his creative works available to the public through exhibitions, screenings, and educational programs.

While The Jim Henson Company focuses on creating new content and characters, these sister organisations ensure that both Jim's personal artistic contributions and his commitment to advancing the art of puppetry continue to thrive.

THE PATH TO DISNEY

By the late 1980s, Jim Henson was looking toward the future of his characters. He entered negotiations with Disney not just as a business deal, but as a way to secure the Muppets' legacy while freeing himself to pursue more experimental creative projects. The proposed deal would have given Disney ownership of the Muppets while allowing Jim to focus on new creative endeavours like fantasy films and technological innovations. He envisioned Disney's resources and reach giving the Muppets opportunities he couldn't provide alone, while he could step back from day-to-day Muppet operations to explore new creative frontiers.

Jim's death occurred before the Disney deal could be completed. The company's path then took several turns. In 2000, the Henson family sold the entire company to German media group EM.TV for $680 million. This sale included everything: the Muppets, the Creature Shop, *Sesame Street* characters and other properties.

However, EM.TV's ambitious expansion (which included buying into Formula One racing) led to financial troubles. During their brief ownership, they made one significant move that would shape the future of the characters: selling the *Sesame Street* characters to Sesame Workshop. This separated Big Bird, Ernie, Bert and their friends from the rest of the Henson universe for the first time.

By 2003, EM.TV sold the company back to the Henson family for $84 million. This set the stage for the next big change: in 2004, Disney finally acquired the Muppet characters and properties, creating three distinct branches of the Henson legacy:

- The Muppets → Disney
- *Sesame Street* characters → Sesame Workshop
- *Fraggle Rock*, *The Dark Crystal*, etc. → The Jim Henson Company

This split explains why you might see Kermit on Disney+ but

won't find Big Bird there, or why *Dark Crystal* projects come from Netflix rather than Disney. Each branch continues to develop new content while honouring their shared heritage, though in ways that might be different from what Jim originally envisioned when he first approached Disney in the 1980s.

THE EVOLUTION OF A LEGACY

Now that we've met the key people and organisations, let's explore how the Henson legacy evolved through different creative eras.

THE SESAME STREET YEARS (1969–PRESENT)

This educational series proved television could both teach and entertain. While the Muppets were just one element of this ambitious project, characters like Big Bird, Cookie Monster and Bert & Ernie became cultural touchstones. The show established that puppetry could have a meaningful educational impact while remaining entertaining.

THE MUPPET SHOW ERA (1976–81)

After an interesting detour into adult comedy with *Saturday Night Live*'s (1975–) Land of Gorch sketches, the Muppets found their perfect showcase in this variety series. Filmed at ATV Studios in England, it combined sophisticated humour, musical numbers and celebrity guests, establishing the Muppets as global entertainment icons.

EXPANDING TO FILMS (1979–84)

The team successfully transitioned to cinema with *The Muppet Movie* (1979), showing Kermit's journey from swamp to stardom.

The Great Muppet Caper (1981) and *The Muppets Take Manhattan* (1984) followed, each pushing the boundaries of what was possible with puppet performances on film.

THE FANTASY YEARS (1982–86)

The Dark Crystal (1982) revealed a completely different side of Henson's creativity, a darker fantasy world populated entirely by puppet creatures. The Creature Shop's technological innovations made this ambitious project possible. *Labyrinth* (1986) combined these advanced animatronic characters with Henson's characteristic warmth and humour.

INTERNATIONAL AMBITIONS (1983–89)

Fraggle Rock (1983–87) was conceived as a show that could help promote world peace by creating a truly international production. While the main Fraggle world segments were filmed in Toronto, each broadcasting country produced its own unique "human world" segments with local actors, sets and writers.

In North America, the human character Doc was an inventor in his workshop; UK viewers saw a lighthouse keeper played by Fulton Mackay; French audiences watched a chef in his kitchen; and German viewers enjoyed a similar set-up to the North American version. This innovative approach allowed children everywhere to see their own culture represented while sharing the universal Fraggle world, making it one of television's most ambitious international co-productions.

The Storyteller (1987–89) continued this international spirit by adapting European folk tales with sophisticated narratives and creature effects, showing yet another facet of what puppet television could achieve.

INNOVATION AND EXPERIMENTATION (1989–90)

The Jim Henson Hour (1989) attempted to showcase the full range of Henson's creativity, from traditional Muppet comedy to technological innovations and serious dramatic pieces. While short-lived, it showed Jim's constant desire to push boundaries.

CONTINUING THE LEGACY (1991–PRESENT)

Even after Jim's passing, his creative team continued exploring new territory. In the 1990s, several ambitious projects honoured his creative spirit:

- *Dinosaurs* (1991–94) broke new ground with sophisticated full-body puppet suits and animatronic faces to tell the story of a working-class dinosaur family.
- *Muppet*Vision 3D* (1991), Jim's final directed project, brought the Muppets to Disney theme parks in a mix of film, audio-animatronics and in-theatre effects.
- *The Muppet Christmas Carol* (1992) proved the characters could adapt classic literature while maintaining their unique charm, leading to another adaptation in the shape of *Muppet Treasure Island* (1996). *Muppets from Space* (1999) deviated from the adaptation path and was the last big screen outing for the characters for over a decade.
- *Muppets Tonight* (1996–98) attempted to update the variety show format for a new generation, introducing memorable new characters like Pepe the King Prawn, Bobo the Bear, and Johnny Fiama, while giving previously minor characters like Clifford a chance to step into the spotlight as the show's host.

- *Farscape* (1999–2003) represented one of the Henson Company's most ambitious ventures into science fiction, combining live actors with sophisticated alien creatures created by the Creature Shop.

The early 2000s were a transitional period for the Muppets, with the characters appearing primarily in television movies and specials:

- *It's a Very Merry Muppet Christmas Movie* (2002) took inspiration from *It's a Wonderful Life* (1946), exploring what life would be like if Kermit had never been born, and marked the first Muppet film produced after the characters were acquired and then returned by EM.TV.
- *Kermit's Swamp Years* (2002), a direct-to-video prequel, explored Kermit's childhood and his journey from the swamp to the wider world.
- *The Muppets' Wizard of Oz* (2005) continued the literary adaptation tradition with Ashanti as Dorothy and Kermit as the Scarecrow, featuring Queen Latifah and Quentin Tarantino in supporting roles.
- *A Muppets Christmas: Letters to Santa* (2008) returned the characters to their family-friendly Christmas special roots, with guest stars including Uma Thurman, Nathan Lane,and Whoopi Goldberg.
- *Studio DC: Almost Live!* (2008) paired the Muppets with Disney Channel stars of the era including Miley Cyrus and the Jonas Brothers, attempting to introduce the characters to a new generation.

After Disney acquired the Muppets in 2004, they eventually returned to prominence with:

- *The Muppets* (2011) and *Muppets Most Wanted* (2014)

brought the characters to a new generation of moviegoers.

- ABC's *The Muppets* (2015) TV series experimented with a more adult, mockumentary approach.
- Disney+ series like *Muppets Now* (2020), *Muppets Haunted Mansion* (2021) and *The Muppets Mayhem* (2023) have explored new formats and storytelling styles.

Away from Disney, *The Dark Crystal: Age of Resistance* (2019), a 10-episode prequel to the 1982 film, showcased the Henson Company's continued commitment to puppetry. Netflix's investment enabled the creation of this ambitious series, which combined traditional puppetry with modern digital effects to build on Jim's original dark fantasy world.

In 2022, *Fraggle Rock* made an unexpected comeback in the form of *Fraggle Rock: Back to the Rock*, with The Jim Henson Company reimagining the series for a new generation on Apple+.

KEEPING THE CHARACTERS ALIVE

One of the most remarkable aspects of the Muppet universe is how the characters have lived on beyond their original performers. This careful transition of beloved characters has helped maintain their legacy while allowing them to continue entertaining new generations. Some of the key character transitions are:

- Kermit the Frog: Jim Henson (1955–1990) → Steve Whitmire (1990–2016) → Matt Vogel (2017–present)
- Miss Piggy & Fozzie Bear: Frank Oz (1976–2000) → Eric Jacobson (2001–present)
- Ernie: Jim Henson (1969–1990) → Steve Whitmire (1993–2014) → Peter Linz (2017–present)
- Dr Teeth: Jim Henson (1975–1990) → Bill Barretta (1991–present)

- Rowlf the Dog: Jim Henson (1962–1990) → Bill
  Barretta (1996–present)

This passing of the torch represents more than just recasting, it's a careful preservation of each character's soul while allowing them to evolve naturally with time. The current performers often studied for years with the original artists, learning not just voices and movements, but the deeper essence of each character.

THE HENSON PHILOSOPHY

Throughout all these changes and transitions, certain principles have remained constant:

- Never talk down to your audience
- Embrace both humour and heart
- Foster creativity and collaboration
- Push technical boundaries
- Create entertainment that makes the world better

As you read through the interviews in this book, you'll discover countless details about how these remarkable artists created their magic. Whether you're most interested in the technical innovations, the character performances or the creative process behind specific productions, there are fascinating insights waiting for you.

Feel free to jump around based on your interests—each interview stands alone while contributing to the larger story of how Jim Henson and his creative family changed entertainment forever.

FRAN BRILL

ACTRESS AND PUPPETEER

"I think I learned how to be a person from Jim."

AFTER JOINING *Sesame Street* in its second season as the show's first female puppeteer outside of Jane Henson, Fran Brill brought life to beloved characters like Prairie Dawn and Zoe.

* * *

Long before she became known for her work on *Sesame Street*, Fran Brill had her sights set on a very different path in entertainment. The future puppeteer discovered her passion for performing at an early age, though not through puppetry, but through a comedic role in a Brownies production.

"Some of the Brownies were playing teenagers, which was quite glamorous, but I got cast as Great Aunt Ella," she explains. "I had a grey wig on, and what am I, seven... I got a lot of laughs. Seeing this little girl try to play old was so silly, and I really loved the applause and laughter."

That early taste of performance led Fran into school plays and regional theatre. Her devotion to the craft was apparent early on—at

16 years old, she convinced her doubtful parents to let her take part in summer stock theatre. However, they struck an important deal: she could pursue acting, but only after completing her college education.

This arrangement led her to the Boston University School of Fine Arts, known for its strong drama programme. While Fran notes that her formal training may not have been the most crucial element of her education, she gained valuable experience working alongside talented peers. "I think most of what I learned was working with good actors and seeing what their approach was."

Fresh out of college, Fran's career took an unexpected turn when she landed a role in a politically charged production in New York. *Red, White and Maddox* was a bold musical satire targeting Georgia Governor Lester Maddox, specifically his segregationist policies at his restaurant, the Pickrick, where he refused service to African Americans. The show had garnered significant press attention during its Atlanta run before making the leap to Broadway.

Living out of a hotel room during the production, Fran experienced both the excitement and harsh realities of Broadway theatre. The show opened during a blizzard and received mixed reviews, ultimately running for 41 performances. However, this brief run had brought her to New York sooner than anticipated, sharing a flat with a stranger while she lived the life of a struggling actress.

Fran began making the rounds with agents, armed with the traditional 8x10 glossy headshots. It was during one of these meetings that an agent made an observation: "You have a really interesting voice... just quirky. You should look into voice overs."

Fran was soon voicing numerous TV commercials in New York, and when not pursuing acting opportunities she'd find comfort in watching television, specifically, *Mister Rogers' Neighborhood* (1968–2001) and a new children's programme called *Sesame Street*. "Fred Rogers would talk to the camera and say, 'You're special, you're this, you're that,'" she says, noting how his gentle reassurance helped lift her spirits after long days of job hunting.

Watching *Sesame Street* in its first season, Fran believed her vocal talents might land her work with the show. "I thought, *I can do accents, I can do all sorts of voices. Maybe they'll hire me to be a voice person*," she says, admitting she was unaware that Muppet performers provided both the puppetry and voices simultaneously. "It's not a two-person job. You talk while you lip-sync with the puppet."

An opportunity arose when Jim Henson organised a puppetry workshop to prepare for *The Great Santa Claus Switch*, a musical special that represented one of Jim Henson's early attempts to reach a prime-time family audience, years before *The Muppet Show*, would perfect this formula.

Fran joined a group of "wannabe puppeteers" for what would become an intensive crash course in the Muppet performance style. The training was challenging, particularly mastering the precise lip synchronisation required for Muppet characters. "Every lip flap is a syllable. It's not easy when you first try it and the camera image is reversed. So you're talking to a puppet here, but your hand is over there. It's a nightmare."

The workshop ran for two weeks, with participants being eliminated after the first week. Fran made it through the initial cut, spending the second week working with mirrors and different puppets. After completing the workshop and taking part in *The Great Santa Claus Switch* filming in Toronto, Henson approached Fran and fellow workshop graduate Richard Hunt about joining *Sesame Street* for its second season, though the latter ultimately didn't join the series until 1972.

Initially hesitant, Fran responded, "Jim, this has been fun, but I'm an actress. I want my face to be seen." However, Jim's persuasive nature and promise to work around her schedule eventually won her over. The timing was fortuitous, as the show had been receiving criticism about its male-dominated puppet cast. "There'd been a lot of complaints from the outside world that all these characters were being played by men, even the girls were played by men. They would go up into their falsetto. It was laughable."

Fran's arrival on *Sesame Street* in the 1970–71 season made her the first female Muppet performer on the show outside of Jane Henson, and came at a pivotal time in children's television. The show had debuted a year earlier, pioneering research-based educational programming for preschoolers.

"It's like so many jobs in life, you trip and fall into something, and it all works out," says Fran of her *Sesame Street* job. "Never in a million years would I have thought this was the way I'd spend most of my life." Despite being the sole woman among the performers, Fran quickly found her place in the group. "I was the only female, so it was sort of an adjustment for them to be around, but I got along with the guys really well."

EARLY DAYS AND EVOLUTION

Constant innovation and experimentation characterised the initial period of *Sesame Street*, not only in educational content but also in the methods of puppetry. Fran continued to balance her puppetry work with acting and voiceover jobs, made possible by the show's production schedule. "It used to be an all-year commitment," she says, but it was eventually condensed into just a few months of concentrated filming.

The physical demands of puppeteering were considerable, with performers often working in awkward and uncomfortable positions. "Back then, it was quite crude in terms of what we sat on or laid down on, because they were inventing the wheel."

In the early years, puppeteers often worked lying flat on rolling platforms, manoeuvring between sets like Hooper's Store and 123 Sesame Street. This setup made vocal performances difficult, as actors had to project while in awkward positions. Over time, performers raised concerns about comfort and vocal quality, leading to the development of cushioned seats mounted on caster wheels. This transformed how Muppets were performed, allowing greater ease and flexibility on set.

The show's unique requirements stemmed from its interaction with child performers. Unlike the later *Muppet Show*, where puppeteers could stand, *Sesame Street* required performers to stay below the height of the children on set. "The set wasn't elevated. I don't know what they were thinking. They just didn't know." This experimental approach reflected the show's broader mission. "When *Sesame Street* was created, all they knew was they wanted it to serve the underserved community. Impoverished children, children who weren't white... that's really who the show was aimed for, so that they could learn from the cartoons. They could learn how to read, learn the letters, learn the numbers, how to treat other people."

Even with improvements in performance techniques, some scenes still required creative solutions and physical dedication. Fran recalls a particularly challenging moment with Elmo performer Kevin Clash on the set of 123 Sesame Street: "They had to drill a hole in the steps so that we could get our arm up... we had to be in the worst position under the steps, with our hands coming up." Such situations were common, requiring performers to, as Fran puts it, "solve the solvable problem".

CREATING PRAIRIE DAWN AND ZOE

The path to creating Muppet characters was far different in the early days of *Sesame Street* compared to today. "Now they have these kids who go to college and learn how to puppeteer and they audition for *Sesame Street*," Fran notes, contrasting with her own experience of learning on the job.

After joining the show, she initially provided female voices for group scenes dominated by male characters. About six months into her tenure, Jim Henson approached her with a specific challenge: to develop a sweet, docile little girl character. He gave her a puppet called Little Pink, who would eventually become Prairie Dawn.

"I started off with a high, whispery voice, very innocent. She wore a little smock dress, and she was very sweet. I even carried a hanky." However, the character evolved organically through the scripts, growing stronger and more assertive over time. Eventually, Prairie Dawn became known for directing pageants featuring her male counterparts like Grover and Cookie Monster, complete with her endearingly poor piano accompaniment.

Bringing Prairie Dawn to life came naturally to Fran. "I work well if you just hand me a puppet that's already made. It's hard to explain. I don't know where the characters come from, but I can just channel them." The character clearly meant a great deal to Fran—when she retired, she was presented with her own Prairie Dawn puppet, now displayed in a display case on her wall.

The process of creating Zoe, another of Fran's signature characters, was quite different from Prairie Dawn's evolution. "That was an idea from a new producer to have a female pal for Elmo." The character was conceived as Prairie Dawn's opposite, moving away from the "sweet and sugary" personality that had defined her earlier creation. The development process involved improvisation sessions with Kevin Clash to explore the dynamic between the characters.

Finding Zoe's voice proved to be a challenging experience, especially under the watchful eyes of the production crew. "When I first hit the set with her, I sounded like Carol Channing... her voice was up here, but it was very, very wide. They wanted her energetic, and I was jumping off the walls. It was so bad, I was so loud."

To refine the character, Fran conducted real-world research, visiting nursery schools in New York and observing children of the target age group. This attention to detail led to authentic touches in Zoe's vocabulary. "I picked up 'Don't joke me' from somebody's child. Instead of saying 'Don't fool me', he would say 'Don't joke me.'"

The early days of *Sesame Street* had an interesting approach to character creation. Each morning, performers would arrive to find a table laden with "Anything Muppets", basic puppet forms that could be customised with different features. The creators deliberately designed these puppets in non-human colours to avoid racial cate-gorisation. "They didn't want people to say, 'Oh, that's a black puppet, that's an Indian puppet, that's a white puppet.' They were multicoloured, which I thought was a clever idea."

These versatile puppets served as a creative playground for the performers. "You could take the eyes off, and the eyebrows, and put different lips on, a different nose." Performers would choose a puppet and develop a voice and personality on the spot, often for background characters or group scenes that would be inserted into the show's daily narrative.

Sometimes, these improvisational performances led to the creation of beloved recurring characters. Fran cites the example of Baby Bear, who originated in a Goldilocks sketch. "Dave Rudman did that character, and he was so cute and funny as this Baby Bear that he became a regular principal character for a while. You either did something terrific with your Anything Muppet, or you didn't."

LEARNING FROM JIM

When asked about Jim Henson's influence, Fran is quick to reply: "I think I learned how to be a person from him." She describes Jim as a "messiah-like human being" whose leadership style was marked by gentleness and restraint. "He talked in this very low voice. He never yelled at anybody, no matter what happened."

In all her years working with Jim, Fran witnessed him lose his temper only once, when a performer struggled with group choreog-raphy while attempting characters beyond their principal role. Even then, his frustration was contained. "He never, ever would raise his voice or hurt your feelings. He might give you a note, but not in front of anybody. He was just too kind."

THE ROAD NOT TAKEN

While the Muppets became her life's work, including appearances in many Henson productions including *The Muppet Show*, *Dog City* and numerous *Sesame Street* spin-offs, Fran's resume also boasts roles in films such as 1979's *Being There* and 1988's *Midnight Run* plus TV series including *Law & Order* (1990–) and *Third Watch* (1999–2005). She particularly cherishes her role as the lead in a stage adaptation of Edith Wharton's *The House of Mirth* in the 1970s. Her theatrical career brought her into contact with notable performers, proudly noting that she's "probably the only actress that has ever worked with both Roddy McDowell and Malcolm McDowell".

For all her success with the Muppets, Fran occasionally wonders about the path not taken. "I love the theatre, if I could do it all over again I'd still be acting, but whether it was with the Muppets... I would love to have done something on the London stage, but you have to play with the cards you're dealt. My life just hasn't gone more in the acting way, it's ended up more in a Muppet way, but that's a good thing, nothing wrong with that."

Now retired, except for occasional talks, Fran reflects on how her experiences have shaped her. "I think personally I've changed a great deal over the years... I'm totally happy now." She continues to share her experiences through unpaid speaking engagements, though she maintains a humble perspective about her career: "When it's your life, it's not that big a deal." Her fondest memories centre on the collaborative spirit of the Muppet performers. "Working with the Muppets was just a wonderful thing. We would just laugh, and these are funny, smart people, very quick. I just love them all."

Fran remains passionate about sharing the Muppets' history with dedicated fans. She discusses *Muppet Guys Talking*, a 2017 documentary featuring several key Muppet performers including herself, Frank Oz, Jerry Nelson, Bill Barretta and Dave Goelz. "They rented a loft in New York and we all just sat around and talked about Jim, talked about memories we had. It's really quite sweet."

Long before environmentalism became mainstream, Jim Henson was advocating for ecological awareness and planetary stewardship. This forward-thinking approach was documented in a book compiled by Cheryl Henson, Jim's daughter, titled *It's Not Easy Being Green*. The book contains drawings, quotes from Jim and reflections from those who worked with him. Fran shares one revealing quote from Jim about his creative process: "Many of the things I've done in my life have basically been self-taught... I think we as the Muppets broke new ground because we approached puppetry from a different angle. I had never worked with puppets when I was a kid, and even when I began on television, I really didn't know what I was doing."

Through Fran's memories, it's possible to get a glimpse not just of the technical and creative aspects of bringing puppet characters to life, but of the profound impact Jim Henson had on those around him. "I think we're all little seedlings of Jim," she smiles. "Whether or not we're cognisant of it, we have all taken that and passed it around, because the world would be a much, much better place if everybody could be like him."

She remembers moments in New York City taxis where, despite visible frustration with terrible traffic, Henson maintained his composure. "Not a word. He would never, ever yell at somebody." Even today, decades after his passing, Fran finds herself guided by Jim's example. "I say to myself all the time, if I'm in a difficult situation, I think, *OK, how would Jim handle this?*" The answer invariably comes back to the qualities that made him such an exceptional leader and human being: "He was always incredibly kind, generous, thoughtful, patient... he listened, he didn't think he was better than anybody."

JOHN STEVENSON

ARTIST, DESIGNER AND DIRECTOR

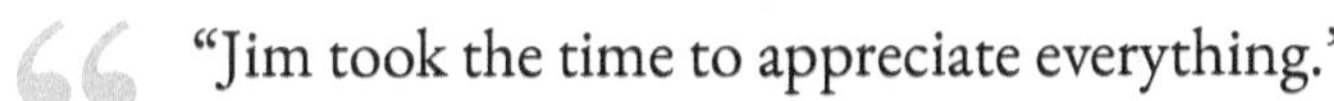 "Jim took the time to appreciate everything."

STARTING as a teenage Muppet fan who drew puppets in his spare time, John Stevenson became one of the key artists helping define the look of the Muppets in print and other media. His time with Henson would influence his later career as an animation director on films such as the Oscar-nominated *Kung Fu Panda* (2008).

* * *

Watching *Hey Cinderella*, Jim Henson's 1969 TV special, marked a turning point for young John Stevenson. This Muppet retelling of the classic tale captivated the puppet-enthusiast. For a boy who'd always been enthralled by puppetry—even running a puppet club at school—the Muppets were a revelation, igniting a passion for storytelling that would last for the rest of his career.

"They weren't your typical stiff marionettes or hard-faced Punch and Judy characters," John says. "The Muppets were soft and flexible. Normally on English television at that time, puppets were sort of locked into a proscenium arch, moving left and right while a voice-over said, 'Tell me what you did today Andy Pandy' or whatever it was. The Muppets were using the whole space of the studio."

But it was one particular character that captured John's heart: Kermit the Frog. "Of all the crazy puppets, I just fell in love with this frog. I just thought his personality, the way he looked, his voice, everything about Kermit just felt magical." This spark of fascination soon blazed into a full-blown passion. John soon pored over listings magazines *Radio Times* and *TV Times*, hunting for any mention of upcoming Muppet specials like *The Frog Prince* (1971) or *The Muppet Musicians of Bremen* (1972).

Fast forward to 1977. A 19-year-old John, working as a runner in a London ad studio, stumbled upon a classified ad that would change everything. "There was a magazine featuring various advertising campaigns and at the back there was a Jobs Available section. One said, 'The Muppets are looking for an artist', which stopped me in my tracks." Despite the late hour, John took a chance and dialled the number. To his astonishment, he reached the Muppet office at ATV Studios. Even more incredibly, they invited him for an interview the very next morning.

Little did John know, he was about to step into the world he'd been dreaming of for years.

John travelled three hours from Sussex to ATV's Borehamwood studios for his interview. "I stayed up all night drawing Muppets from memory on the kitchen table, threw whatever I'd done into a Sainsbury's carrier bag, and started to schlep up to Borehamwood at six in the morning to get there." Though he knew he didn't have the five years of experience they wanted, he wasn't discouraged. "I knew I'd be found out but I didn't care." His motivation was refreshingly simple: "I just wanted to see the puppets."

Upon arrival, John came face-to-face with Jane Henson and executive producer David Lazer. "Jane was the sort of wonderful earth mother kind of person. She came in and smiled, which made me feel better. But I saw David Lazer's face when he saw me, it was like,

What a waste of time. However, Jane said 'Would you like to go draw the puppets?' and she had somebody take me out to the soundstage where they shot *The Muppet Show*."

What John discovered was a testament to the show's ambition and scale. "One of the things that people don't realise is that *The Muppet Show* was the most expensive television show on the air at that time, and it was made in the biggest studio in Europe. ATV had this huge stage, and it was built for them to have a live audience. They would do these big variety shows where they were getting Perry Como or Julie Andrews or somebody to come along, and it would look like an American show."

As the day unfolded, John found himself in the heart of Muppet creativity, the puppet workshop. The room was a wonderland of fabric and fur. "There were hundreds and hundreds of Muppets, three or four rows deep on racks all wrapped around this big room. There were three big tables in the middle of the room for puppet costume makers and puppet builders. There were boxes full of puppet bits, eyeballs and fur. It was amazing."

In this bustling workshop, John experienced firsthand the warmth and generosity that would come to define his time with the Muppets. Puppet builders like Rollie Krewson, Amy Van Gilder and costume designers Calista Hendrickson and Polly Smith took the young artist under their wing, providing him with materials to continue his sketches on the backs of old Muppet scripts.

"For some reason, somebody introduced Jim Henson to me. I was nobody, nothing and he's the producer and main star and creator. Why is he going to spend five minutes talking to me? He came over and chatted to me and looked at my drawings." During this impromptu review, Jim noticed a detail in John's sketch of Waldorf, one of the cantankerous balcony hecklers. "Jim goes, 'Oh, this isn't right, you've drawn Waldorf with a wonky eye." This observation led to a memorable moment where Henson personally investigated the puppet, discovering that one of Waldorf's eyes had indeed slipped. The puppet was promptly fixed, but this small interaction left a lasting impression on John, who wonders if it played a role in Jim remembering him later on.

As lunchtime arrived, John found himself still free to explore the Muppet workshop, amazed that no one had asked him to leave. The puppeteers, returning from their performances on the studio floor, filled the room while live feed monitors scattered throughout the workshop provided a glimpse of the on-set action. John was fully immersed in the world of the Muppets, even getting the opportunity to hold and touch the puppets as he drew them. However, as the afternoon turned to evening, he suddenly realised that the workshop had emptied and he assumed that everyone had gone home for the day.

In reality, the Muppet team was simply taking a tea break out on the studio floor, a necessary respite during their long shooting days that often lasted from 8am to 8pm. Leaving his drawings on one of the tables, John made his way out of the studio, his thoughts filled with the incredible experiences of the day. "All I'm thinking is, *I touched Kermit, I saw Fozzie, I was with the puppets, I saw them.* I just spent the day seeing, touching and being around the Muppets and that was fantastic," he says, content with the once-in-a-lifetime opportunity he had been given.

Just a few days later, he received a call from executive producer David Lazer, offering him the position of a junior artist on *The Muppet Show.* Knowing that Jim Henson and his team could have hired any artist for such a prestigious job, John was stunned. In reflecting on the reasons behind his hiring, he believes that it was his genuine love and passion for the Muppets that set him apart from the other candidates. "I think Jim and Jane saw that I loved the Muppets, that I would have shown up for no money just to be with them."

John also considers the possibility that his physical resemblance to a young Jim Henson, along with Jane Henson's motherly nature, may have played a role in their decision. "[I was] tall, thin, awkward and geeky and there might have been a little bit of like, 'He's sort of weird and awkward, but he's got something.'"

WORKING WITH THE MUPPETS

John officially joined *The Muppet Show* in 1977, continuing to endure a daily six-hour round trip to his parents' home. "At the time, the company was pretty small, around 30 people, and half of them were in the UK and half were in Manhattan. So it was the builders, the puppeteers, Jerry Juhl, some of the key writers, and David Lazer. But basically, all the main people from the Muppets spent six months in the UK and then they spent the other six months back in the US."

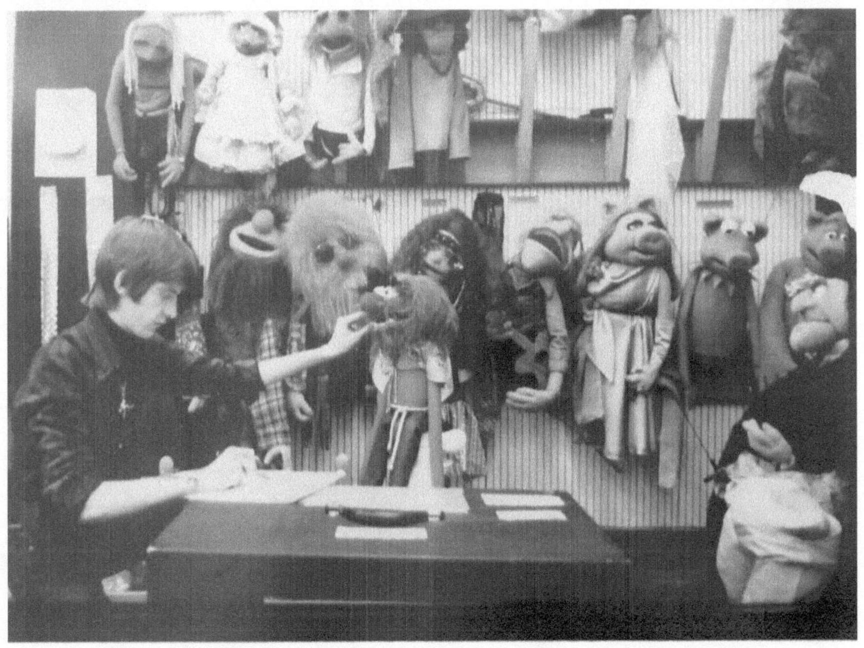

John and friends in the Muppet workshop. Photo courtesy John Stevenson

As the newest member of this creative tribe, John's first major assignment was to create a style book for the Muppet characters. "There was a lot of merchandising blowing up at that time, and mostly it was terrible because there wasn't any good reference. People would use some terrible picture of Piggy with her arms in a weird way and you'd get that looking sort of wonky on t-shirts. It looked awful. So Jim wanted a good style book."

But John's task wasn't just about perfecting existing designs. He faced an unusual challenge that would test his imagination and artistic skills. "The other main thing I had to do was give them legs, because they didn't exist below the waist. So if somebody wanted to make a doll, or a little plastic figurine or comic strip, people would say, 'What do the legs look like if they're walking?' So I had to figure that stuff out."

While tackling these projects, he was part of the vibrant, creative atmosphere of the Muppet workshop. "I talked to the puppeteers when they had tea breaks. That's how I kind of got to know Jim, Frank, Richard, Jerry Juhl, the builders and later Louise Gold and Steve Whitmire."

As *The Muppet Show* grew more popular, Henson's team needed more space in London. They moved into a Victorian workhouse on Downshire Hill, which became their creative hub and home to *The Dark Crystal* development. The art department settled on the first floor, sharing the building with the embryonic Creature Shop. This wasn't just an office, it was a place where innovation thrived. The art team expanded to include Bruce McNally as art director, veteran graphic designer Les Skinner and Sue Venning, a young artist Jim Henson reportedly selected personally.

The conversation then turns to the memorable experience of being called upon to help with large crowd scenes during the filming of *The Muppet Show*. "If you were in the workshop, and they needed people to sort of wave chickens, you would get roped in. I wasn't anything like a puppeteer the way the main puppeteers were, but they could give me a main character like Fozzie or the Swedish Chef for a crowd scene and I would make sure that the eyeline would be right." This privilege came with its own challenges, as the main character puppets were often much heavier than the background puppets. "I remember my arms breaking holding Fozzie up for hours. He's a heavy, heavy bear."

John goes on to describe the physiques of the Muppet performers, who had developed incredible upper body strength from years of puppeteering, "except Dave Goelz, who had a different physique. Jim and Frank had these lanky bodies with massive upper body strength. They'd have narrow waists and bad posture, but their biceps were like bowling balls. If you hold that weight 12 hours a day for 20 years, you're gonna get really strong."

Discussing the physical demands of performing some of the larger Muppet characters, such as the giant blue Thog, John notes that they may have looked impressive, but that they weren't fun to wear. "Just moving in those things was incredibly hard, never mind trying to give a performance and bring it to life. [Puppeteers] needed a lot of massage and body treatments, because doing big things with Muppets was tough."

The typical workflow of a *Muppet Show* production week found each day dedicated to a specific aspect of the show. "I think Monday they would record the music, so all the songs that were going to be on the show. They would do everything to playback, but they would record all the music with the guest stars on Monday. Tuesday, as I remember, was the primary guest star day, which often ran into Wednesday. And then Wednesday and Thursday were the rest of the show. Friday was theoretically a day off for the puppeteers. But often they would shoot promos and pickups and things on Friday. Saturday was editing, and Sunday was read-through and rehearsal."

Though the hours were long and the schedule demanding, John's passion for the Muppets and the creative process kept him coming back, even on his days off. "I'd be getting up early and getting home at nine or 10 in the evening, quite often later, because I just liked staying [in the studio]. I would come in and do some work on Saturdays, for no reason other than I just liked it, and sometimes Jim would let me come and sit in on the edit."

The off-season, however, brought a stark contrast. With the Muppet performers and writers back in the US, John found himself alone in the London workshop. "At the beginning, it was very lonely and weird. It was just me in the puppet workshop for six months," he explains, adding that he would occasionally be visited by maintenance staff. "The Creature Shop didn't exist at that time. So it was just me coming to work in this big puppet workshop. Most of the puppets were kept there for the next season, so occasionally a puppet would get looked at. It was kind of cool, but it also was kind of lonely."

A LEARNING EXPERIENCE

The Muppet Show also attracted a wide array of celebrity guest stars, and John relishes the opportunities he had to witness some of these performances firsthand. "I remember when Blondie was on the show and I designed a kind of punk band. I love Blondie and I got to go and watch Debbie Harry record. John Cleese was on the show. I love *Monty Python's Flying Circus* [1969–74] and *Fawlty Towers* [1975–79], so I was allowed to go out on the floor and just look around at John Cleese being John Cleese."

John puts this inclusive atmosphere down to Jim Henson's leadership style. "It was the most expensive and most popular show on television, and it was very stressful with time constraints, but there wasn't the stress of people shouting. Jim never shouted, and he didn't like people shouting around him. Even if it was to move lights or something, he just found that very psychically disruptive." This calm and supportive environment extended to the creative process as well, with Jim encouraging experimentation and learning from failure. "It was okay to screw up on *The Muppet Show*. If you tried something and it failed, whether it was me doing drawings or designs or a joke or whatever, that was fine. You weren't punished for screwing up. It was a learning experience."

John reflects on the long-term value of this approach. "Maybe something would come out of it later, maybe that joke didn't work, or that puppet design didn't work now, but maybe there's something that we could take later on and use. You were never worried about getting fired or shouted at for taking a risk. It wasn't until I left the Muppets and went out into the world that I realised, 'Oh, most other places don't work like this, never mind the level of creativity—everybody's yelling and shouting and stressed.'"

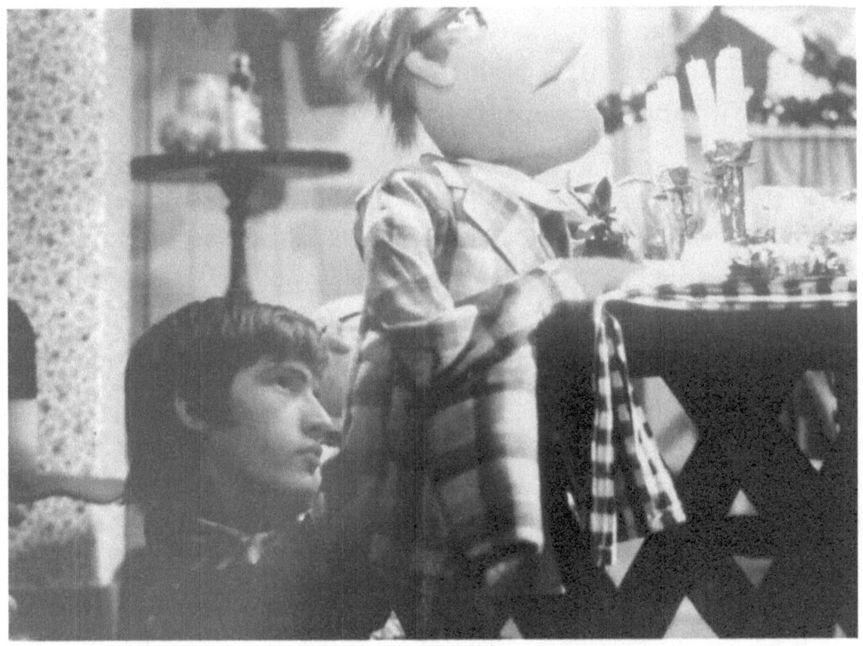

John with the Guy Smiley puppet. Photo courtesy John Stevenson

The lack of ego and hierarchy within the Muppet team was another striking feature. "There was no doubt in anybody's mind whose empire we were in. It's Jim's creation, he's the boss. Everything comes from Jim. He never had to assert his authority. If somebody came up with something that he liked, he would always give credit."

For the team, pleasing Jim Henson was the ultimate goal. "The main motivation for all of us was to make him happy. The best thing you could ever get if you were working for Jim, whether we showed him any kind of creative work—a script, a drawing, a puppet, whatever—was that he would laugh. If you disappointed him, he would never get angry. He would just look at it kind of quizzically and he'd say, 'Okay,' then he would just sort of walk away, and you'd just be like, 'Ah, I've disappointed him.' And then you'd work three times as hard to make Jim laugh because he kind of lit up the place with his big wheezy laugh. That was better than any kind of bonus or anything like that. That was the reward."

John marvels at Jim's ability to embark on new and ambitious projects with apparent ease. "If Jim was ever stressed or unhappy or challenged by something that was causing him upset, he never showed it to anybody. He would come in and say, 'We're going to do this thing.' Suddenly we'd be doing a giant thing. And we would just take it as accepted."

This was particularly evident in the development of *The Dark Crystal*, which marked a significant departure from Jim's previous work. "At the time Jim did *The Dark Crystal* he was at the height of his fame and popularity with *The Muppet Show*. It's a huge left turn and I don't know how easy it was to get the money to make *The Dark Crystal* from being the guy who did *The Muppet Show* and *Sesame Street*. 'Yeah, give me 25 million dollars.' 'Oh, sure.' I don't know whether it was that, or if it was a huge amount of frustration."

John emphasises the profound impact Jim had on his life and career. "Everything I've ever learned of any value, professional, personal, I learned from Jim Henson. I think everybody who has worked with Jim one-on-one tries to carry some version of 'How would Jim do this?' into our lives." This commitment to Jim's legacy intensified after his death in 1990. "Particularly after Jim died, some of us went out into the world and worked for people who didn't know what it was like to work with Jim. Whatever that experience was that we had with him is sort of... it's finite. And it's limited to not that many people who knew Jim intimately. I'm not claiming to be one of Jim's closest friends, but I'd say we were friends. Jim was very kind to me and I stayed at his house and had dinner with his family and he tried to help me become a better version of myself. And he was doing this for everybody."

With candid self-awareness, John acknowledges the challenge of living up to Jim's example. "I'm nowhere near as kind and patient and forgiving and gentle as Jim. I'm a cranky asshole and I have to work very, very hard every day to be a reasonable human being. But when I am in charge of a project, whether it's *Kung Fu Panda, Sherlock Gnomes* [2018] or a short film I made with students that got nominated for a BAFTA, I try as hard as I can to do it in a way that Jim would approve of. And to try to take whatever I've benefited from—from knowing him and being mentored by him and seeing his example—and pass it on."

John believes Jim aimed to harness his team's full creative potential, creating an environment free from fear or distraction. "If you worked at the Muppets, you were chosen by Jim. Other people might meet you, but in the end, it was Jim's choice. So if he invited you in he wanted 100% of your brain working for him on whatever it was that he had chosen for. He didn't want 40% of your brain, because the other 60% is worried about getting fired or shouted at. So the environment was like; 'What do you need to be creative? Do your work, take risks and fall on your face. It's all fine. Just bring me things that make me happy.' And that got the very, very best out of everybody."

Comparing Henson to another visionary, John reflects, "I think Jim was a genius like Walt Disney was a genius. I don't know what Walt Disney was like as a person, there are stories that he was not the easiest person to work for. Jim *was* the easiest person to work with. But easy or difficult is neither here nor there. The point is, those people completely changed popular culture by the power of their imagination."

John elaborates on the seismic shift brought about by Disney and Henson in animation and puppetry. "Before there was Walt Disney, there were animated films, but they weren't like Disney animated films, they were like Felix the Cat, sort of simple things. Disney brought a different approach to making that stuff and elevated it beyond what anybody could imagine. And by doing so, suddenly things which had never existed in the world before became lodged in the consciousness of everybody around the globe. There's a point in the world where there is no Mickey Mouse. And then there's a point in the world where there is Mickey Mouse and everybody in the world knows Mickey Mouse."

Similarly with the Muppets, "There was a point in the world where there were puppets that were marionettes or Punch and Judy, or whatever, and then there are the Muppets. And nothing is ever the same again once the Muppets come in. They are different from everything. Not only do they look fun and interesting, but the writing is really smart."

John credits head writer Jerry Juhl for the Muppets' intelligent humour, noting that "*The Muppet Show* never talked down to their audience." He recalls a sophisticated joke from the first season: "Fozzie's joke was, 'Did you know that Toshiro Mifune means no smoking in Japanese?' Not a kid's joke. That is not a joke that even most adults get. That was a statement joke, 'If you're not smart enough, you're gonna have to keep up with us. We're not talking down.'"

This commitment to never underestimating the audience, especially children, was central to Jim's philosophy. "Jim always believed that kids would rather reach up to something they didn't quite get than have somebody reach down and give it to them. So he would never dumb anything down on any of the stuff he did. He wouldn't put in anything offensive, but if it was an intellectual idea that people thought might be too hard for kids to get, he'd be like, 'If they're interested, they will want to find out what it means.'"

According to John, Jerry Juhl was "the heart and Jim was the soul of the Muppets. There would be no Muppets without Jim. I think Jerry's big contribution is the fact that *The Muppet Show* is a dysfunctional family, like all great comedies. The characters in *The Muppet Show* are very eccentric, and basically, they all need each other. They may get on each other's nerves, but without each other, they don't work. They may be frogs and pigs and chickens and what have you, but they care about each other. There was not a mean-spirited laugh in the Muppets when Jerry Juhl was the writer, and I think that was something that Jim and Jerry both believed, which is you can get just as good and bigger laughs without being mean-spirited or sarcastic. I think Jerry Juhl was the key to that, that the Muppets care about each other.

"You see little moments in *The Muppet Show*, and there are moments in the movies, where it's not funny or somebody's hurting emotionally. It's just a cloth bag, and yet you sort of feel something, this character is having an existential crisis. Without that, I don't think the Muppets are as powerful or meaningful. If they were just doing good goofy stuff, even if it was beautifully crafted, I don't think it would have resonated or lasted. I think it's those little moments where you sort of get a sense that these guys have an emotional inner life. And that's Jerry Juhl."

A LITTLE BIT OF IMMORTALITY

One long-standing rumour surrounding John Stevenson is that he inspired the character of Beaker, the nervous, red-haired assistant to Dr Bunsen Honeydew. "Bunsen didn't have an assistant on the first season, he appeared shortly after I showed up on *The Muppet Show*. And he looked exactly like me. It's hard to tell now, but at the time, I had big, shocking bright red hair and I was rail thin, I had a 29-inch waist, and I was very nervous," says John.

Muppet performers and writers would often be immortalised as puppets themselves, though at the time John never directly asked about his connection to Beaker. "The puppet builders would make caricatures of Jim Henson, a puppet of Frank Oz, and Jerry Juhl had a puppet. My friend [writer] Kirk Thatcher confirmed that he talked to Jerry Juhl and he confirmed Beaker was inspired by me. So I have a little bit of immortality," John laughs.

While John didn't work on 1979's *The Muppet Movie*, he played a role in the moment Kermit's legs are seen when he stands in the film. He explains that while Kermit had been shown with legs in a few shots of the 1975 *Muppet Show* pilot *The Muppet Show: Sex and Violence*, there was a longstanding rule against depicting the famous frog standing on his own two feet. "I think [Jim] made these kinds of wooden rod-operated legs, so Kermit could be seen sitting on a surface with crossed legs." The rule against showing Kermit standing was reportedly enforced by Michael Frith, the overall Muppet art director.

John, in a moment of youthful audacity, decided to challenge this rule by creating drawings of Kermit walking and standing hand-in-hand with his nephew, Robin. "Michael was a good guy and a very good artist, but he didn't like it. He didn't want me to show Jim." Undeterred, John took his drawings directly to Jim Henson. John then adopts an impression of Jim's voice, saying, "'I don't think we want... we don't do that... oh, that looks nice.' After that point, Kermit was allowed to be seen standing. When I saw Kermit standing as an animatronic puppet in *The Muppet Movie*, I thought, *He wouldn't be doing that unless I'd done those drawings and shown them to Jim.*"

Though the development of full-body Kermit scenes was a collaborative technical effort, John's story offers a fascinating glimpse into how his artwork helped spark a creative turning point.

John was more involved in *The Great Muppet Caper*, which was filmed in the UK, explaining that while Jim Henson already had a storyboard artist in Bill Stallion, he also asked John to work on some storyboards. "Stallion knew how to do storyboards for movies, but he didn't really know the Muppets." He goes on to explain that Stallion's storyboards tended to treat the Muppets as interchangeable, rather than distinct characters with their own quirks and mannerisms. "They all kind of looked the same, they just kind of blurred together. Jim wanted me to help show their correct designs and personalities."

Stallion's guidance helped John understand the limitations and possibilities of camera work in filmmaking. "Sometimes I would draw stuff and Bill Stallion would say, 'The camera can't do that.' I mean, this is the old days, cameras were on dollies or cranes, and he'd say, 'Where's the camera? How are you going to shoot that? The camera can't be there.' So it made me think about things I've never thought about before."

In addition to working with Stallion, John had the opportunity to learn from another renowned storyboard artist, Ivor Beddoes, thanks to an introduction from Jim Henson. "One evening Jim took me to see Ivor, I think he'd been in the art department on *The Red Shoes* [1948]. He had the glass paintings from *The Red Shoes* in his front room, and he was doing the storyboards for *Star Wars* [1977]."

Beddoes provided John with a crash course in storyboarding for films, emphasising the importance of screen direction and the challenges of depicting complex scenes. "I remember him asking me, 'What do you think the hardest thing to storyboard is?' I said something stupid like, 'A giant space battle' and he said, 'A dinner party with eight people.' There's a conversation going on between eight people at a dinner party and you're trying to keep the geography straight. [He's talking about] screen direction and the 180-degree rule of crossing the line and all these terms and I have no idea what he's talking about."

John's many positive memories of being in Jim Henson's orbit includes one from his time on *The Great Muppet Caper* that he says "tells you a lot about Jim, and probably tells you a lot about me". He sets the scene, describing how he had stayed overnight at Jim's home in Hampstead to accompany him along with his daughter Cheryl and son Brian to the set early the following morning to film the technically challenging sequence of the Muppets cycling through the park. "I'd had dinner with him and Cheryl and Brian. Jim had said, 'Come and hang around on the set and watch this big thing.' I didn't need to be there, I wanted to be there."

As they drove to the set in Henson's Kermit green Lotus Eclat, John sat in the back alongside Brian Henson. "At some point in the journey, I said something stupid. It would have been me complaining about why I wasn't getting to do something; selfish, self-obsessed 19 or 20-year-old behaviour as Jim's driving to the biggest, most technically complex scene on the show. I can suddenly tell I pissed him off. He didn't say anything, but I can tell by a certain tension in his neck and shoulders. I realised I'd just stepped in it."

Arriving on set, John found himself grappling with the consequences of his actions. "It's now uncomfortably quiet and I realised I made a huge mistake and we're driving up towards this freaking huge film crew of 50 or 100 technicians with a giant crane for this massive, technically complex scene. They're all waiting for the director and producer to show up with a bazillion questions and it's my first day. And I'm arriving with Jim and I've just made him angry."

John expected to be scolded publicly, but what happened next spoke volumes about Jim's character. "As soon as the car parks, Cheryl and Brian race to get out, they don't want to be any part of it, and I'm waiting for Jim to give me what for, which I entirely deserved. I just wish it wasn't going to happen in front of dozens of professionals."

Instead of publicly chastising John, Henson took him aside for a private conversation, shielding him from any potential embarrassment in front of the crew. "Jim puts his arm around my shoulders and he walks me away. Jim had hands the size of dinner plates and he was gripping my shoulder. I could tell he was angry. I'm paraphrasing [but he said] 'It's not very respectful when someone's done you a favour to be so ungrateful.' I was absolutely demolished by him because he was right. I'd just been a spoiled, entitled, selfish little prick. I felt horrible that I made him unhappy, and I realised how selfish I'd been. He had all this stuff on his mind about shooting this huge scene and suddenly he's got this whiny twit behind him complaining about something trivial, distracting him from what he needs to do.

"What I felt was not what the crew saw. What the crew saw was the producer-director arriving in his fancy Lotus with this guy they'd never seen before. And before they can all ask their important 'What do we do today, director?' questions, he puts his arm around this guy and they walk off for a little private conference where he was talking to my ear, very intimate, nothing to do with them. And then he comes back again. Even though Jim was angry with me, he protected me. The crew never knew Jim was angry and I was treated well by everybody for the rest of the day."

John contrasts Jim's handling of the situation with his own occasional lapses in patience on set. "I'm not that nice when people have stepped in it on movies I've done. I've taken their heads off," he admits. "I've regretted it instantly and I apologise. I don't do it that often, but it does happen when I get very tired and stressed. I'm not as good as Jim at hiding my feelings and I spend a lot of time cleaning up my mess because I've made people feel bad and I hate myself for doing that."

John remembers being amazed by the technical intricacy of filming the bicycle scene. "There was a gigantic crane with a specially built platform for the puppeteers to marionette Kermit and Piggy, and there was a squad of puppets kind of welded together as a group that was remote controlled. But when Piggy and Kermit are doing figure eights, they're being puppeteered and the strings are like 20 feet high."

An industrial-sized crane was used to create a stable environment for the puppeteers' precise movements. "With a cherry picker or a smaller crane, vibrations get magnified as they travel up the arm. So if you're on there trying to puppeteer and you need to control something with precision, any vibration like that is going to come down to the puppet. So for Brian Henson and whoever was up on the platform doing Kermit, that platform did not wobble or vibrate and that didn't get down to the puppets."

THE DARK CRYSTAL

John's involvement with *The Dark Crystal* began during his time on *The Muppet Show* when he first encountered fantasy illustrator Brian

Froud. "I remember when Brian came around the Muppet workshop, I knew him from [his 1977 book] *The Land of Froud*, which had made Jim want Brian to be the designer of *The Dark Crystal*. So when Brian was there I knew something was up, but nobody was talking about it."

Intrigued by the project, John managed to secure a role. "I kind of became a pest and I got put on *The Dark Crystal*. Brian was designing the world, the creatures, the characters and the environment... he was sort of the global world designer. My job was to illustrate key scenes from the script, like production drawings." John's work on *The Dark Crystal*'s storyboards provided a unique insight into the co-directors' different approaches.

He worked separately with Jim Henson and Frank Oz to develop their individual visions for each scene. "That was very weird and interesting because I'd do the Jim version of the scene, then I did the same scene with Frank, and they wouldn't talk to each other about their approaches."

John notes that Oz typically had a more visually inventive and cinematic approach compared to Jim. The two versions would then be merged in a Saturday meeting, with John creating a composite storyboard based on their preferences. These initial storyboards served as a foundation for more detailed production boards, later developed by artist Mike Ploog. John humbly acknowledges, "Mike was an infinitely better story artist than I was. I think I was just helping Jim and Frank get their ducks in a row."

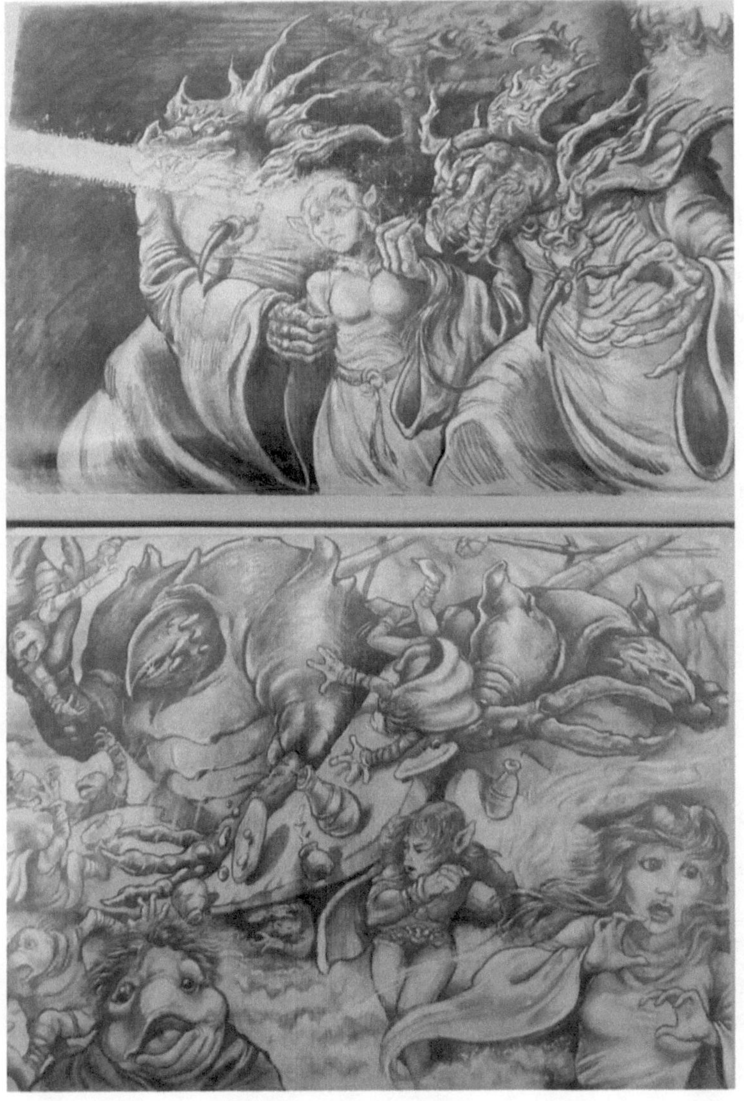

John helped Jim and Frank visualise the world of The Dark Crystal. Image courtesy John Stevenson

By the time production began on *Labyrinth*, John had left Henson Associates to pursue a career as a freelance artist but continued to collaborate with Jim on various projects. "I could see where I could become institutionalised at the Muppets, so I went off to become a freelance artist." Although no longer a full-time employee, John maintained a close connection with Jim, who would periodically reach out to him for various projects. "I would always know when Jim was going to call me, I'd get this weird feeling in my gut. It might be an hour later, or it might be a day later, Jim would call."

Jim later called John back to work on character development for *Labyrinth*. Though Brian Froud returned as the main character designer, John's job was to create detailed expression sheets—similar to those used in animation—that would guide the puppet builders.

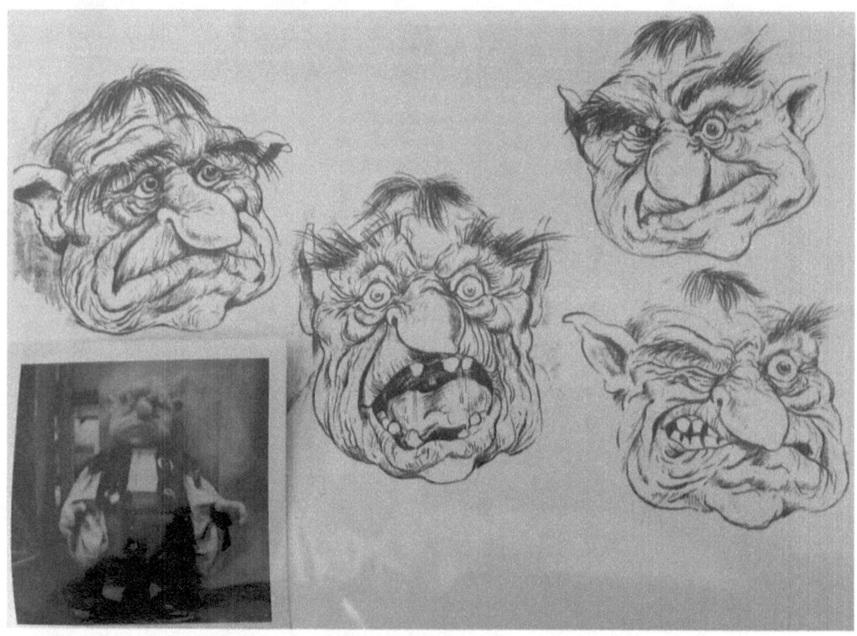

An expression sheet for Hoggle in Labyrinth. Image courtesy John Stevenson

"Because we'd usually just get one painting from Brian, the puppet builders needed to know, 'What happens in profile, what happens behind the character? What does Hoggle look like when he's angry, when he's licking his lips?'" These detailed plans helped builders understand when they might need to create different puppet heads for various expressions, with Jim reviewing all final designs.

LITTLE SHOP OF HORRORS

Around the same time John was working on *Labyrinth*, he also accepted the opportunity to be part of Frank Oz's 1986 film *Little Shop of Horrors*, which featured puppets created by the Henson Creature Shop. John worked with production designer Roy Walker to develop mouth charts for the film's plant creature, Audrey II. "I remember doing all the vowels and consonants, mouth shapes for the plant," John says, his role key in ensuring that Audrey II's movements would be able to accurately mimic human speech when the plant grew larger.

John also worked on conceptual sketches for the film's climactic sequence, initially envisioning a global invasion by Audrey II before the scope was narrowed down to focus on New York City. He developed ideas for the plant attacking famous landmarks like the Brooklyn Bridge and the Statue of Liberty, and even recalled a specific direction from Frank Oz, who wanted the character of Seymour (Rick Moranis) to be eaten "like a hot dog".

After investing significant time and resources in bringing the original ending to life, including a year of special effects filming and a substantial portion of the film's budget, the original ending was ultimately cut when test audiences reacted negatively to the dark conclusion. Years later, he finally had the opportunity to see the sequence he worked on fully realised when the restored director's cut was released on Blu-ray and screened at the British Film Institute. "That was a nice closing of the loop, to finally see this thing I started doing drawings for in Roy Walker's office up on the big screen, and it looked amazing."

For 1987's *Inner Tube* pilot, John designed several characters for what was planned as a more adult Muppet show. His creation "Crasher" was inspired by Vyvyan from *The Young Ones* (1982–84), "a full-body costume that John Henson could wear and smash things up because he had a habit of doing that in real life". John Stevenson also created TV repairman Muppets and a band with New Romantics styling.

When the project evolved into *The Jim Henson Hour*, John received an unusual assignment directly from Jim. "Jim did this weird thing where he paid me to come up with 10 concepts for things we could do on the show. A blank canvas." Among John's ideas was *Hurting Something*, a parody of *Thirtysomething* (1987–91) with monster yuppies that played on Jim's fear of spiders: "Because I knew Jim hated spiders, I wrote this sketch where a monster couple are going to bed and the wife goes into the bathroom and finds that a little human is running around in the bath and freaks out, so he carries it outside."

For all its creative talent, *The Jim Henson Hour* struggled to find a cohesive identity. John believes the show's high-tech approach worked against it: "Jim was always very interested in technology, in computer animation and computer puppetry and things like that. There was always a kind of push to make things that weren't *The Muppet Show* in a TV studio with video screens and things. But there's something kind of cold and dead and antiseptic about the show. The theatre in *The Muppet Show* was a lo-fi, organic space, with little rooms that people go in. [*The Jim Henson Hour*] was caught up in a TV studio with cameras and monitors and things and it's sort of cold. I think every time any Muppet thing tried to be too high-tech, it kind of worked against the simple organic nature of the puppet characters themselves."

LOSING A FRIEND

The first episode of *The Jim Henson Hour* was broadcast in April 1989, just 13 months before Jim Henson died at the age of 53 in May 1990. At the time, John was working on an animated series called *The Dreamstone* (1990–95) in the Philippines, far from his colleagues and friends in the Henson company. "The way I found out was I was looking at the local newspaper and there was a picture of Jim

Henson. It was in Tagalog, but I knew what that meant. You don't have a picture of Jim Henson on the front page of a Filipino newspaper unless it's bad news."

The distance and the difficulty of communication at the time left John feeling isolated and unable to properly grieve with his colleagues and friends. "I'm trying to call people and either I can't connect or when I do get through people aren't there. People went to the Muppet offices in Manhattan and grieved, then they went to the memorial. I was on the other side of the world in the Philippines. I couldn't go and I couldn't find out what was happening, so I felt very alone and lost. So I was kind of dealing with that on my own and I found it very hard. It took me a long time and I probably still haven't quite come to terms with it."

Years later, John found some solace by watching a bootleg DVD of Henson's memorial service. "I cried my eyes out and kind of finally got closure. Knowing the people there, one of the things that I find amazing is that they were functioning at all, that they could do the performances and sing the songs at a time of being bereft and grieving. I can't imagine how hard it was for those guys to not just come up and say how much Jim meant to them, but to put on a performance. It was important for Big Bird and for those characters to pay tribute and say goodbye and it must have killed those guys to do that."

Reflecting on the current state of the Muppets, John draws a parallel to Disney's struggles after Walt Disney's death. "Disney lost its way for a long time after Walt Disney died. People didn't know what to do. Most of the animated films made just after Walt Disney's death are OK, they're technically good, but they don't have the same kind of cultural impact as *Snow White and the Seven Dwarfs* [1937], *Pinocchio* [1940] and *Dumbo* [1941]. Then they make a lot of weird choices. Then they had a renaissance with *The Little Mermaid* [1989] and found a formula that brought them back. Most people are nostalgic about the body of work done up until Disney's death."

He notices a similar pattern with the Muppets, where Jim

Henson's directly supervised work remains the most memorable. "There was this huge body of work guided by Jim that is interesting, fun, crazy, whatever. And then after Jim dies it all kind of dissipated. Disney owns some stuff, Henson owns some stuff, and it's all in different places being run in different ways. There's no unifying glue, creative or emotional."

John notes that writer Jerry Juhl's passing in 2005 may have marked the end of the Muppets' golden era. He draws a parallel to Pixar's creative dynamics, emphasising the importance of a unified team under a single vision. "Pixar's golden days were definitely with John Lasseter, who was probably the biggest name at the time. Then there was Joe Ranft, who was kind of like Jerry Juhl, Pete Docter and Andrew Stanton. There's a collection of key people, all on the same wavelength, this collection of brains is unified by one mega brain. This satellite system of really powerful, creative thinkers gets you the best Pixar movies up until Joe Ranft dies. I think it's kind of the same with the Muppets. When Jerry and Jim and Frank were bouncing ideas off each other, you get the best Muppet stuff. Then one huge bit gets removed, and it's less. And then another bit gets removed, then it all evaporates."

JIM'S LEGACY

While most people didn't have the opportunity to know Jim Henson personally, John believes that the ripple effect of his influence, carried forward by those who did, has the potential to make a positive impact.

"Most of the world did not have one-on-one access to Jim. I mean, he had good days and bad days, but he never got angry. He was never mean, he was never grumpy. He was just a wonderful, inspirational human being." According to John, those who worked with Jim each took a bit of him and pushed it out into the world in different ways. "Maybe it gets diluted a bit more by other people taking some of that, and maybe it keeps getting diluted. Maybe it also keeps rippling out. So what started in the very small, tiny bubble in Manhattan, or Borehamwood, is now maybe bouncing around the world in a somewhat watered-down version, but that's still better than not being there at all. I would still rather work for someplace that was using some version of Jim's methodology, even if it was a watered-down version."

On his time spent working with Jim and the Muppets, John acknowledges the profound impact it had on his personal and professional development, in a career that has seen him move into directing and which saw *Kung Fu Panda* receive an Oscar nomination.

"I've been lucky a couple of times in my life. The first one was Jim. Everything of any value I've learned personally and professionally, I believe I got from Jim. Jim showed me when I was an annoying, irritating, thoughtless, grumpy, poorly behaved 19-year-old how to be a good person. I try to do what I can to pass on what I learned and fail very often, but I keep trying. There's always that weird thing of thinking, *What would Jim think of this? Would Jim think I was doing a good job? Would Jim be happy with the way I'm doing it?* For anybody who knew Jim, I think it matters to us that we do stuff that Jim would go, 'Yeah. You did a good job with that. And you treated people well, and that was good.' So we have Jim's spirit kind of sitting on our shoulders, filtering our behaviour and hopefully making us more benign, better people."

John notes that Jim's simple act of expressing appreciation and gratitude had a profound impact on his creative environment. "He appreciated everything, whether it was a nice carpet, a tree, a design for a puppet, a joke in a script or his dinner. If you were with him on a walk and he would look at a tree, he would tell you, 'Isn't that a great tree?' If you were with him at dinner, and he was enjoying his sandwich, 'This sandwich is great. I love this sandwich.' And he would tell the chef, 'The sandwich was great.' If he liked what you'd done, he would tell you that he liked it. Jim took the time to appreciate everything.

"That's one of the biggest things that I try to do if I'm in charge of something. This is like the simplest piece of people management advice in the world that costs absolutely nothing and takes 10 seconds and nobody ever does it. Somebody comes up with an idea to fix a problem or make something better or whatever and somebody goes, 'Oh, yeah, great. We'll do that.' And they don't say, 'Thank you for that idea. That's a great idea, that will help make the show better.' How long did that take? Five to 10 seconds? And it costs nothing."

John shares a final anecdote about an impromptu evening spent with Jim Henson. "I was showing Jim some work after hours when Jim decided he wanted to see Peter Brook's film *Meetings With Remarkable Men* [1979] that was playing in London. I remember we barrelled downstairs and jumped in Jim's Kermit green Lotus Eclat." The two drove to a cinema to catch the film. On leaving the cinema and realising it was too late for John to catch the last train home, Jim invited him to stay the night at his place in Hampstead.

Back at Jim's home, the two flipped through television channels and stumbled upon a Tod Slaughter film. "Jim was pissing himself laughing, running this sort of *Mystery Science Theatre 3000* [1988–99] kind of commentary throughout the film," laughs John. The next morning, Jim prepared grits for breakfast, a childhood favourite of his, and drove John to the studio. "Those are two memories nobody else has."

LOUISE GOLD

FIRST BRITISH MUPPET PERFORMER

"If we weren't filming, and there was a camera and monitor free, then we were encouraged to play."

WHEN LOUISE GOLD auditioned for *The Muppet Show* in 1977, she was a 20-year-old stage actress with no puppetry experience. She would become not only the first British Muppet performer but a vital bridge between the American and British puppet traditions, later helping establish the long-running *Spitting Image* (1984–96).

* * *

Before she became the first British on-screen Muppet performer, Louise Gold was treading the boards of regional theatres across the UK. A graduate of the prestigious Arts Educational Schools, London, where she'd balanced her studies with performing arts from age 11, Louise had carved out a promising career in traditional theatre, touring with productions of *Joseph and the Amazing Technicolor Dreamcoat* and *Hair*, while taking on various understudy roles.

It was while touring with a 1977 production of *The Land of the*

Dinosaurs that fate intervened in the form of an unexpected audition call for *The Muppet Show*. The catch? It conflicted with a scheduled performance. "I said, 'I can't audition. I have a show. There are no understudies. I can't take a show off.'" But fortune smiled in the form of the play's director, Ken Hill. When Louise reluctantly approached him, his response surprised her: "We'll make it up without you. The girl playing your sister can take your lines."

This allowed Louise to attend what would become a life-changing audition. Thanks to the sets being built to allow puppeteers to stand up, *The Muppet Show* was in search of a tall woman to join the cast for its second season. When Louise's agent learned that actors' union Equity had encouraged the producers to hire someone from the UK, her agent suggested she audition. At just 20 years old, the 5' 9" Louise soon found herself at Elstree Studios.

Despite having no prior puppeteering experience, Louise's natural talents shone through. Her singing voice impressed the Muppet team, including Jim Henson, Frank Oz and Richard Hunt, with Louise recalling an early challenge: "The very first show I did, they asked me to sing 'Chanson D'Amour' in three-part harmony with myself. I went home crying and said to my mum, 'I don't know if I can do this.' When I went back they said, 'Oh my God, that's incredible. None of us could do that.' So my singing voice was something that they really valued. With the puppeteering I said, 'I don't know how to do this' and they said, 'Nobody does what *we* do, we'll teach you.' At that point, they were the only people doing that style of television puppetry."

A WARM WELCOME

Louise's initiation into the world of puppetry was gradual, starting with simple tasks like manipulating chickens crossing backstage "and when I was doing the singing, someone else would work the puppet". She then progressed to being a right hand for more experienced performers like Jim or Frank, gradually getting to do more puppeteering.

"On *The Muppet Show*, we performed standing in holes for much of the time, our arms were constrained as we operated the puppets. For me, the weird thing was watching Jim, Frank, Jerry and Dave Goelz and thinking, *Oh my God, these people are geniuses. I can't do this.* I'd always wanted to be an actress, and I spent a lot of my early years trying to get my face into shot and forgetting about the puppet. It took me a long time to realise the puppet needed to be animated, not me."

Louise soon found herself welcomed into the Muppet family. "Jim and Frank were amazing. Watching them together was like watching Laurel and Hardy or any of the great comedy double acts, the rapport of Kermit and Piggy or Kermit and Fozzie. For me there was always a slight feeling of, *They're really good at this, I can't do this.* But I would do the singing and they respected that I could hold a tune. When Steve Whitmire came in, he was also very musical."

She adds, "I never felt out of place, even though I was only 20. The team never made me feel like, 'Sorry, what are you doing here? You're the young one. You don't know what you're doing.' Richard Hunt, who became my best buddy, sort of dragged me into it all. I was part of the gang from the start. It was an amazing place to work and we laughed all the time."

While the core puppeteer group was predominantly male, Louise emphasises that there were many women involved in other aspects of production, including Muppet designers Amy Van Gilder and Rollie Krewson, while Kathy Mullan later joined the team as a puppeteer. The gender imbalance among puppeteers didn't feel deliberate, but rather a practical consideration due to the height of the set and the physical demands of the job, while Louise's outgoing personality helped her fit in with the men. "There was a slight feeling of 'Why are the men doing all the female parts?' and I'd try to do more. Back then I was rather loud. Some people say I haven't changed. I was able to hold my own."

The close-knit nature of puppeteering created a unique working environment, with Louise noting that "you've got your head in somebody's armpit and your arm around them if you're being a right hand". Though Jim was often busy with a schedule of performing, directing and taking meetings, Louise remembers bonding with fellow puppeteers Jerry Nelson and Richard Hunt. "Richard took me under his wing and would shout at me and tell me off for doing things wrong. He'd be watching out for me."

Working with Jim Henson was a unique experience, partly thanks to his hands-off approach to teaching: "One time he was performing a character, and I was blinking the eyes. I was thinking, *I don't know what I'm doing. I've never done this before. Help me!* Jim was very much, 'You'll be fine. Just blink.' It was, 'Just get on with it, jump in.' If we weren't filming and there was a camera and monitor free, then we were encouraged to play. There were monitors on the floor and mirrors on the wall, so we played with those."

She reflects on how different things were then compared to now: "Today, people can much more easily go away and rehearse using their iPhones and computers. But in those days, they were big cameras on pedestals. I look back at some of the stuff I did as a puppeteer and it's not very good. But we were doing things so quickly and we just had to get on with it."

PIONEERING PUPPETEERS

Louise Gold offers an interesting perspective on the evolution of Muppet performances, noting that while newer performers who have learned through watching may be more technically skilled, there was something special about the original team.

"If you watch *The Muppet Show*, it's quite rough, but the life of the characters is extraordinary because the people operating them were all the creators. Jerry Nelson may not have been as technically polished as some, but his character voices were brilliant and versatile, and he was a wonderful singer. His characters are beautiful and he brought soulfulness and heart to everything he did. Jim appeared to be quite quiet and then his characters would be anarchic and wild."

It's often suggested that Jim was the Kermit of the Muppet crew, attempting to keep some semblance of sanity among the madness. "That's absolutely true," says Louise, "I felt he was the daddy of the company. He was very gentle, trying to hold the thing together." She notes that Henson often relied on executive producer David Lazer to handle more difficult administrative tasks, allowing Jim to maintain a certain distance from the "bad stuff".

As a junior member of the team, Louise didn't always have direct input into character development, but she observed how others, particularly Frank Oz, helped shape their characters. "Frank certainly had feedback on Piggy and his characters, he was very involved in that. I would always try to get some English accents in and Jim would say, 'Try this character' and they'd always end up with an American voice."

Louise highlights the creative spontaneity that often emerged during production, particularly in the "backstage crosses" scenes. These moments allowed for improvisation and character exploration beyond the scripted dialogue. She remembers one instance where Frank Oz's improvisation with a snake puppet turned into an entire scene. "Gradually his character took over just by improvising and the dialogue was irrelevant to Frank playing about and being wonderfully funny."

As the success of *The Muppet Show* grew in the UK, Louise and her colleagues sometimes escaped the cramped confines of the studio. "It was an incredible thing to be part of, it was so huge. We were invited everywhere and it was all very exciting. We were sort of the toast of the town."

However, in a pre-internet age, the performers weren't necessarily keeping track of their popularity around the globe. "You never really knew because you were just going into the studio and having fun doing it. There'd be a time in the week we'd go and sit in Jim's office and watch the most recent show edited together. We had no idea what it was like going out, but we did know that all those huge stars were coming in and they all adored Jim and his direction. They were treated very well and got to do whatever they wanted. Jim loved working with talent. He really admired and thrived off it and wasn't jealous of other people's talent, whereas some people are threatened by it. He surrounded himself by people whose work he loved."

Louise also notes Jim's support for other team members' ambitions, particularly Frank Oz's desire to direct. "Frank obviously wanted to be more than a puppeteer and despite having created these extraordinary characters, wanted to go off. Jim supported him."

As *The Muppet Show* progressed, Louise sensed a growing desire from Jim Henson and the team to explore new creative territories. This, coupled with the changing landscape of variety shows, led to a feeling that it was time for something new. "*The Muppet Show* was harking back to variety theatre, which was not really in existence in the 1970s. It was a great formula, but we'd had all the stars... where do you go next? I think there was definitely a feeling of, 'It's been absolutely brilliant, lovely, great. Next!' And Jim wanted to go on and explore other things. He wanted to do *The Dark Crystal* and we did *The Great Muppet Caper*, which was lovely."

MORE THAN MUPPETS

Throughout her time with the Muppets, Louise was eager to pursue other acting opportunities, with Jim Henson supportive of these endeavours. "In the last season of *The Muppet Show* I got offered *Godspell* in Leatherhead and it meant missing the final two episodes, but Jim let me go because he knew that was what I wanted to do. He was so kind. He came and saw the show and was so supportive and generous. At various times, ever since working with the Muppets, they've always let me do things when they come up."

This support continued throughout Louise's career, with Jim inviting her back for projects like *The Dark Crystal* and *Labyrinth*. "For *Labyrinth*, Jim asked me to be in the bubble sequence with

David Bowie, he thought it would be fun. I was always thrilled. The last thing I did for Jim was *The Ghost of Faffner Hall* [1989]. You thought, *I can't let Jim down.*" Jim would also attend Louise's performances outside of the Muppet world, even the less successful ones. "I did this huge flop, *Ziegfeld* at the London Palladium, and Jim came to the first night and Richard was there. Jim was obviously trying not to say, 'Oh, my God, this is a disaster', but being so supportive and lovely."

Louise's journey with puppetry continued in 1984 when she helped set up and perform in the hugely successful satirical series *Spitting Image*, which saw famous faces of the day represented by caricatured puppets. She discusses a period when she thought her puppeteering days were over because of a repetitive strain injury sustained during a production of *Mary Poppins*. Thankfully, after working with a trainer, she found herself drawn back into the world of puppets.

For all her extensive work with the Muppets, Louise admits she long struggled to identify as a puppeteer. "For many years I never really thought of myself as a puppeteer. I was always leaving and thinking, *I don't want to do this, I'm an actor, I want to get out there and do things.* The wonderful thing about Jim is that he supported me with that because he knew how important it was to me. Then I realised I could come back and do both acting and puppeteering."

It was after meeting a younger puppeteer that Louise had a moment of self-reflection: "I thought it was a little bit arrogant of me not to be a puppeteer if I've done all this work with these incredible people, and *Spitting Image*, which I helped set up. So I thought, *Oh, I guess I am.* Richard Hunt always wanted to perform. He was very much conflicted about being a puppeteer and wanted to act, but he was stuck in an incredibly well-paid, wonderful job. But he felt a bit trapped in it."

Though deeply committed to his work with the Muppets, Richard also harboured ambitions that extended beyond puppeteering. Notably, he directed several productions, including an episode of *Fraggle Rock* and *Sing-Along, Dance-Along, Do-Along* (1988).

Louise's appreciation for the dual nature of her work has grown over time. "The puppeteering skills feed into my acting work and my acting work feeds into the puppeteering. I'm doing a workshop for a new musical in a couple of weeks. I helped out [puppeteer] Warrick Brownlow-Pike with *Dodge's Pup School* [2024–] last week. I did something on *The Count of Monte-Cristo* [2024] TV series. I was helping Ryan Dillon, who does Elmo now, a couple of weeks ago, he was over and I was assisting him. It's amazing, I feel very lucky," says Louise.

"Jim worked so hard. One of my memories about *The Muppet Show* is laughing. Laughing and laughing and laughing. Jim would always have the heaviest puppet. He would be there longer than anybody else." She paints a picture of Henson's tireless work ethic: "He'd fly on Concorde to New York for meetings in the lunchtime. He'd be over at Elstree Film Studios for meetings, which was across the road from ATV Elstree Studios where we filmed *The Muppet Show* [now the BBC Elstree Centre]. He worked and worked, but it was joyous."

Looking back at *The Muppet Christmas Carol*, Louise explains that filming without both Jim and Richard Hunt "was heartbreaking in one way, but it was also a celebration of all that Jim had created. I talk to people today who think it's the best *Christmas Carol* and love that film. I've always felt how lucky I was for *The Muppet Show* to be one of my very early jobs and to work with Jim, who cared so much and brought joy to people with his work, but had joy *in* his work. That's what I try to remember when I'm really tired and thinking I hate whatever the job is. That's what I try to pay forward, the spirit of Jim and the joy in his work. But he bloody well worked harder than anybody else as well. He didn't skate through anything."

Another Henson production that continues to attract new fans is *The Dark Crystal*, leading to a prequel series, *The Dark Crystal: Age of Resistance*, being commissioned for Netflix and Louise taking on many roles. "It's a miracle that we did a puppet series of *Dark Crystal* all these years later with this fantastic production that was not a total success, but the original film wasn't a total success either. But the work and the skill that went into it, and the love and the Frouds being involved, it was incredible. I've done a couple of *Dark Crystal* conventions and to hear people talking about what it meant to them, to have been part of that and hopefully take forward something that Jim taught me is kind of my mission."

Louise particularly notes the strong female presence both behind the scenes in producing roles and among the puppeteering team on *Age of Resistance*. "We had a puppeteering team with a lot of women, and although the height differences—there were some short men too—made things a little tricky, the women were brilliant and so able to cope with the huge physical demands of the show."

CHANGING THE WORLD WITH LOVE

According to Louise, Jim Henson was aware of his position and the tools at his disposal: "I always felt he knew he had this unbelievable toy set, the tools to make these joyous things, and he loved it. He knew how lucky he was, he didn't take it for granted. I'd often be his right hand in Link Hogthrob or Rowlf and we'd been sitting there for hours. One time I made some fatuous comment about something going on in world politics and said, 'Jim, what do you think about it?' He said, 'That's not really what I do. This is what I do.' With *Fraggle Rock* he tried to make the programme that would bring peace, but he was doing it in his way. He wasn't a politician, but he wanted to do his bit in the way he could. He wanted to change the world with love."

The spirit of collaboration that Jim fostered extended well beyond the studio. When Louise first moved to Kentish Town, settling into what she describes as "a rather rickety, rubbish flat", she found herself part of a close-knit creative family. Henson, who had just purchased a house on Downshire Hill in Hampstead, would regularly host parties, eager to share his success with the team.

"What I loved about Jim was how joyous he was," says Louise, adding that this joy manifested in unexpected ways, from whisking her and Jim's daughter Lisa off to Germany in a helicopter for a TV appearance with Rowlf, to encouraging both women to go shopping when Louise needed something to wear for a post-appearance evening out. "I said, 'I haven't got anything to wear.' He said, 'Well, we're going to buy you something.' I went out with Lisa and bought some silly T-shirt. It was the idea of 'This is no fun unless we all play and work together,'" she says, remembering trips in his Kermit-green Lotus and the infectious excitement he brought to everything.

Regarding the dynamics of the Muppet performers and characters, Louise describes them as a "dysfunctional family": "They love each other and would kill for each other, but they also hate each other and they drive each other mad. But deep down, they would do anything for each other. And that's kind of the message. There's a great deal of love in it all."

Louise reflects on how the performers' personalities infused their characters: "It only struck me when we were doing *Muppets Most Wanted* that Dave Goelz was the only one left doing his character. I looked at Bunsen and Gonzo and I thought, *They're all Dave*. I'd sort of not been aware of it. Those original performers were so defined in who they were. Jerry Nelson *was* Floyd. That was part of him. He *was* Robin. My little Annie Sue Pig, who was very ambitious, young, talented and overjoyed to be there. I thought, *That was me. How silly am I? It was all of us.* Those performers are in the characters; their fallibility, their vulnerability, their idiosyncrasies."

For Louise, it's important that new puppeteers are encouraged to find their own voice. "Do your thing. Don't do Jim's thing. Everyone has something special. That's what you have to find. You're special. Don't make a Kermit, make a *you* thing."

MIKE QUINN
MUPPET PERFORMER

"Jim could see potential in people, let them find their way and find out who they could be."

FROM TEENAGE MUPPET fan to professional performer, Mike Quinn's determination to join the Henson team led to a career spanning four decades, including work on *Star Wars* films as the performer of Nien Nunb.

* * *

Born and raised in London, Mike Quinn's love affair with the Muppets began at the age of 13, coinciding with *The Muppet Show*'s explosion in popularity across the UK. "I became this obsessive Muppet fan, trying to figure out, *How do they build these things? How do they move?*" This fascination drove him to study the puppets' movements and mechanics with an intensity that surpassed casual fandom.

In 1977, Mike's dedication led him to a pivotal moment. Learning that the Muppet performers would be appearing on Kenny Everett's Saturday show on Capital Radio, he saw an opportunity he couldn't miss. Spending his precious pocket money on bus fare, Mike and a school friend made their way to the radio station, clutching an issue of *Look-In* magazine. The back cover featured a photo of the puppeteers—Jim Henson, Frank Oz, Dave Goelz, Richard Hunt and Jerry Nelson—holding their famous creations.

"I waited in the lobby," Mike remembers, "and sure enough, they showed up a bit before the show, the main five guys, and I intercepted them on the way in. They all signed my picture." The day's excitement didn't end there. "Then I met Kenny Everett afterwards and he signed my autograph book." Years later, Mike would learn the significance of that day extended beyond his own experience: "I hear that was the same day that Louise Gould had her audition for the Muppets as one of the puppeteers, so I guess that was quite a historic day in many ways."

This encounter only fuelled Mike's passion. He began investing all his spare cash and time into his craft. "I started spending my pocket money on bits of foam, fabric, fleece and stuff, just trying to figure out how to build these things. Also practising in front of the mirror, sort of mimicking the moves, trying to work out the techniques of how they did stuff. I was doing my own schooling and studying, but to me, it was just fun. I didn't realise I was training myself for the rest of my career."

As the second season of *The Muppet Show* aired, Jim Henson's creativity left an indelible mark on Mike. "I used to record all the shows on tape and listen to them all week long and memorise all the routines and everything. So I got really immersed deeply into that Muppet culture and how they all moved and sounded and the comedy of them as well."

His perseverance led to him attending the royal premiere of *The Muppet Movie* in Leicester Square in 1979. Displaying the resourcefulness that would serve him well in his future career, Mike phoned the office of producer Lew Grade directly to purchase two tickets with his hard-earned pocket money. "It was just the most amazing thing to walk the red carpet." Dressed in a borrowed black suit and bow tie, he attended with his mother, rubbing shoulders with the entertainment elite. The evening brought unexpected encounters, including a meeting with Muppet performer Richard Hunt and comedy legend Spike Milligan, who had likely just finished filming his guest appearance on *The Muppet Show*.

The experience left such an impression that Mike found himself overcome with excitement. "I was sick the next day, I just was too excited to go to school."

As Mike entered his final years of schooling, he firmly set his career aspirations on puppetry and the Muppets, finding creative ways to pursue his passion within the confines of the education system. "A victory that I won was I wanted to make puppets at school and at home, so I opted to take what they called needlework, sewing." Breaking gender norms, Mike became the first boy in his school to take the class, using half his time there to craft puppets.

In 1980, Mike's persistence led to a significant moment: a visit to the set of *The Muppet Show* at ATV Studios in Elstree during his school's work experience programme. Leveraging his father's business connections, the 15-year-old found himself on the hallowed ground of Muppet production. Dressed in a custom-made Dr Teeth t-shirt adorned with Muppet badges, Mike witnessed the taping of an episode featuring Lynda Carter, famous for her role as Wonder Woman. His focus, however, was entirely on the puppeteers. "I completely blew her off because I was just obsessing over the Muppet guys, Jim and everyone talking to me about my t-shirt and whatever I'd made."

This visit offered Mike invaluable insights into the Muppets' world. "At the side was a workshop, where they would dress and then repair the puppets and do a bit of puppet building." The puppet builders, noticing his enthusiasm, even allowed him to try on Kermit. This hands-on experience only deepened his admiration for Jim Henson and his team's artistry, with Mike's ingenuity soon making him a regular fixture on set. "I visited every other week. I'd bring along chocolates and cigarettes to give to the accountant as a kind of bribe to keep letting me into the studio."

Mike's persistence continued to pay off, granting him unprecedented access to the world he so admired. During his regular visits to *The Muppet Show* set, he could interact directly with Jim Henson and the other Muppet performers, who generously encouraged the aspiring puppeteer. "I'd bring a puppet I'd made to the studio in bin liners and Jim would put them on and work them and do voices. This was my first glimpse into seeing more of who he was. I was nobody, I was a 15-year-old kid, but he still stopped and spoke with me and appreciated what I was trying to do."

JOINING THE MUPPET FAMILY

As *The Muppet Show* wrapped up its last season in 1980, Mike found himself at a crossroads. With his formal education coming to an end and production about to begin on *The Great Muppet Caper*, he found a way to turn his dream into reality. After an initial letter to ATV proved unsuccessful, Mike took a more direct approach. He prepared an envelope for Jim himself, including a heartfelt plea for a job, photos of his puppets and a local newspaper article about his unusual hobby.

Determined to deliver his pitch in person, Mike embarked on a quest to find Jim on location for *Muppet Caper*. He arrived just as the crew was wrapping a scene with Robert Morley in a duck pond, coincidentally on Jim's 44th birthday. Mike seized the moment, presenting Jim with the envelope containing his puppetry ambitions.

Two weeks of anxious waiting followed before Mike received a call that would change his life. Producer David Lazer asked if he'd like to do some background work on the film. "That was it basically," Mike says, still sounding slightly amazed. "Jim had read the letter and passed it on to everyone. I heard years later that he took pity on me and said, 'Well, if he's going to be around anyway, why not have him do some puppets?'" Without a formal audition, Mike worked as a background puppeteer on the set of *The Great Muppet Caper*. What started as a week-long gig soon turned into something more permanent. "They just kept me on."

Mike's unconventional entry into the world of the Muppets was a testament to Jim Henson's approach to nurturing talent. "It's not meant to happen that way," Mike reflects, still somewhat in awe of his good fortune. "There's supposed to be auditions and years of training. I was self-taught, I didn't know how to work with cameras and monitors, with acting beats and timings on camera, how to scale the performance to film... I was going from nothing. With anyone other than Jim that would never have happened. He could see potential in people, let them find their way and find out who they could be. He was never one to tell people what to do."

As Mike began his work with the Muppets, Jim took on the role of mentor, guiding him through various roles and challenges. This hands-on approach helped Mike develop the diverse skill set needed to bring the beloved characters to life. "He was very patient with me. He would try me out with different things. Sometimes he'd have me doing Rowlf's hands for him while he was doing Rowlf, or Kermit's hands while he was doing Kermit and assisting. That led to Frank [Oz] using me a lot for helping with Miss Piggy and Fozzie Bear and doubling up for the main characters."

This progression required Mike to master the subtleties of puppet movement. "I had to learn the mechanics of how their muscles and arms would move, so I could mimic their movements in wide shots, then they would come in and do the close-ups with their own voices for commercials and the movies and some TV."

Mike also explains that Jim's patience extended to on-set mishaps. "I was doing Rowlf's right hand and the end of the fuse hit Rowlf's face. It kind of fizzled and smoke came up and they had to stop shooting and repair it, but Jim knew it was an accident. He didn't get mad and didn't make me feel bad. Lesser men would have gone a bit crazy over that or made some comments. He understood and probably thought it was kind of funny. They fixed it and it was fine."

LEARNING FROM THE BEST

Mike's journey with the Muppets quickly evolved from his early background roles. He started as an assistant puppeteer, operating parts of established characters like Sprocket on *Fraggle Rock* for the international versions.

"Duncan Kenworthy, [puppeteer] Dave Barclay and myself were involved in the co-productions. So we did the UK, France and Germany. Sometimes we would do the same episode three times over, in three different languages. I went through a bunch of different jobs on those productions. I think I started out being Sprocket's bum and right hand and ears, so the assistant for Sprocket. Then I graduated to doing Gobo coming through the hole. Jerry Nelson was the main Gobo puppeteer in the tunnel parts of the story, and the voice. We'd have to match the continuity on the postcards and the costume and the speed with which he went through the hole to match the edit for the Canadian version. I was also rigging and repairing puppets. Sprocket's face would get a bit manky and I had to rebuild and repair that. I worked Uncle Matt in the UK and France, in the studio and on location. For the UK versions, Dave Goelz would have to dub what I what I'd done.

"One time I was in Downshire Hill, which was the Henson International Television office, gathering up all the bits of puppets for an upcoming shoot and making sure everything was there. Jim Henson came in, I think he was doing some some production work on *The Storyteller*, and he was confused at seeing me in there: 'Michael, what are you doing here?' He had no idea because his companies were so huge and I had to explain, 'I'm gathering up all the Fraggle bits for an upcoming shoot.' I guess he didn't quite realise the boring minutiae of how the co-production ran. Every once in a while, he would show up at events. We'd be in Paris for *Fraggle Rock*, so he'd fly in by a helicopter or Concorde or goodness knows what else to be at a press event for an opening of a *Fraggle* series in France. He was always everywhere at the same time."

According to Mike, Jim was always observing and he would test people out. "He'd throw something at someone just to see how they would do with it and how they would cope." This approach led to Mike's first speaking part in *The Tale of the Bunny Picnic*, a BBC special filmed in the old *Muppet Show* Studio D stage.

Jim's mentorship went far beyond teaching technical skills. "He had this natural gift to bring out the best in people and everyone somehow wanted to be the best they could be for him. I saw that again and again, not just in myself, but in many other people. He was such a calm, gentle man, he never yelled at people. He'd make the odd quiet comment and leave it at that if somebody wasn't behaving themselves. He had a lot going on, yet he always had time for everybody, whether it was some kids visiting the set, or someone needing an interview."

What struck Mike most was Jim's approachability and patience, even amid high-pressure projects. "He was directing *Labyrinth*, and I had some stupid questions that I was bothering him with during the shoot. He was approachable, no matter how trivial or silly it might be." This democratic approach to leadership made a lasting impression on Mike. "He never made people feel silly or bad or little. He made everybody feel valued no matter how old or young or how important they were. Everyone was equal to him. I've not seen anyone like that before or since."

Jim's calm demeanour and gentle leadership style created an environment where creativity flourished and team members felt valued. "Jim was a good advocate of the Arts and of other people doing puppets and other creative things. He encouraged other people to find their own voice. He was a great supporter of other styles of puppetry and other puppeteers and other people doing things. He enjoyed sharing that with people.

"Around the time of *Dark Crystal* I was hanging out with Jim quite a bit, assisting him on a lot of things. There was one evening he went to see Sergey Obraztsov, who was the most famous puppeteer from Russia's State Central Puppet Theatre. He was performing in London and Jim took me with him to see the show and of course they met afterwards. Jim introduced me to Obraztsov and said, 'This is Michael, he's one of our new puppeteers' and treated me as though I was the most important person in the world. It had nothing to do with Muppets, he just wanted to go and witness this great puppeteer and share that."

As Jim Henson's creative empire expanded throughout the 1980s, Mike observed a growing weight of responsibility on his mentor's shoulders. He draws an insightful parallel to a scene in *The Muppet Movie*, where Kermit the Frog has an introspective moment in the desert, contemplating the responsibility of bringing various characters along on his journey.

"I always felt that was kind of like Jim. As his company grew, especially during the '80s with *Fraggle Rock*, he had all those different companies. He had quite an extensive empire and was doing well with almost everything, animation and *Fraggle Rock* and goodness knows what. I think he felt the burden somewhat of the size and the breadth of the other companies in different countries. He was still involved in a lot of stuff in Canada."

Despite these pressures, Jim's dedication to his creative vision and his collaborators remained unwavering. Mike suggests Jim used his characters, especially Kermit, as an emotional outlet. "Kermit was an extension of him. Kermit could say the things that Jim couldn't say and act in ways that Jim couldn't really act. Every once in a while, Kermit would lose it and Jim would never really do that, but through Kermit, I guess he could."

BEYOND THE MUPPETS

Mike's observations reveal that while Jim Henson deeply loved the Muppets, he was constantly looking to push creative boundaries.

"He had a healthy respect for the characters and a love for them. And certainly a respect for the audience that loved them and also a respect for what those characters had enabled him to do at that point in the early to mid-80s, *The Dark Crystal*, *Labyrinth*, *Storyteller*, *Fraggle Rock*, all those other things. But he was always 10 projects ahead of what was going on.

"What people don't realise now with Muppets is that back then, Jim was always trying new characters, new puppeteers, new puppets, new ideas, and sometimes they wouldn't work and they'd get dropped after an episode, or they'd take a little while to find themselves. But Jim was never stuck on this one dynamic, this one core group of characters, he was always looking for new stuff and had they continued with Jim in that way, we would have seen quite an evolution."

This willingness to adapt and evolve extended to accommodate the changing needs and aspirations of his collaborators, such as Frank Oz's desire to pursue directing. "He knew that Frank wanted to go off and direct films and so he would have lightened the load on Piggy and Fozzie and found other characters. They could have filled their shoes differently so that Frank could be free and new puppeteers could do things with new characters."

Well ahead of his time, Jim envisioned embracing emerging technologies like CGI for innovative puppetry productions. "I remember around the time of *Dark Crystal*, hearing about CG becoming a thing one day, and that he had an idea for a TV show where the puppeteers would perform these CG characters in real time. I'm pretty sure that was in 1981 or thereabouts, nobody even knew what this was at that time and of course the technology wasn't there yet, but he knew that one day it would be. Then he got to do it for the first time with the Steve Whitmire character in *The Jim Henson Hour*, Waldo, named after the Waldo control mitt. Then we did it a few years later for Tizzy the bee with Karen Prell on *The Animal Show*."

Jim's creative ambitions extended to theatrical realms too, with

Mike recalling hearing about early concepts for fantasy-themed Broadway shows.

Mike pinpoints Jim's work in the 1980s as being what he thinks of as "Jim being in his sort of purest form, where that little kid inside him would come out. On *Labyrinth* he was like a kid in a toy shop, he loved directing so much. He was at his happiest when he was performing, because when he was on set he didn't have to be a producer or a businessman. He could just become that performer."

This became obvious even in unexpected moments, like impromptu singing while playing a dog character in *The Tale of the Bunny Picnic*. "One of us would start singing this stupid song between takes and then he couldn't stop himself... I think we were doing 'I'm Just Wild About Harry' and he would do it in this dog voice and he was just so happy."

Mike's fondest memory of Jim Henson perfectly captures the joy and camaraderie that defined the Muppet team. During the filming of a Playhouse Video VHS release in the early 1980s, Mike witnessed a moment of pure, unscripted delight between Jim and Frank Oz.

"Jim and Frank were with Kermit and Fozzie in this attic set," Mike recounts. "Something happened where one of them just got the giggles. Then the other one did, and that was it." The laughter proved contagious, spreading to writer Jerry Juhl. "They just set each other off and tears were running down Jim's face with laughter. It was the best thing I've ever seen in my life. Jim and Frank, just having fun with puppets and getting to play and make each other laugh. It was amazing to see, and I'll never forget it."

This playful spirit was a cornerstone of the Muppet production process, though it sometimes puzzled outsiders. Says Mike, "Often-times, directors and outside people would think, *Who are these crazy people? They're not very professional, they're just farting around.* They didn't understand that if we all had to nail the scene in one take, for the most part, we could and often had to. When it was time to work, everybody worked hard and did amazing things."

The key, Mike suggests, was that this hard work sprang from a place of genuine joy and creativity. "It came out of that spirit of play and child-likeness and innocence," he reflects. "There was an innocence to it all. There was never anything cynical about Muppets or Jim, and that's part of the appeal, even to adults."

WORKING TOGETHER

Mike's skills, honed under Henson's guidance, have taken him far beyond the Muppets and into the *Star Wars* universe. In *Return of the Jedi* (1983), Mike brought to life the memorable character of Nien Nunb, co-pilot to Lando Calrissian in the Millennium Falcon. His portrayal of the Sullustan rebel was so well-received that he was invited back to reprise the role in the sequel trilogy films, *The Force Awakens* (2015), *The Last Jedi* (2017) and *The Rise of Skywalker* (2019).

Reflecting on his experience, Mike shared a conversation he had with Frank Oz at the premiere of *The Last Jedi*: "I was telling him about my puppetry academy and how everything that I'm doing now, even in *Star Wars* and beyond, I learned from those first few years from Jim and Frank and all those guys on the *Muppet Caper* and *Dark Crystal*." Mike expressed his gratitude, but Frank deflected, saying simply, "It's all Jim. It's all Jim."

Mike acknowledges the strengths both Jim and Frank brought to their work, particularly in co-directing *The Dark Crystal*: "I did learn a lot from Frank and still do, he's such a superb actor, performer and puppeteer. He's meticulous and plots and plans everything out. That's his strength. He was very different from Jim in that sense. When I was in the Skeksis, one would come around and sometimes the other, and for Jim, everything was much more sort of general about the world and the feel of the thing. Jim had a different approach to a scene and where the fun and joy were in that scene. For Frank, it was a lot more about specifics and beats and motivations. At the time I thought they were contradicting each other, but I now look back and they were complementing each other."

Mike also highlights Jim's generosity in supporting his collaborators' ambitions: "I think Jim gave Frank *Dark Crystal* as co-director to help launch his directing career because he knew Frank wanted to direct. He could have that under his belt as a feature film directing credit. That was a gift that Jim gave to Frank. A powerful theme that ran through everything Jim did was that we were always better together than apart. We all need to work together to become something greater. You can see that in *Fraggle Rock* and probably to a lesser degree *The Dark Crystal*, there was sort of that spirit behind there. That's definitely something that Jim wanted for us all."

Even small moments revealed Jim's joy in the creative process. One example found him instructing Mike to walk in front of a blue screen wearing his blue Muppet Stuff sweatshirt. "Jim was sitting in the chair in front of the monitor as they were setting up the key for the blue screen and he was like [puts on Jim voice] 'Michael, why don't you just walk in front of that camera there?' He just wanted to see me disappear so I could just be a head walking around on screen. He thought that was the best thing ever. He started giggling and really enjoyed that, just such a simple, stupid thing. But it gave him so much joy."

On *The Storyteller*, Mike observed Jim's directing style on 'The Soldier and Death', for which Mike puppeteered the devil who runs from the sack and the devil on Bob Peck's shoulder: "Jim was very confident and very 'in the moment' while directing; very laid back, relaxed and just enjoying the process of making this TV show." This was despite the technical complexity of the production, which Mike notes was "advanced for its time and a lot of fun".

At a banquet during the filming of *The Ghost of Faffner Hall*, Jim shared a playful reflection on ageing: "He commented on growing older and growing up and what was maturity? He answered that maturity to him was something that he never reached, that it was always just out of arm's reach. I don't think he enjoyed having to be an adult too much. He liked throwing parties and inviting people to them and having fun. He was a a remarkably generous man, I've heard people tell me he would give them very large tips, he wanted to share what he could with everybody."

Although perhaps reluctant to embrace the responsibilities of adulthood, Jim's caring nature made him a father figure to many of his collaborators. "I don't think that was something he chose to be at all, it just sort of happened, but many people saw him as that, in as much as Kermit is to the Muppets. But he enjoyed what he had. I think he enjoyed what it afforded him. He enjoyed his lifestyle and his clothes and his cars and his properties and just being able to go and see things. His hot air ballooning was a big thing for him as well, he would go off and recharge. He enjoyed life as much as he could. But he also wanted that for everyone else, too."

In Mike's opinion, Jim's decision to sell the Muppets to Disney was driven by a desire to focus on the creative aspects of his work. "He wanted to be done with the business side of things [that I think] were consuming him. I don't believe that he wanted to spend his time being a businessman. He wanted to be a creator and a performer and a director and all the things that he enjoyed about it all. It could have been a great partnership."

Jim died before completing the Disney deal. "The very last thing I ever said to Jim was in London at his HIT offices. I said, 'Congratulations on the Disney deal' and he hadn't quite signed it all yet, although it was happening. Next thing I know, I'm in the offices in New York at the memorial after the service, standing next to Michael Eisner. Weird. And then, of course, they backed out of the deal because they didn't have Jim. I think when they bought Muppets, they were mostly just buying the catalogue, and the characters happened to come along with it."

Mike's recollections of learning about Jim's sudden passing in 1990 are a reminder of the profound impact that he had on the lives and careers of those who worked with him. Mike was directing a children's television puppet show in London with fellow performers Dave Barclay and Karen Prell when he received the devastating news from a colleague. Though shaken and aware he owed his entire career to Jim, Mike knew he would want them to complete the day's shoot first. Mike suggested they "do this one for Jim", revealing the tragic news only after they wrapped. Days later, Mike and his colleagues made the solemn trip to New York for Jim's memorial service.

The service itself was an intensely emotional experience for Mike and his friends. "Being part of that memorial service was the hardest thing I'd ever had to do, without question. I thought Jim's family handled it with such grace, they were all very kind to us all about it. Jane [Henson] was a sweetheart. It was an amazing experience, very hard, but also uplifting. I don't think we were all ever the same again."

Even with the challenges faced by the Muppets in the years following Jim's passing, Mike remains confident in the enduring appeal and potential of the characters. "Had Jim been alive, we would have all been extremely busy and made a hell of a lot of TV shows and films, and there would have been a lot more franchises out there. Things would have been very different and that kind of mostly left with Jim."

HONOURING THE VISION

Jim Henson's philosophy of encouraging individuality, creativity and collaboration significantly influenced Mike Quinn, who now strives to pass these values on to the next generation of puppeteers and performers. "I'm starting to mentor other people now and advise them a little bit, in much of the way that I would have wanted when I was starting out, passing on that knowledge, information and work ethic, but also that play ethic. It's not about jealously guarding secrets, which can be a thing for some people. It's about sharing and coming together."

Following Jim's death, Mike and his fellow collaborators have worked to honour his legacy. "As [writer and producer] Jocelyn Stevenson put it in the memorial, we'd all become "Jim seeds", and that's true, but I never feel that we've ever quite been able to do him justice with all our various projects. But we try to do him proud."

According to Mike, some have even reported feeling Jim's presence watching over them as they continue their work. "I've heard from at least three people who have said that they've seen Jim since his passing. They won't admit it because they're afraid of being considered crazy, but I'm beyond that. Different people have said they've seen him around and looking in, usually it's on a shoot. He's kind of just looking in and seeing what's going on."

Mike himself experienced a poignant moment during the filming of *The Muppets* with Jason Segel. "We were shooting on Hollywood Boulevard, hundreds of extras and puppets surrounding us. Looking down from a flagpole was a photo of Jim with an accompanying quote. In that instant, it became abundantly clear, a true 'Rainbow Connection' moment. Jim was happy this film was being made because he wanted us to keep working and keep enjoying our craft."

Mike believes that Jim's primary concern was for the wellbeing and creative fulfilment of his performers. "He wasn't precious about Kermit or any specific characters. His desire was for the performers to thrive, to embrace individuality. If he could speak to us now, I know he'd say, 'Work, have fun, be the best version of yourself and keep creating.' That's what he'd want more than desperately trying to keep the Muppets alive for tradition's sake alone. We all have dozens of new characters inside us, yearning to be developed and workshopped. His message was, 'Don't worry about anyone else, do your thing, have fun doing it and do it well. Somewhere in the middle we'll come together and meet at some point."

Ultimately, Mike feels that the best way to honour Jim's memory is to embrace the values and approach to life and work that he embodied. "He wants us to be happy. He wants us to enjoy our work and to create, and if we can do that, then we're honouring him and we're honouring ourselves and each other. Collaboration was important to him. He enjoyed that and that's something that I'm trying to push towards more in my future, working less in isolation on my own things and collaborating more with great people. It's another lesson from him I'm still trying to put into action."

BRUCE MCNALLY
ART DIRECTOR AND DESIGNER

"Jim's rule was if the creative guy disagrees with the business guy, the creative guy takes precedence."

Initially reluctant to take a full-time position, Bruce McNally transformed from freelance illustrator to the creative force behind much of the Muppets' visual identity, overseeing everything from merchandise designs to the Jim Henson logo.

* * *

The year was 1976, and while most of Britain was tuning into *The Muppet Show*, Bruce McNally was busy missing out. Sceptical of puppets and buried in freelance work, he seemed an unlikely candidate to join Jim Henson's creative revolution.

Bruce's introduction to the Muppet phenomenon came through an enthusiastic office mate. "This guy kept raving about this new puppet show. It was on every week at seven." But Bruce, often working late or decompressing at the local pub, remained unconvinced. "I must say I was prejudiced against a puppet show. I thought that sounded a bit naïve. As soon as I saw it, I realised the depth of it and the humour in it."

Fate intervened while Bruce was on a freelance gig in France. His persistent colleague, now aware of an art director opening at the Muppets studio, urged Bruce to make contact. Reluctantly, Bruce called, but with an unexpected twist. "I spoke to the production secretary and said, 'I don't want the job that you're advertising, but what I would like is the illustration generated by it.'" The production team, possibly unfamiliar with Bruce's unique request, took his name and number with the promise of getting back to him.

A month of silence followed before the studio reached out, inviting Bruce for an interview. However, the life of a freelance artist is rarely conducive to scheduling, and Bruce found himself in the awkward position of declining, not once, but three times. "I was mortified," he confesses. "I didn't want to be rude or offhand with them, but I was stuck with deadlines."

When Bruce finally made it to ATV Studios, he met with executive producer David Lazer. As Lazer flipped through Bruce's portfolio, mostly filled with sleek advertising work, his interest seemed to wane. That is, until his eyes fell upon a series of illustrations Bruce had created for Jolly Green Giant, a famous advertising mascot for the Green Giant vegetable brand. "I'd animated a pea, a bean and a carrot. The runner bean was depressed, the pea was angry, the carrot was disillusioned and nobody cared about them in favour of sweetcorn."

At that moment, Bruce noticed a monitor in Lazer's office displaying a feed from the studio floor, where the puppeteers were setting up for a segment featuring the Swedish Chef. "All the puppeteers were operating cabbages and carrots and beetroot. I pointed and said, 'That's exactly the kind of stuff I do.' He said, 'Oh, you understand that vegetables can talk?' and I said, 'Yeah, of course,' because I'd been keen on animation since I was about 10. He asked if I wanted to do a test and draw the characters and he said, 'Our art director in New York says that the characters cannot be drawn because they were created for television.' I said 'I don't think anything has been created that cannot be drawn. You put life into it in a different way to compensate for the different medium.' Anyway, I went down, I drew the characters and he liked them."

After his vegetable-inspired breakthrough, someone ushered Bruce onto the studio floor, where he met Jim Henson and the puppeteers including Frank Oz, Dave Goelz and Richard Hunt. "Quite honestly, I nearly fell through the floor. I couldn't believe I was meeting this guy, he was this big tall, smiling, gentle guy and that's how he always was," Bruce fondly remembers of his first encounter with Jim.

Bruce's talent caught the attention of the Muppets team, and they offered him the job on the spot. However, he reiterated his desire to focus on illustration work rather than taking on the role of art director. "I didn't want to sit in meetings and argue the toss about things. I just wanted to create characters and illustrate." David Lazer, sensing Bruce's potential, explained that the Muppets' skyrocketing popularity had led to a flood of licensing requests for new merchandise. Bruce agreed to take on illustration work, but remained hesitant about accepting a full-time position.

NEW SURROUNDINGS

For three months, this arrangement continued smoothly. The Muppets were riding high on a wave of success, with their blend of sophisticated humour and lovable characters capturing audiences across the UK and beyond. But as the franchise expanded, so did the need for dedicated, full-time talent.

David Lazer approached Bruce again, pressing him to reconsider the full-time position. Bruce, still protective of his freelance lifestyle, responded, "I've got a very good business, it's very varied, I don't want to get tied down to one thing." He admits now that his response might have been "pretty arrogant" in hindsight. Lazer, however, was persistent. With the foresight of a seasoned producer in a rapidly evolving entertainment landscape, he insisted, 'This thing is going to be much more involved than you could ever imagine.' I asked how and he said, 'I can't explain it to you, but trust me.'"

The early days of *The Muppet Show* coincided with a transformative period in television. The variety show format was evolving, and Jim Henson's creation was at the forefront of this change, blending adult humour with family-friendly puppetry in a way that hadn't been seen before. Sensing the potential for something truly revolutionary, Bruce finally agreed to take the job, but on his own terms. He negotiated for the creative freedom to run things his way, maintaining the artistic focus that had made him successful as a freelancer. "I thought I'd give it six months and see how it went, but from the first minute, it was fantastic."

Bruce's tenure with Jim Henson's company was a stark contrast to the typical corporate entertainment structure of the time. "There will never be another company run the way Jim ran his, it just doesn't happen anymore," he says, highlighting the creative-first approach that defined Henson's leadership. "Jim's rule was if the creative guy disagrees with the business guy, the creative guy takes precedence. That's unheard of today."

This philosophy fostered an environment that was not only productive, but genuinely enjoyable. "He wanted everyone to have a nice time. And we did. I think it was the most incredible place that any of my team ever experienced."

Bruce's early days at ATV Studios were a whirlwind of activity, reflecting the Muppets' rapidly growing global popularity. "I had six phones in my office and at any time all of them could be going off at the same time. It could be America, Germany or France. Holland was a big one, Germany was a huge market."

Initially, Bruce's team comprised himself and a part-time secretary, but as the workload increased, he advocated for additional support. "The first thing I got was a secretary. Then there was a guy there who they had already hired [John Stevenson], who was more or less a student, and he spent his time in the workshop, drawing bits and pieces. He was then sent up to my office, which he wasn't very keen on because it wasn't very glamorous compared with the world of the workshop, where all the women were mothering him and looking after him."

As the workload intensified, Bruce's department grew from a one-man operation to a bustling creative team. Among his key hires was Les Skinner, the very colleague who had first introduced him to *The Muppet Show*. Bruce's recruitment pitch to Les mirrored David Lazer's earlier persuasion: "Drop the job you're doing, they don't appreciate you, come here, it's gonna be great, trust me." Together, Bruce and Les would make an enduring impact on the Muppets' visual identity. Their collaboration on the official logo, which incorporated Jim Henson's handwriting, exemplified the perfect balance of personal warmth and professional polish that characterised the Muppets' aesthetic. "I got Jim to write his signature several times and then I took it and drew it out before Les lettered it."

Bruce's experience at the Muppets studio was a blend of creative freedom and organised chaos. His role constantly shifted between managing international business relationships and spontaneous creative work. "I could be arguing with a German licensee who wants to go into production without approval on some bedding line that he'd created, and he would say to me, 'Trust me, it looks just like your drawings,' and I'd say, 'No, send it in, send it in,'" Bruce explains. "But then I might get a call from the workshop or from Jim to say, 'Could you go down, they're having trouble designing some sheep,' so I'd go down and work with the puppet builders and create a load of sheep or monsters."

One of Bruce's significant contributions was his work on the *Muppets Annual*, a popular UK-specific publication. "We took over creating the 64-page book and we used to make up cartoon strips, games and puzzles." His creative influence extended far beyond the printed page. Bruce's character designs would often make unexpected journeys from his sketchbook to the screen. "Often, unknown to me, Jim would go down and hand that to the builders and say, 'Build that guy there,' some huge beast, and it was a tremendous privilege."

Bruce recalls Jim praising him after they completed work on the first annual. "Jim was actually in Hollywood working on the first Muppet movie and he saw a copy of the finished annual. We had Telex in those days before fax, and he sent me a Telex saying how delighted he was and to take the guys out for a meal on him."

The Muppet Show's ability to attract top-tier talent from across the entertainment spectrum—from country music stars to Hollywood action heroes—spoke to its broad appeal and cultural impact. Even with his gruelling commute from Kent to ATV Studios, Bruce would occasionally stay late to glimpse the stars. However, he admits to some regrettable misses: "Sometimes if I finished about seven I might phone down and say, 'Who's the guest star?' I can remember them saying, 'Oh, it's Kris Kristofferson and Rita Coolidge,' and to my horror today I'd say, 'Nah, can't be bothered,' I'd go home. I missed Sylvester Stallone because I thought, *I don't want to see that guy in that boxing film*. What an idiot."

However, there were moments of pure joy when he interacted with the guest stars. "I got to see my idol, Buddy Rich. It was fantastic. The place was packed. Then there were Raquel Welch and Danny Kaye, I had a brief chat with him."

One of Bruce's most cherished memories involves operating a puppet alongside a true icon of Hollywood's golden age. "It was the first character I ever designed and had built completely from scratch, a character called Angus McGonagle, the Argyle Gargoyle. My family's Scottish, so I said to Jerry Juhl, the writer, 'Please let me design that character.' He was a mad Scotsman with a red beard, a big long tongue like a gargoyle and so I got to operate him on 'Singin' in the Rain' with Gene Kelly. I looked up from the monitor that I had on the ground. I had my arm up with Angus and he gave me the most fantastic smile. It's just a silly little moment, but I've never forgotten it. Julie Andrews was the same, a beautiful beaming smile from somebody who's just about to go on stage just because I was standing there looking. Wonderful stuff. It was magical."

Beyond the studio, Bruce's role extended into the world of Muppets merchandise. He worked with many licensees on products ranging from bendy toys to plush characters and toy vehicles, reflecting the Muppets' expanding commercial reach. This period—the late 1970s and early 1980s—witnessed a boom in character merchandising, with the Muppets leading the charge. Bruce made significant contributions to the Muppets' publishing initiatives as well, demonstrating the collaborative spirit that Jim Henson cultivated. Speaking about *Muppet Magazine*, which ran from 1983 until 1989, Bruce notes he collaborated on developing the format with Jane Leventhal, Vice President and Director of Jim Henson Productions' publishing division, and her editing team.

"We set up the format and worked out the regular features. I drew the logos for each section and we created the look of the front cover and the masthead. I was down as art director, I think. But because it was created in New York, after that I didn't have any day-to-day involvement with it. I know that the people in the photographic workshop over in New York, East 62nd Street, had a lot of fun. They would have Diana Ross come in for photo shoots and Christopher Reeve, which was a great thrill for them which I envy because I would have liked to have been involved in as art director, but not to be in a different country."

Bruce is proud of the children's books he worked on in collaboration with author Jocelyn Stevenson, titles that allowed fans to experience new adventures with their favourite felt friends. "The first children's book that was illustrated was 1980's *Robin Hood*. I was looking at a couple of *Muppet Shows* and the big production number was Robin Hood and they had fabulous costumes. I said to Jocelyn, 'Why don't we take that Robin Hood idea and make a 48-page children's book of it?' So we did. That's how things were done. We'd say, 'Let's do this,' and we did it. Random House looked at it and said, 'Absolutely, just do it.' I designed and illustrated the whole thing. It was the first book I'd illustrated, and we put it out and it was a great success."

The next title was 1981's *The Muppets Go Camping*, which was also illustrated by Bruce and written by Jocelyn. "We would sit down and come up with an idea. Jocelyn would write it and I would design it and illustrate it. I did those things while I was doing other work," he says with a smile. "It was just all fun."

Bruce's wide-ranging role saw him frequently travelling between England and the United States, particularly New York, where he worked closely with the publishing and licensing divisions. His involvement in character design, production, and corporate branding meant that he was an integral part of the creative process for many of Jim's projects.

"I designed a lot of the corporate logos later on. There used to be a lot of company names, the main company in New York was Henson Associates, which was HA! with an exclamation mark, and when I started the company in England it was lowercase h, lowercase e, exclamation mark, he!, which was Henson Enterprises. And then, I think as much for fun as anything else, Jim came up with Henson International, which was HI!, Henson Universal Music, which was HUM!, Henson Organisation which was HO!, so you had this HE, HUM, HI, HO, HA stuff going on and I worked on most of these, designing corporate logos or suggesting things."

Bruce's recollections of Jim Henson's venture into more ambitious projects like *The Dark Crystal* highlight the sense of wonder and excitement that surrounded these productions. "Jim came in with Frank Oz and Brian Froud, who had designed it, and I was there because I had things to check out with him all the time. It was a wonderful moment, because it was like he was a little kid. He looked around and said, 'Wow, this really is big-time movies,' and it was such an innocent thing to say."

GETTING ANIMATED

As the 1980s progressed and the initial Muppet mania cooled, Bruce found his department fully staffed but with a dwindling workload.

"I remember when we finished *The Muppet Show* after five years and 120 shows, with all those fabulous guest stars. Jim had the best of the best, and he didn't want to drag it out for the sake of dragging it out, he wanted to do new projects. I went to him one day and said, 'What if we animate the characters so that you're not directly involved?' I quoted *Yellow Submarine* [1968] and said, 'The Beatles were never involved in it, and yet it was a massive success and ground-breaking in a way that was unheard of at the time.' While Jim didn't pursue that exact concept, it sparked the idea of depicting the Muppets as their younger selves in the long-running *Muppet Babies* [1984–91]. "Rather than commit the puppeteers to another puppet series, it was animated. So we worked on designing the characters as babies, and that was great fun."

Bruce's creative influence extended to another Henson creation, *Fraggle Rock*. "I think Jim got about 30 people around a table in Sterling Forest in New York State, and we brainstormed this idea." The show's multi-layered concept was ambitious for children's television, featuring three interconnected worlds: the giant Gorgs, the Fraggles and the Doozers. "It was a terrific concept of three different stories running simultaneously, but all having an impact on each other."

During the show's development, Bruce's personal passion for composting found an unexpected home in the show's universe. "I said, 'There's got to be a compost heap,' and I explained it was all about recycling and the writers could do a lot with that," Bruce adds, reflecting on the discussions during the show's development that led to the creation of Marjory the Trash Heap.

While Bruce didn't design the Fraggle characters, he was a vital part of their transition to the printed page. "I'd designed hundreds of books by then for Henson, then *Fraggle Rock* came along and I did many dozens of books for that. I used to travel to New York, work with Jane Leventhal, and I would always give the artists the chance to design the things, but they would say, 'If you can design it, we'll illustrate it.' So I'd design everything page by page, brief them out and then I'd come back to England, go back three months later and approve all the artwork."

Bruce's problem-solving skills came to the fore during the production of the British segments of *Fraggle Rock*, particularly in dealing with actor Fulton Mackay's appearance as the lighthouse keeper. "Fulton was quite a tricky character to work with. I know they were at their wit's end because they wanted him to grow a beard and his beard wasn't thick enough. I came up with a drawing and showed it to Duncan [Kenworthy], saying, 'Why don't you kit him out like this? Get him a false beard and a bit of a wig, and tog him up with an Aran fishing jumper, a blue heavy serge coat over the top of that.' He went for it immediately, so I went with him to the wig people in London, and we fitted him out with a wig and the hair and he was happy as Larry after that."

Bruce's involvement with *Labyrinth*, adapting the film's story for a children's book, shows the company's approach to storytelling across different media. "I was on set every day and I was phoning New York every day, talking to Louise Gecko, who was the writer for the children's book. We were taking the movie story and looking at how we could do it as a picture book. We had to change certain things, but always keep the essence of it. I was involved with a lot of the photography stuff and publicity shots with David Bowie and Jennifer Connelly."

When asked about his impression of Bowie, Bruce admits the musician was "very distant". He recounts a moment during the production when Bowie arrived on set with a severe hangover, causing the crew to be stood down. "Of course, he was being guarded in this room where he was sitting. I like to think he was feeling kind of ashamed of himself really, stopping the entire production for a hangover. But he approved all the illustrations I had done that had his image in them for the book, and I suppose he must have been feeling pretty crap but he didn't comment on them, just nodded, signed them and we went our separate ways."

Bruce encountered challenges in attempting to transition to a new role within the company. "I could never get into production full time with Jim because there was a kind of glass wall that I couldn't get through. I could do bits, but I couldn't become production. I remember one lawyer in New York saying to me, 'Jim's got his people where he wants them, and it's very hard for you to move from one place to another.'"

Despite his success in publishing and licensing, Bruce felt a pull back towards production work. "I'd done everything I wanted to do with publishing. I used to work on the big coffee table books with Abrams in New York, children's books with Random House and Reinhardt Winston, fabulous prestigious companies, but I wanted to go back into more challenging stuff."

Bruce's post-Muppets experience reveals an interesting irony in his career trajectory. It was only after leaving the company that he received the opportunity he had long sought, designing characters for 1989's *Dog City*. Dubbed "*On the Waterfront* [1954] with dogs" by Jim Henson, it was a high-concept idea that blended familiar genres with the Muppets' unique sensibility. The later adaptation of Bruce's character designs into an animated series proves the lasting quality of his work. "I like to think the characters were so well designed, kind of three-dimensional when I gave them to the puppet builders, that they worked as animation."

GETTING OFF THE ROLLERCOASTER

For all the success of the Muppets, Bruce muses that the administrative burden of running an ever-expanding company may have weighed on Henson in the later years of his life. "Through the five years of production [on *The Muppet Show*] it was wonderful. It was a rollercoaster that got faster and faster, the shows got more and more sophisticated and the budgets for the sets and the characters went up, up and up. He could take it because it was all success."

By 1990, Bruce suggests Jim was "getting very bogged down with the administration of it all. I know at one point in the New York office they reached over 100 people. I used to work with half a dozen guys in New York and nobody thought about titles, or who was senior to who, we were all caught up in this wonderful excitement. My office was pretty simple. I ran it, and there was very little admin on, or what I call bullshit, going on. We didn't have that many meetings. I used to decide things, and they got done. But in America, it was much more committees, and committees about committees, and that's what Jim was not keen on."

Jim's planned creative contract with Disney, which would have allowed him to focus on his own projects while Disney handled the licensing of the Muppets, never came to fruition because of his death. Bruce, who was in New York on Henson business, had a rare one-on-one lunch with Jim just days before his passing.

"Although he and I were friendly and never had any fallouts, if he had anything to discuss, he always used to invite somebody else to lunch, so you had this funny triangle of people, which deflected what you were trying to talk about. This particular time, it was just him and me, which I thought was very unusual. I said, 'You know, in England and in New York, we're like *The Muppet Show*, you are Kermit and you've got all these dysfunctional people cloying for your attention and it must be such a pain in the arse.' I apologised to him for my part in bogging him down with things when he just wanted me to run with them. I was working on a production in New York when Jim died. I'll never forget the phone call with the terrible news. I just couldn't believe it."

Through the subsequent outpouring of shock and sadness from the public, Bruce admits he learned more about the impact of Henson productions than he did when he worked on them.

"I remember a little Hispanic boy saying, 'I love *Sesame Street* because it made me feel part of the world, whereas before I thought I was not involved.' It was because Jim's characters were crazy and diffi-cult in different ways. And they were all different, like Gonzo. Even Dave Goelz never knew what Gonzo was, and he was the puppeteer. He was a thing and was deranged. People identified with them, think-ing, *If he can get by and be accepted, maybe I can.* And I never even knew that. I was so busy going through the working day that I didn't see the bigger picture."

In the years following Jim's death, Bruce witnessed a shift in the entertainment industry's focus, with CG and other technological advancements overshadowing the art of puppetry. "In the 1990s, when I was returning to the world I used to be in before Muppets, it was already at a stage where I couldn't talk about Muppets or puppetry because it was already so old-fashioned. It was all CGI and nobody was into it. They were interested in Aardman Animations, but not the Muppets."

Bruce highlights several key aspects of Jim's management style and creative philosophy. His rule that "in any disagreement the creative guy prevailed" fostered an environment where individual talents could shine. "Everybody had a special place, that's what Jim allowed," Bruce adds, emphasising the importance Jim placed on nurturing creativity and allowing his team members to thrive in their respective roles.

Looking back on his time with the Muppets, Bruce's sentiments echo those of many who worked closely with Jim Henson. "Knowing Jim was such a magical experience that it changed my life. He directly changed the lives of everybody who worked for him, certainly at my level."

The impact of those years continues to resonate with Bruce and his former colleagues. "I still see my artists and keep in touch with them. At some point, we always say what an amazing time we had which will never be seen again. We all had freedoms that today are unheard of."

AUSTIN PENDLETON

ACTOR, MAX IN THE MUPPET MOVIE

> "He calmed the set down just by his presence, just by what he gave off, what he emitted."

A RESPECTED STAGE and screen actor, Austin Pendleton's suggestions helped shape his character arc in *The Muppet Movie*, demonstrating Jim Henson's willingness to collaborate with performers to enhance their roles.

* * *

In the late 1970s, *The Muppet Show* had taken the world by storm, so when the news came that the Muppets would make their big-screen debut in director James Frawley's 1979 film *The Muppet Movie*, fans eagerly awaited the chance to see their favourite characters embark on a grand cinematic adventure.

Among the cast brought together for the film was Austin Pendleton, a seasoned actor known for his work on stage and screen in the likes of *What's Up, Doc?* (1972) and *The Front Page* (1974). Austin portrayed Max, the reluctant sidekick to Charles Durning's villainous Doc Hopper.

"Well, let's see. I don't think I had to audition for that one. I think they called me before I'd even heard it was going to be made. I remember I had been going to do a play and it had just fallen through. And then they called about this and I read the script."

Austin found himself somewhat underwhelmed by the character of Max as originally written. "I went and met with the director, and I told him I thought the part was kind of undeveloped. The character didn't change in the script I read. I was disappointed that I wouldn't be in the play that I wanted to be in, so I thought, *Why should I go out there and spend a long time making a movie with a character that doesn't develop at all?*"

The feedback led to a significant transformation in Max's character arc. "I think the way it used to start was that Max went along with everything Doc Hopper wanted, and he stayed that way throughout the movie. And I said, and this is going to sound very funny, 'He should be like the guy in *On the Waterfront* who changes his entire perspective during the movie.' So he wrote three or four scenes to make that happen."

Austin's request for script changes took his agent somewhat by surprise. "My agent kept saying to me, 'Do you want to do it?' And I said, 'Well, I'm asking them maybe to rewrite the part a little bit.' My agent said, 'What?!' I said, 'It's not a part that's very interesting to me and maybe if we just wait, something more interesting will come along.' Instead, he made me have a change of perspective during the movie and I became more sympathetic to Kermit and Piggy. So I did it. It took a while, and it also made it a longer part, so I was out there for quite a while working on it. It was a very good experience. I was slightly arrogant, but I hadn't made an important movie in a few years, so I wasn't in a position to behave like that."

ON-SET TENSION

As a fan of *The Muppet Show*, Austin was thrilled at the prospect of acting alongside Kermit and the gang. "I had watched the show and then I wondered what it would be like acting opposite the Muppets." The experience took some getting used to. "They are, after all, pieces of cloth. The thing I liked the most was I was going to be acting with Charlie Durning again. I was in the original cast of the Broadway original production of *Fiddler on the Roof*, and Charlie had a part in that when we were out of town, in the trial period. We got close, we would hang out together.

"Before *The Muppet Movie*, there were two or three other films we were in, one was *The Front Page*. And now here I ended up with him in this Muppet movie. So many scenes were us in the car, and sometimes in the middle of the night in the lot at night. Between the camera setups, we would drive around and talk about our personal lives. It was just awfully nice being with him."

Austin's connection with Durning extended beyond their time on the set of *The Muppet Movie*. "I called him from the airport in Los Angeles when I was gonna fly back to New York after it was over, just to say I enjoyed seeing him again and he said: 'I'm about to be in another movie, I think you should audition for that movie.' And that was an Alan Pakula movie called *Starting Over* [1979] with Burt Reynolds. So that phone call led me to my next film. If I hadn't been in *The Muppet Movie*, I never would have been in the Pakula movie."

Despite the warmth that radiates from the screen in *The Muppet Movie*, Austin reveals that the atmosphere on set was not always as lighthearted. "It was tense. Jim Henson and Frank Oz were lovely. The director was going through a really hard time. He was a terrific director, but he was nervous and highly strung, so there was just a lot of tension on the set. It's belied by the atmosphere of the movie, which is very sweet-natured, but he did a great job directing."

Perhaps James Frawley felt pressure directing puppets? "Let's put it this way: Jim Henson or Frank Oz directed the next few Muppet films. That was the only time they used a director from outside their own complex. I think possibly the director was feeling the pressure of that," Austin explains. "It's the most utterly benign film I think I've ever been in, but it had one of the tensest atmospheres, so that's always interesting to me. That shows you how good the director was because he could create this thing even though he was having a rough time. I don't think he was having a rough time with Jim Henson and Frank Oz. He just hadn't been part of the whole Muppet experience."

Did Austin ever witness Jim or Frank Oz offering advice or guidance to James Frawley? "I certainly never saw it happen. I don't remember that we ever had to reshoot it. That's when you could tell that there's behind-the-scenes tension, when you shot a scene and then a week later you have to shoot it again, and then a week later you have to shoot it again. That didn't happen at all, at least in anything I had to do with it, so there was the feeling from both Jim Henson and Frank Oz that they seemed very relaxed and supportive of what was going on."

Regarding Charles Durning having to re-record his own voice throughout the film, Austin notes that Frawley "pressured Charlie to go over the top and do a very extreme performance. Then when he saw a rough cut of the film he said, 'Charlie's way too high, it's too much.' So we had to loop every scene I was in. I think that's the only film I've ever been in where that was the case. Sometimes you have to loop an occasional line, but this was like every scene. I think I was in the looping room a few months after we made the film for hours and hours and hours and hours."

One highlight of Austin's time on the film was working with actor Mel Brooks. "That was wonderful. He made up his own lines. I want to say he was on the movie for a day or two. I knew him because I'd been in a play with his wife Anne Bancroft, so I knew her pretty well. The two of them would come and see shows I was in and we would go on afterwards, so it was terrific when he came on board. What he said had very little to do with the script, but it was inspired."

A UNIQUE PERSPECTIVE

When asked about the challenges of working with the Muppets, Austin acknowledges the complexity of the process. "It was pretty smooth running. Jim Frawley was extraordinarily helpful to me, but he was jumpy. It was a technically difficult thing to shoot, it's sort of like an animated film with real actors in it. I never felt there were delays because of the technical difficulties. It wasn't a set where people fought with each other. From my experience, the heart of it was working with Charlie Durning."

For Austin, being part of such a film with such a devoted fanbase came as something of a surprise. "I don't think I've ever been in a film that had that kind of success, where a big thing was made out of the 40th anniversary, probably because so many kids have seen it in the intervening years. But it's a lovely movie.

"It didn't exactly set the town on fire when it first opened. It did well, it wasn't a flop and a lot of people went to see it. But when people started calling me up to come and do interviews or speak to groups of people and I said, 'Why do you want me to?', they'd say, 'Well, this is the 40th anniversary of *The Muppet Movie*,' and I thought *And?* I've never been in a movie that had celebrations on its 40th anniversary. *The Muppet Movie* was a movie that people wanted to take their kids to, and that people enjoyed. But it wasn't like an event, but that's also what's so appealing about the movie. It's very unassuming and it doesn't feel like it's trying to be a big deal."

Austin notes that Jim Henson "was a marvellous man. There was a spirituality about him and he also had an ever-ready sense of humour. He calmed the set down just by his presence, just by what he gave off, what he emitted. He calmed the waters a lot. I was shocked when he died. It was unbelievable because he was this utterly healthy guy. He was a lovely, lovely person."

When the word "genius" is brought up in relation to Jim, Austin doesn't hesitate to agree. "I would use that word, and I don't throw that word around. People use the word genius just for someone extremely talented, but a genius is a very particular thing. A genius is someone who has a perspective that nobody else has on the world, and that was Jim Henson."

TONY CHARMOLI

DIRECTOR

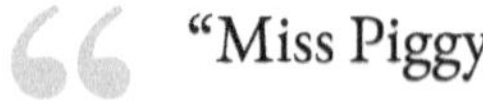 "Miss Piggy was a handful."

AN ACCLAIMED TELEVISION director known for his work with variety shows and specials, Tony Charmoli brought his expertise to the much-loved TV special, *John Denver and the Muppets: A Christmas Together*.

EDITOR'S NOTE: It was in 2019 that I first reached out to Tony Charmoli about his time directing 1979's *John Denver and the Muppets: A Christmas Together*. I received a swift response from Paul Manchester, the co-author of Tony's 2016 autobiography, *Stars in my Eyes*, in which Tony had written a chapter about his time with the Muppets. Paul explained that Tony wasn't well enough for an interview, but he kindly gave me permission to reproduce the chapter here. Paul has written a few words to give some context to the chapter. Tony sadly passed away on 7th August 2020.

* * *

Tony Charmoli was born in the small town of Mount Iron, Minnesota and moved to New York City after WWII once he finished his college degree. He began dancing on Broadway and soon gained notice for staging productions for early TV, shows like *Can't Stop The Music* and *Your Hit Parade* (1935–59), among many others.

Over his career, Tony won three Emmy Awards (*Your Hit Parade* (1951–54), Shirley MacLaine's *Gypsy in My Soul* (1976) and Mitzi Gaynor's *Tribute to The American Housewife*, 1974). But he always said that he was most proud of his many Directors Guild Awards, one of which was Best Director for *John Denver and the Muppets: A Christmas Together*. Directors Guild Awards were voted on by his fellow directors and were therefore more meaningful to him.

One of Tony's greatest strengths (aside from being extremely well organised and having a consistently pleasant approach on set) was that he excelled at making women look great on camera. After decades of working with many of the greatest stars of the 20th Century, it was only natural that he would be called on to direct Miss Piggy.

What follows are his own reflections on his time with the Muppets.

* * *

I thought a Christmas special starring John Denver and the Muppets was a great idea. I had worked with John when he guested on the Doris Day special a few years earlier, and I was very fond of the Muppets from the first time I saw them on TV. I grew even fonder when I had the opportunity to direct this wonderful TV Christmas Special.

There was a lot of holiday pageantry going on, and Miss Piggy was in her dressing room getting all primped up for the next scene. She was powdering herself vigorously and I thought it would look better from a different angle, so from the director's booth I said,

'Miss Piggy would you turn a little more to the right while you're powdering yourself?'

She turned to Jim and coolly asked, 'Mr Henson, WHAT is the director's name?'

He replied. 'Tony, his name is Tony.'

Miss Piggy turned to me as directed, then in a crisp undertone added, 'Anthony, you're treading on thin ice!'

It cracked me up. She was a handful.

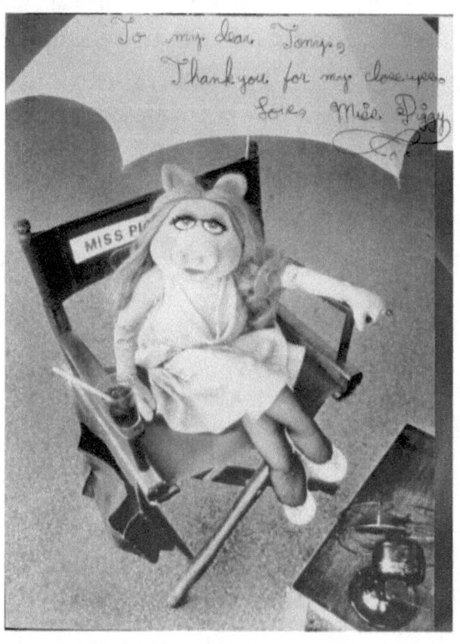

Miss Piggy's signed photo to Tony. Courtesy Paul Manchester

John Denver seemed to fit in easily with the Muppets, as he did in a big number set in a town square. I surrounded him with real dancers and singers doing an up-tempo winter holiday production number. Having done so many appearances alone with his guitar, John seemed energised when supported with singers and dancers. It appeared he was fully enjoying all the extra help.

Later in the show, he sang 'Have Yourself A Merry Little Christmas' with Rowlf the Dog at the piano and it was very touching and sentimentally slushy, but wonderful and deeply heartfelt. It's difficult to accept we will never get to see that combination in performance again.

The tableau of the holy birth done Jim Henson style was a treasure. I added some gossamer angels floating above the manger scene to Jim's approval and delight.

The topper was that the Directors Guild of America honoured me with a Best Directors Award for this special. That night we celebrated with a late dinner in Beverly Hills. Coincidentally John was also having dinner in the same place. I was still so excited from the win I went over to his table to show him the trophy.

I was so disappointed with his non-reaction. He seemed so unenthused he didn't even congratulate me. I don't know what might have happened prior to my getting there, but even a slight acknowledgment would have been appreciated... but none? What a bummer. We had a good time at our table anyway. That was the last time I saw John and was shocked when I heard about his fatal plane accident. I still have my Directors Guild Award to remind me of the wonderful time we had working together.

I ran into Kermit a few years later while I was on a shoot for a pageant at a high end hotel in some exotic locale I can't quite remember. We had a shoot scheduled for the pool area that day and when I got there, Kermit was lounging on one of the pool lounges in the midst of another shoot.

I said, 'Kermit! What the fuck are you doing on my set?'

Kermit was of course very polite and explained that their shoot was running long, but they'd be finished momentarily. He was much more respectful than Miss Piggy. He called me 'Mr Charmoli.'

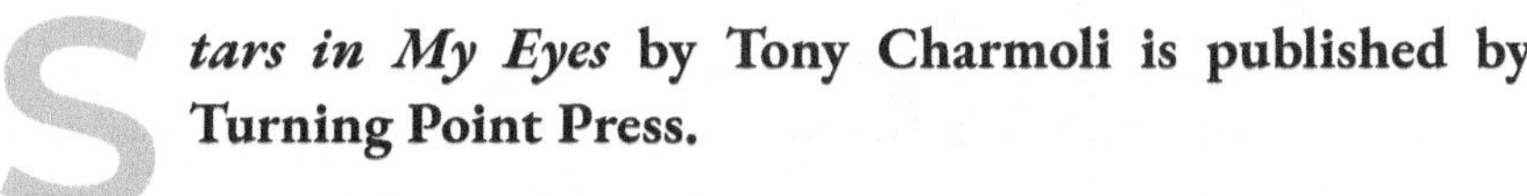

S*tars in My Eyes* **by Tony Charmoli is published by Turning Point Press.**

JOCELYN STEVENSON
WRITER AND PRODUCER

"It was heaven to have this experience so early on. It completely informed the rest of my career."

STARTING at *Sesame Street*'s publishing division, Jocelyn Stevenson became a key creative force in developing *Fraggle Rock*'s vision of promoting world peace through entertainment.

* * *

"If you want to change the world, start with kids." This epiphany, born in the halls of Stanford University, set Jocelyn Stevenson on a path that would revolutionise children's education and entertainment. From a $1-a-week daycare centre to one of the creative forces behind *Fraggle Rock*, Jocelyn's story is a testament to the power of persistence, creativity and the belief that television can be a force for good.

Her journey began in earnest during the late 1960s and early 1970s at Stanford, where she shifted her focus from medicine to child psychology. This change aligned perfectly with the growing preschool movement of the time. After graduation, she joined a small group that started a daycare centre with a unique approach. "If people were going to bring their kids to this daycare centre, they'd just pay what they could. Some people could only pay $1 a week, that kind of ethos." The centre's progressive philosophy attracted an eclectic group of parents, including folk singer Joan Baez.

It was during her time at this daycare that Jocelyn had her first encounter with *Sesame Street*, a moment that would alter the course of her life. "It was one of those days where I was the last teacher there and I was with the kids and I was also trying to sweep the floors so I turned on *Sesame Street*, and they were riveted and so was I, the floor did not get swept that day." The experience was transformative. "I couldn't believe what I was seeing. They're doing for 9 million kids what we're trying to do here for 30. I've got to get to New York!"

Inspired by what she saw, when Jocelyn eventually moved to New York, she walked into the Children's Television Workshop (CTW), determined to be a part of this revolutionary approach to children's education. "I have to work here," she told them, only to be met with scepticism. "They looked at me like 'Yeah, you and a million other people.' When I gave them my very scant CV, I could practically see them throwing it in the circular file as we used to say, right into the bin."

Jocelyn's persistence paid off when she secured an interview through a friend of a friend connection. However, her first encounter with the publishing department head, who had *Sesame Street Magazine* in her remit, was far from smooth. "I sat in the lobby waiting for her, all dressed up ready for my interview, and she'd forgotten. Oh my God, it was just horrible. You sit there watching all these people come in and out, and you know that feeling when everybody else belongs there but you?"

The situation took an unexpected turn when the interviewer, realising her mistake, took Jocelyn out for lunch, during which she was offered a secretarial position. "My soon-to-be boss apologised, saying I was overqualified for the job. Are you kidding?! I jumped at the opportunity, telling her I'd empty waste paper baskets, whatever!

I didn't care, just as long as I could get in." Her determination paid off, and within two weeks, she had become not only the secretary but also the assistant editor of the magazine.

Jocelyn's role at CTW soon brought her into contact with Jim Henson and the world of the Muppets. She describes the meticulous process of creating the magazine: "In those days, you took all the mechanicals for the magazine over to Henson's. We had tracing paper over the top of all artwork that included Muppets. These needed to be approved by Jim Henson. He himself at that point was doing all of the vetting of every drawing of a Muppet, and would use the tracing paper to blue-line his corrections. Lesson number one, quality control. Jim didn't want 20 million representations of the Muppets out there. He protected the essence. He used to call Don Sahlin, who was one of his designers and chief puppet makers, his 'essence checker'."

The day Jocelyn first went to the Henson offices carrying the magazine's mechanicals, it was raining. In fact, that's why the person who normally did that job had opted out. "But that was another opportunity I wasn't going to miss. By the time I travelled across town to the Henson offices, my bell bottom jeans—the fashion of the day—were soaking. The water had wicked up to about my knee. So I sloshed into this impressive office and these big wooden doors opened and there was Jim, sitting behind his big desk. I stood there like a drowned rat, and then he looked up, saw the humour in the situation and I liked him immediately."

This encounter marked the beginning of a long-lasting collaboration. "He was a creative mentor, and I had the opportunity to talk to him over the years and we agreed on so many things, most significantly on how important screen-based media is and how much potential it has for educating kids." Jocelyn notes that in those early days of *Sesame Street*, they were still grappling with the fundamental question: Can TV educate children?

As Jocelyn's role at the magazine evolved, she began to explore her creative side. "I started to write little poems, and I liked to write little Muppet stories." These pieces often featured characters from *Sesame Street*, allowing her to delve deeper into the world she had admired from afar. The magazine's approach was not just creative but also scientific. "We were using the same research tools for the magazine to research print literacy that they were using on the show."

Jocelyn's fascination with the educational potential of children's media is clear when she describes a particular revelation: "You have a pre-literate kid, a kid who can't read, who looks at a page in the magazine with a number of things on that page. At the top of the page is a picture of Count von Count. Without being told what to do, the child knows that they're supposed to count the objects. To me, that was mind-blowing."

The conversation then turns to the international reach of *Sesame Street*, particularly its presence (or lack thereof) in the UK. Jocelyn explains the cultural dynamics at play: "There was always a battle here because you had *Play School* [1964–88]. It was the BBC saying, 'Well, we've got *Play School* and we've got our own thing. *Sesame Street*'s very American."

Despite these challenges, there were efforts to create a British version of *Sesame Street*. "They were doing different versions of *Sesame Street* all over the world. Why not a British version?" Jocelyn ponders. She mentions that this effort eventually resulted in *The Furchester Hotel*, which ran for 103 episodes from 2014 to 2017 on CBeebies in the UK. The unofficial *Sesame Street* spin-off featured some appearances by the likes of Big Bird and Count von Count, while some *Furchester* characters also appeared in *Sesame Street*.

STARTING A NEW CHAPTER

Jocelyn's life took an unexpected turn when she met and married a Scotsman, leading to her moving to the UK. Faced with the prospect of leaving *Sesame Street Magazine*, she approached Jim Henson with her news. His response was characteristically supportive and opened a new chapter in her career: "'Well, you can come work for us at

Muppets.' Because I'd been in the publishing department at CTW, it made sense that I worked with the Henson publishing department. For a while I was doing Muppet annuals, Muppet books, *Muppet Show* characters for kids." She found this work to be "a really good exercise in learning character writing".

Jocelyn shares a conversation with Jim that illustrates his approach to leadership. When she informed him that she wouldn't be living in London, his response was both surprising and empowering: "'I don't care where you live as long as you get the job done.' That was genius, because then it puts it all back on you, right? So I did everything in my power never to make it a problem that I didn't live in London."

Jocelyn introduces a key figure in the Henson Company's international expansion: Peter Orton. "Peter headed up the distribution arm of the Henson company, eventually it became HIT, a separate company." Orton's role was crucial, as he had been responsible for international deals for *Sesame Street* and understood the global appeal of *The Muppet Show*. "He knew that *The Muppet Show* was one of the most popular shows internationally and that puppets are easy to dub. Peter's wife Sue was my husband's sister, so I was kind of vaguely related to him."

When Jocelyn's first son, Freddie, was born, she asked Jim Henson to be his godfather. "Jim said yes, and he was christened up in Scotland, because we were living in East Lothian at that time." Sensing an opportunity, Peter Orton arranged with Jocelyn to sit next to Jim Henson at dinner the night before the christening. Orton's message to Henson was clear: "You have a once in a lifetime opportunity to create a show for children that is internationally co-producible." Adds Jocelyn, "*Sesame Street* was difficult to do in other countries as so much of it involved real humans."

Jim immediately grasped the potential of this idea. "He called it 'The international children's show'. You have to appreciate that Jim was a creative. While he was supported by good business people, he was the one who ran that company. So he starts to think about the international children's show and says to us, 'We can reach kids globally... I want you guys to create a show for kids that will help stop war.' I love that he would get so excited about that. Of course, all the rest of us were getting excited."

The first step was for Jim to organise a meeting with various company members and creatives to consider the concept. "A lot of the discussion was that people don't see other people's perspectives, nobody was saying, 'What are the toys gonna be?' It was a high level discussion: 'What level can the kids understand these ideas and how can we do this?' I think it was Jane Henson who came up with the idea of the three species and that they would be different sizes, the big Gorgs and the little Doozers and the Fraggles. That immediately gives you a different perspective. Then we just went from there."

This meeting led to the formation of *Fraggle Rock*'s original creative team: Jocelyn, Duncan Kenworthy, Michael Frith, Jerry Juhl and Jim. "He put us in a room together. There was no, 'We have to have a Bible and two scripts done by MIPCOM,' there was none of that." The team would work all day at Henson's house in Hampstead, soon realising that "the most important thing to a Fraggle was figuring out what's for lunch and how to sing about it. I learned so much from Jerry Juhl. What an opportunity to learn from him. He was such a goofball."

Jim would join them in the evenings due to his commitments to *The Dark Crystal*. "I remember Jim on the floor in tears, he was laughing so hard. It was such a good release for him to come and work on this goofy thing. We laughed all the time."

Fraggle Rock marked a shift in Jim's involvement with his productions, with Jocelyn noting that it "was the first thing he did that he didn't have to be there every day." By placing what he called his "A Team" in charge—Dave Goelz, Steve Whitmire, Richard Hunt and Jerry Nelson—Jim was able to focus on other projects while still contributing to *Fraggle Rock* by directing early episodes and performing characters like Cantus, Jocelyn's "favourite character ever." She describes the working environment on *Fraggle Rock* as "totally vision driven. [Producer] Larry Mirkin said, 'We were all in the service of the best idea.' It didn't matter whose idea."

On the subject of how the name *Fraggle Rock* was chosen, Jocelyn explains, "We discussed various ideas and Jerry Juhl said, 'Well, we had these characters [on *The Muppet Show*] we never really used called Frackles.'" The team didn't like "Frackles," but it led to "Fraggle," which clicked with everyone. "It was no one person's idea. You've got to trust the process."

AN INTERNATIONAL PRODUCTION

The production was spread across multiple locations: California, Toronto, London and New York. To manage this global collaboration, they turned to emerging communication technologies. "I was one of the first people in the UK to use the internet as a private user." Jocelyn describes the early days of what would become the internet, then called Telecom Gold, primarily used as an intranet for British Telecom. "Jerry Juhl was always interested in what you could do with technology, he knew about modems, and we could send our scripts to each other. At that time you had to have the same hardware and software, this was 1980."

Though she hadn't written for television, Jocelyn was keen to write for *Fraggle Rock*. "I said to Jerry [Juhl], 'Would you mind mentoring me, teaching me the skills? Do you think I could write *Fraggle Rock*?' He said, 'You're gonna be fine; you know how to write character.' That was his secret, being able to write character." When she expressed her desire to write for the show to Jim, he replied: 'That's great. And if it doesn't work, you can always go back to heading up the publishing.' Again, enlightened leadership. It makes it safe for you to take a risk because he didn't frame it as a risk."

A steep learning curve marked Jocelyn's transition into screenwriting, particularly regarding industry terminology. She recalls a time when she was unsure about the meaning of a "two shot". Confused, she called Jerry Juhl for clarification: "I said, 'Jerry, I know this might be a stupid question... what is a two shot?' And Jerry's [response was], 'It's a shot with two people in it.' He said, 'You're making this a lot harder than it is. It's very simple.'"

One standout memory for Jocelyn was episode 18 of the first season, which featured the minstrels and Jim Henson as Cantus. As a rookie writer, Jocelyn was grappling with imposter syndrome. Jerry Juhl introduced them all to Linda Seger's book, *How to Make a Good Script Great*. Jerry gifted her a copy with a humorous inscription: *Or in our case, How to Make a Great Script Sublime*. This book, along with Jerry's guidance, taught them about the three-act structure and other crucial writing techniques.

"Three-act structure kept us honest... each episode was like a little play. It's always about wanting the basic idea to be big, but then you have to make it work as a story. Red was a character I felt particularly close to, having created her alongside Karen Prell, the performer, and this story was centred around Red finding her song. That was the first time I felt deeply emotionally invested in the story. I came to it with such commitment. This helped me figure out how to make the script work cohesively, beyond just worrying about technical aspects like what a two shot was."

The collaborative nature of the writing process on *Fraggle Rock* was clear in how they approached each script. "We would all work on each other's scripts. Jerry was the most creatively generous person I've ever known. He'd do a pass on a script of mine, then Jerry, his wife Susan, who also worked as a script editor on the show, Larry [Mirkin] and I would sit down together to go through each script. This is where I learned about giving notes to writers from Jerry, because you've got to motivate people at the same time as saying something isn't working. Jerry would read a script of mine that he'd done a pass on and say, 'I love that joke you put in there, it's hilarious.' I'd say, 'Jerry, that was your joke.' He'd genuinely forgotten he'd added it, and would simply say, 'Yeah, but you set it up, it was fine.'"

Jerry Juhl had his own way of assembling the new writing team. "Jerry did not want kids TV writers on *Fraggle Rock*. Instead, we had bpNichol, a poet; David Young, a playwright; and various other interesting people that did not do kids' TV writing for the show. It was sometimes a question of me trying to teach them the form. The three-act structure we used in the Fraggle world was so flexible."

Since her time on *Fraggle Rock*, Jocelyn has strived to create similar environments, where everybody is serving a bigger idea. "It's not to make money for the shareholders and it's not to see how many toys we can sell and how much more plastic we can put out there." This underscores the idealistic, creative-driven approach that characterised Jim Henson's projects. "I was in my 30s, it was heaven to have this experience so early on. It completely informed the rest of my career."

Working on set with Jim was always a learning experience for Jocelyn. She notes a particular incident: "He was directing and I was standing next to him. In those days, you didn't really have radio mics and people would get all tangled up in their wires with their microphones. It was my script, and we were blocking a scene and Jim said, 'This isn't working,' and I said, 'I know, I'll fix it.' I stood there because I was planning to go up to the office during a break to rewrite the problematic section. But he said, 'Now...' So the other thing I learned was to think on my feet because you have to rewrite on the spot. It was really good training."

The production of *Fraggle Rock* required significant commitment from the team. Jocelyn remembers, "They would help us find a place to live in Canada for the shooting, which began on 9th March, 1982—I remember that because it was my eldest son's second birthday. I had a three-month-old daughter, and we brought a nanny to help. It was a family decision to embark on this adventure, with the mindset that if we could get through this, we could get through anything."

Jocelyn emphasises the importance of music in the show's structure. "The writer had to figure out where the song was going to be, the song had to move the story on. We were working with Dennis Lee and Phil Balsam. Phil, God rest his soul, has left us, we're all sad about it. But they got it. They had to write two songs every episode, and we almost never rejected one. It was such a pleasure to work with them."

The production schedule was demanding, but rewarding. "Our lives kind of fit in around the *Fraggle* schedule, but I was always there as much as I could be. By then, we'd not perfected, but we were getting better at the whole digital way of communicating. It was exhausting." The decision to end the original series came from Jim Henson himself. "We did 96 episodes and Jim just thought *That's enough*. We then started the discussions about ending it. We figured out the whole way the thing ends with that almost tagline, 'You can never leave the magic,' that's so very Jerry Juhl. We were sad for a minute and then looked at it as an opportunity. It's hard work, so we were tired of leaving home for months at a time."

THE TALE OF THE BUNNY PICNIC

Jocelyn's collaboration with Jim Henson extended beyond *Fraggle Rock* to projects including *The Tale of the Bunny Picnic*. "My favourite Jim story about *Bunny Picnic* is how he and Cheryl [Henson] came up with the idea. They loved walking across Hampstead Heath and Primrose Hill at twilight, seeing lots of bunnies out. Being the creative minds they were, they thought, 'What if there was a picnic?'"

Jim asked Jocelyn to write the 45-minute special, a challenge she accepted while heavily pregnant with her third child. "I was literally writing while in labour because I never wanted my personal circumstances to be a problem for production." The writing process wasn't without its challenges. When Jocelyn handed in her script, Jim's initial reaction was unexpected: "I don't like it, but I don't know why." Drawing on her recent zen readings, Jocelyn suggested they review the script together. "This process allowed him to pinpoint what he didn't like and what he did. There was actually more that he liked than disliked.

"Jerry [Juhl] joked that Jim's reaction was because I hadn't included 'that exorcism scene in the third act that he's had in his brain for the last 10 years.'" In the end, Jocelyn feels rewriting the script made it "a billion times better. I'm really pleased with how Bean Bunny's story turned out."

Jocelyn highlights Jim's creative process: "Jim often got these vivid visual ideas, like the Skeksis from *The Dark Crystal*, inspired by illustrations he'd seen. I loved doing stuff for Jim. He had this gift of taking an idea for a character and elevating it. Take the dog in *Bunny Picnic*, for instance. That brilliant dog, you just feel for him, with that mean farmer and all. It scared some kids, but it was powerful."

The special featured puppeteers, like Steve Whitmire and Louise Gold, with whom Jocelyn would continue to work on other projects. She takes pride in one particular line from the special: "Nobody ever said being a bunny would be easy." Reflecting on this, she says, "It's moments like that when you're working with puppets and kids that you stop and think, *Where else could you say something like that?*

The Tale of the Bunny Picnic remains a cherished project for Jocelyn. "It was so much fun to do and Jim was there, he co-directed it. It was a really good Henson experience." The special's enduring popularity is evident in fan feedback: "People still tell me they watch *Bunny Picnic* every Easter with their family."

Another series, *The Ghost of Faffner Hall*, borrowed some of *The Muppet Show*'s showbiz sparkle. "It was done for HBO in the States, because they were kind of our go-to kids producer at the time, and it was Tyne Tees in the UK. Jim asked me to come to dinner with Milt Okun, he was the producer of Peter, Paul and Mary and was the music director of John Denver. Milt told us that in the States there was no money for music education and Jim said, 'Why don't you go create a show about music for kids?' That was my dream."

Jocelyn's research led her to the work of R. Murray Schafer, a Canadian composer and music educator known for coining the term "soundscape". Schafer's book *Ear Cleaning* provided inspiration, with its central idea that "everyone can make music". This concept became the foundation for *The Ghost of Faffner Hall*, a show Jocelyn developed while Jim was working on *The Jim Henson Hour*.

"The first musician who agreed to do it without saying to me, 'How much am I gonna be paid?' and 'Who else is doing it?' was Joni Mitchell. She liked the idea. We had this big brochure we'd send out and she was going to be in Paris anyway, could she come on her way back?" Once Mitchell was on board, other musicians followed suit. "I will always be grateful to her for starting the ball rolling."

GOING BACK TO THE ROCK

While Jocelyn wasn't involved at the executive level on the 2022 revival series, *Fraggle Rock: Back to the Rock*, she has nothing but praise for the team. "Lisa [Henson] and Hallie [Stanford], whom I adore, brought in Max Fussfeld and Alex Cuthbertson as showrunners and executive producers. I absolutely loved working with them. They came from *New Girl* [2011–18], a live action sitcom, but they got, and wanted to get, the whole Fraggle ethos. The energy behind it was really Johnny Tartaglia. He played Gobo and he'd done these little Fraggle shorts during the pandemic that he filmed on his own, and they'd been so popular. His thinking was, *Maybe this will lead to a series*."

The first season was produced during the pandemic, which presented some challenges. "They asked me to be in the writers' room on Zoom for three weeks during the first series and to write one of the first scripts. That was really great. They were in LA, so I couldn't go past nine o'clock at night UK time. I'd start at six in the writers room, and then I could go till nine, and then they had to carry on with it.

"My job mostly was essence checking, because I was the only one who had really worked on *Fraggle Rock*, and then it was also structural. They are comedy writers, and it was so much fun being in a room. I'd never been in an American writers' room before, so this was interesting, how everybody contributes to the scripts. We'd be pitching on a Mokey joke and it's really fun and you're loathe to stop it, but I would just go, 'Guys, guys, it's great, we're pitching a very funny Mokey thing, but this is a Wembley story, and we haven't seen him for two scenes.' And Matt and Alex would invariably say, 'Oh, yeah, you're right.'"

For the second season, Jocelyn's involvement deepened. "They asked me to be in the room for the whole 20 weeks, so I worked on every script for the second season. It was really a nice little vote of confidence for what they felt I brought to the room. It was very Henson in that everyone was contributing. So *Fraggle* then evolved, and the second season has taken it places we just never imagined we would be able to go, but you can because it's *Fraggle Rock*."

As well as her involvement in new *Fraggle Rock*, Jocelyn recently published the first in a new series of books, *The Waterubas*. Initially planned as a streaming series for Netflix, she found herself struggling while working alone and "organised a creative summit in Bath, bringing together eight people I trusted to give honest feedback. Writing a novel for nine to 12-year-olds was a new challenge. I quickly learned that describing scenes in a book is very different from writing for the screen. In a script, you can write, 'Miriam turned into water,' and you have a whole team to figure out what that looks like. In a book, you need to describe what it feels like, what it looks like, what's happening."

Reflecting on the impact of *Fraggle Rock* on her life, Jocelyn says, "*Fraggle* has truly been the gift that keeps on giving. Not only has it provided financial gifts, such as the recent Apple TV+ production, but when I mention my involvement with the show, people invariably know it, so that's nice too."

Jocelyn pauses, thinking back to her time working with Jim Henson. "Jim was really good at sitting in meetings and listening. Then at the end of the meeting he would synthesise what had been said and he made everybody in the room feel as if it was their idea. One idea would come from another idea, it's not like, 'My idea is better than your idea.'"

This method created an environment where ideas could build upon each other, rather than compete. "He was able to put people together that 10 minutes before wouldn't have imagined working together. He was a magnet for people. That's a gift. We were all, as Larry Mirkin used to say, 'in service of the best idea'. It's the idea of the 'Jim seed'—when Jim died we were all seeds blown from a dandelion, planted in different places but still influenced by his approach."

ind out more about Jocelyn's book *The Waterubas* at thewaterubas.com

LARRY MIRKIN
PRODUCER

> "It was always about 'What's the best idea?' that serves the show and the moment in the scene."

Hired to take over *Fraggle Rock*'s production after a brief meeting with Jim Henson, Larry Mirkin helped shape what would become one of Henson's most ambitious international projects.

* * *

Larry Mirkin's life changed forever when he met Jim Henson in 1982, but the seeds of that encounter were planted years earlier.

Larry grew up in Cumberland, Maryland, a small city in the Appalachian Mountains about 100 miles from Washington, DC. Cumberland had an interesting claim to fame: it was an early test market for cable television in the United States. The mountainous terrain made it challenging to receive clear broadcast signals, necessitating this new technology. Among those early broadcasts was Jim's 1950s sketch comedy, *Sam and Friends*.

While Larry was too young to remember *Sam and Friends*, he

does recall the commercials Jim created during that period. However, like most children, he didn't have his future career path mapped out, let alone any inkling he might work with Henson one day. As Larry puts it, "When you're seven, you don't say, 'When I grow up that's what I want to do,' or 'I'm going to work with this guy.'"

In 1975, Larry moved to Canada to work as a story editor and producer in the CBC (Canadian Broadcasting Corporation) TV drama department, but after eight successful years he found himself at a crossroads. "I was getting restless and wondering if I should return to the United States. CBC was facing its first round of budget cuts. I'd just finished a TV movie and had projects in development, but I was uncertain about my next steps." Larry remembers a conversation with a friend where he expressed his concerns about work and his personal life. "I jokingly said, 'There are no women in Canada.' She replied, 'You might not be looking in the right place.'" Remarkably, within the same week, Larry met both his future wife and Jim Henson, dramatically altering the course of his life.

The opportunity to meet Jim arose when Duncan Kenworthy, who had overseen the first 12 episodes of *Fraggle Rock* in Canada, decided to return to Britain to focus on the show's international co-productions. Jim's team needed someone to take over the Canadian production, preferably a local hire with a strong background in working with writers.

"I was recommended to [Executive in Charge of Production] Diana Birkenfield and Jim by Stan Colbert, the Head of Variety at CBC," says Larry. "The show was produced out of the CBC Variety department, not the Children's department. When they said they wanted someone who worked well with writers, I was suggested because that's where my strengths lie. I always approach things from the script outward."

Larry's first meeting was with Diana, whom he describes as "a wonderful woman from Pittsburgh, and in my experience, I've never met anyone from Pittsburgh I didn't like. But she was really special." They connected instantly. "She said, 'I think you should meet Jim.' I flew to New York to meet Jim at his offices in the glorious building on East 69th Street, which also housed the Puppet Workshop, which was filled with a number of Muppet makers, even on a Sunday, and countless Muppet creations. Diana introduced me to Jim and left us to talk. I explained a little bit about my background and how I worked, not only with writers but just in general, that I'm very collaborative and that while the buck would stop with me, I'm a 'best idea wins' kind of guy. We're all there to serve the idea of the show and the 'management structure' is just there to facilitate things."

After a brief chat, Diana returned to check on them. "She said, 'I'm just checking how things are going. Larry's a drama producer at the CBC, and no commitments are being made at the moment.' Jim, having known me for only 20 minutes, responded, 'Well, I'm ready to make a commitment.' I attempted to be cool and producerly, asking, 'Can I have a day to think about this?' and he said, 'Oh sure, take the time you need to think about it.' The only criteria was that I had to go and meet Jerry Juhl. Jerry was what I call the 'literary voice' of the Muppets and a co-creator of *Fraggle Rock* who deserves his own book sometime. In any case, at this point, we needed to meet because if he and I didn't get on, nothing was going to work."

For years, Larry hesitated to share this anecdote about his appointment as a *Fraggle Rock* producer "because it felt like it was about me. But this was Jim in a nutshell. I had the skills he needed, but what he knew, and I didn't know, was that I had the personality to work with this group of people. Because this whole group of people worked together in a very collaborative way. There was no creative tension, or any other kind, on the set. It was always about 'What's the best idea?' that serves the show and the moment in the scene."

Adds Larry, "That's one thing I want to emphasise about Jim, his skill in seeing qualities in people that would benefit the group." He cites examples such as Henson's casting of a young Karen Prell as Red Fraggle and his discovery of Carol Spinney, who would become Big Bird and Oscar the Grouch. "I wasn't there, but the story I've heard many times over the years is this: Apparently, Carol was performing at a public festival and Jim came to see him and what he did was terrible and he knew it. When Jim came up to meet him afterwards, he said, 'You know, I really liked what you were trying to do up there,' and then he hired him to play Big Bird and Oscar. So there's all that kind of quality about how Jim found the right people to work together."

PRODUCING FRAGGLE ROCK

Larry's new role was to take over the work that Duncan Kenworthy had done on *Fraggle Rock*'s first 12 episodes before he'd returned to the UK. "Duncan's episodes hadn't gone on the air. It was produced in I think the spring and summer of 1982 and didn't air until January 1983. So this was November of '82 and I was coming in to do the next 12 episodes and then ended up doing the next 84 episodes out of 96 total."

While some minor adjustments to casting and set design were necessary, Larry feels that the show was in excellent shape. "It was just getting the scripts working better because it's a very ambitious show and had many ideas. As with most shows that have many ideas, in the early days you try to put all the ideas into one episode. Not that those episodes were bad, it was just, 'How do we build from that?'"

Fraggle Rock's premise and international reach placed Larry at the centre of an innovative creative endeavour. "There was an underlying idea about the interdependence of all of us, of all living things and a philosophical principle of having the audience, the kids at home, see this interconnectedness, even when the characters don't usually see it." The show's complex world-building posed challenges and opportunities. "So we have the Fraggles, the Gorgs, the Doozers and the humans, and then we also had the Ditzies which were only in two episodes, and they were something that was in the original pitch document and none of us knew what the hell the Ditzies were.

"But one of our writers, this terrific experimental poet named bpNichol, had this great idea about the Ditzies. The thing we never could figure out, or talk about, was why is there light in these caves? We never dealt with a light source and we all kind of squinted about that for many years. bp came up with the idea that it's the Ditzies who provide the light and they gain the energy to do that from the Fraggles singing. It was a sublime idea, and he wrote a script in which the Fraggles stopped singing and the caves went dark."

These intricate details were all in service of *Fraggle Rock*'s central themes. "It was this notion that if we can see how we are all interconnected and interdependent with one another, perhaps we can reduce conflict. Not that we said any of that directly, but that was one of the big ideas in the show, along with joy and singing and all the interrelationships we showed. When you have a show that espouses these ideas, there's a certain demand on how you produce it. We had to make the show according to the same things we believed in. So it was always very collaborative, the best idea won. You could disagree about something, but we'd always say, 'What would be the better idea?'"

This spirit of collaboration and openness was key. "I always believe that you've got to create an environment where stupid ideas are welcome, because if you can't feel free enough to have a stupid idea, then you'll never have a good idea. So we did that everywhere and we laughed an awful lot. As much fun as you would think it would be to make this show, it was more fun than that. It was exactly as you would hope it would be given what the show was about."

Larry adds that pressure to boost *Fraggle Rock*'s profile in the United States sometimes led to some difficult conversations among the show's creatives. "It was a co-production between Henson Associates and the CBC. I was hired by Henson's, but because I'd worked at the CBC as a contract producer, I also knew the system so I could help translate for both companies. *Fraggle* was the very first series on HBO and they only had about 8 million subscribers at that point, although we tended to get around three million of those. In Canada we were across the country on the CBC, and we would get between two and a half to 2.7 million an episode. We were on Sunday nights against *60 Minutes*, and we would sometimes beat *60 Minutes*, not that we were ratings-driven."

Though there was a large awareness of *Fraggle Rock* throughout Canada because it was broadcast on the public network, Larry notes that in the US "it was on this little thing called HBO that not a lot of people had. It was a movie network basically, and we were the very first original series they commissioned, not just kids' series but any series. So there was a lot of concern about how we could get more publicity in the US. Gobo would get invited to appear on *The Tonight Show* [1954–], for example, and Jerry, Jim, Jocelyn Stevenson and I would talk and say, 'Jim, you really can't do this because the Fraggles exist in this fantasy world and if you bring them out into the real world, first they don't know anything about the real world, and second you're going to undermine the whole thing for our main audience, which is kids, because you're breaking this fantasy.'

"I said, 'You could take Travelling Matt, but he won't understand anything, you could take Doc and Sprocket, but that doesn't help you a whole lot.' Jim said, 'You know, you're right, we won't do that' and he was probably the only producer in the world who would have done that. He had a long view—the original show is still playing all these years later—and that's one of the things that I just admire so much about him."

Fraggle Rock's international co-productions added another layer of complexity. "The way we worked on it with the international audiences in mind was that we produced the bulk of the show in Toronto. The show was constructed so that the Doc and Sprocket workshop scenes were a way for the audience to see themselves in the local, by which I mean national, depiction of Doc and Sprocket. And the workshop was how we entered the world of *Fraggle Rock* through the Fraggle Hole in Doc's baseboard. Wherever the world was in the UK or North America or France or Germany would look like the audience's world, and then once you went through that Fraggle hole you were into the bulk of the show.

"If the show was 24 minutes, I would say we produced 20 to 21 minutes of that material for our versions for North America, then we just had to be careful about how we wrote the ins and outs of those things so that the local people in the UK or France or Germany could make it work."

Larry marvels at the different approaches taken by the international teams. "The Germans did *precisely* what we did in Canada; they designed the workshop to look exactly the way we did. They shot it exactly the way that we did. In Britain, Fulton Mackay became a lighthouse keeper, not an eccentric inventor, and I thought it was really lovely what they did there. Then in France, it was set in the south of France and Doc was a chef and Sprocket was called Croquet, which was pretty funny. Other than making sure that we didn't cause extra problems for the people in these other countries, I had nothing to do with it."

Despite his role as the driving force behind *Fraggle Rock*, Jim Henson's presence on set was relatively infrequent during the show's initial production period. Says Larry, "I didn't have a real appreciation for this until many years later, but he was doing *Labyrinth* a lot of the time when we were doing *Fraggle*. I'm used to running the show and just sort of doing my job, so creatively Jerry Juhl, Jocelyn and I really ran things. In terms of the management of the show, it was me, Martin Baker and Diana Birkenfield. I'm an old-fashioned producer, where you're supposed to know both parts of that profession, the art and the craft of it, so that the craft supports the art. What I didn't realise until many years later was that for the performers *Fraggle Rock* was a big deal, because Jim had left it in particular to Jerry Nelson and Dave Goelz, as senior members of the team, to be the leads on the set." It was the first time that Jim hadn't been on the set most of the time as the leader.

By empowering his team to handle the bulk of the creative work on *Fraggle Rock*, Jim demonstrated his confidence in their abilities and his willingness to step back and let others shine, though Larry notes that Jim's occasional visits to the set were always memorable.

"He performed Cantus and Convincing John and he would

always direct a few episodes every year. I would say he came every couple of months and it was wonderful when he was there. He was there a bit more in the first 12 than in the shows I produced, but he shot the first show that I produced and so he and I were in the edit room together and got to know each other a little better. We had a great relationship, but I had a closer relationship with Jerry Juhl and Jocelyn and he just trusted us to do it. He would come in and give his opinion about things, but he didn't give lots of notes or anything like that. But whenever he came it was an extra energy on the set and he was a wonderful director, particularly for *Fraggle Rock*."

Larry particularly remembers Henson's direction of the episode 'All Work and All Play', which focused on the industrious Doozers. "That was just beautifully done, and I learned a tonne from him because I hadn't done puppets, let alone kids. We didn't think of it quite as a kid's show. We kind of wanted to entertain ourselves and thought of it in the most general sense as family."

Jim's approach to directing left a lasting impact on Larry. "What I learned from him because I came out of scripting and writing was how he led with his eye as well as his performing talents. He asked me questions such as, 'What does it look like?', 'What's the shot going to be?', 'How does that relate to what the story is?' He helped me understand more deeply that transition from the page to the screen. That was independent of everything I also learned about puppetry, which took me some time. The first two or three episodes I kept saying, 'Why are we doing that take again?' and then finally it clicked. I said, 'Oh, I know why we're doing that again, I can see it now.' Jim was very good at the mechanics of the scene in terms of how to make a scene play well. The overarching kind of story points were less important to him, except in the most general kind of way. But it was his eye that you see not only in *Fraggle Rock*, but you see in bigger ways in *Labyrinth* and *The Dark Crystal*."

FINDING THE EMOTION

After proving his value as a creative collaborator on *Fraggle Rock*, Jim offered Larry a staff position with the company. However, Larry declined, preferring to maintain a more flexible arrangement that allowed him to pursue his own projects outside of children's entertainment and puppetry.

Nevertheless, Jim recognised Larry's storytelling skills and was eager to keep him involved in his productions. "Diana [Birkenfield] had said to me, 'Jim doesn't have anybody in the company that has the way of working on story that you have,' so that was probably what he wanted me to do. So in addition to producing, I had separate contracts that were an annual retainer for six or seven years where I would just read and comment on scripts or meet with him and others about stories. That included things that I'm not credited on and things that didn't happen, but also projects like *The Witches*, *Little Muppet Monsters*, the animated *Fraggle Rock*, *Muppet Babies* and all sorts of other things."

One of the most significant projects Larry consulted on was *Labyrinth*. "When I first saw *Labyrinth* he had a first draft from Terry Jones and I hadn't seen the earlier material. I stayed with it from that point on until they got into production in terms of giving notes and having meetings with him and I had meetings with him and with George Lucas, who was the Executive Producer. I did not meet Terry Jones or Elaine May."

Larry's involvement focused on refining the script and strengthening the emotional arc of the story. "If I remember this correctly, the first draft had many of the things that are in the movie now, but the kind of emotional line of the show we didn't think was strong enough. So Laura Phillips was brought in, who had written a lot of emotional shows on *Fraggle*, to add that 'heart element' to it and she did several drafts that got a lot stronger but some of the other funny stuff kind of got lost, which I think would have come back anyhow, it just was sort of where it was in the process. Jim gave it back to Terry

Jones at that point, and he only kept a bit of what Laura had and went back to a lot of stuff that was in the first draft. Then they were near production, and I was doing *Fraggle Rock*, so I wasn't involved with the Elaine May rewrites and I'm not quite sure what was involved there."

While Larry praises the casting of David Bowie and the film's stunning visuals, he feels that there was still room for improvement. "The only thing I said to Jim later and the only thing that surprised and bothered me—and I think it's a wonderful movie and people love it—but I still think there was more to make of Sarah's story. Sarah doesn't have a song, and it's her show. Now, I think that might be because who knew if Jennifer Connelly could sing or not, but it always struck me as off balance that she didn't have a song that revealed more of what was going on for her. I think it would have brought even more heart into the picture."

Beyond these minor critiques, Larry remains a fan of the film and its intricate world-building, which he likens to the attention to detail found in *Fraggle Rock*. "All of those details are very Henson-y. Like on *Fraggle* there's all the Doozer stuff that's happening in the show that was never scripted. We'd need to have Doozer constructions around the basic scenes, but these weren't written. Faz Fazakas— another genius in the group responsible for all the radio-controlled puppetry among other innovations—and Tom Newby and the rest of Faz's team would talk about those by themselves after the production meeting.

"They and their team would figure out what needed to be in each of those shots, but it wasn't confined to just some random background activity. They'd have huge stories about who the characters were, what they were doing, etc. They had this whole other world in their heads, which none of us knew about, but if you look at those background characters, there's always something happening. Again, that's another example of how collaborative and creative the world is, because you can't do all this by yourself. You can't have one person say, 'You have to do this or you have to do it this way,' and this was always about making it possible for everybody to contribute. Otherwise, you deprive your artists and crew of any creative agency."

This commitment to excellence and collaboration, Larry believes, was a direct reflection of Jim's approach to his work. "It was never said this way, but there was a demand for excellence always in anything we ever did and that's just because that's how Jim was, how we all were. You wanted to do the very best you could. *Fraggle Rock* was like a repertory theatre. We did an adventure story one week, we did a little sentimental story the next week and we did a farce the next week. We had all these puppets and sets and props and nobody complained no matter what the hours. We were just trying to make it wonderful."

Jim Henson's generosity and appreciation for his collaborators were legendary, as Larry discovered firsthand. "I had this retainer and I read whatever was sent to me and sent notes out. One of those things was the *Fraggle Rock* animated series. Jerry and I, and maybe Jocelyn, met with the head writers only once and they did a very good job with the show. I think I made comments on the first 10 or 12 scripts, but they knew what they were doing. A few years later, out of the blue, I got this little cheque for my work on the show. Jim gave me half a per cent of the net income from *Fraggle* animation just because he thought I should have it. We never talked about it. That's just the kind of guy he was."

Jim's approach to production was equally unconventional. "He had this belief, unlike other producers, that you should live where you want to live and live your life the way you want. We'll get everybody on a plane and go to someplace, whether it's Toronto or wherever, and we'll make the thing. Jocelyn told me that he would pay long-distance bills if you called your family." These gestures, while seemingly small, had a profound impact on Henson's team. "He was in a position where he had the wherewithal to do these things, which a lot of producers don't, but he just did this stuff for everybody because he appreciated them. That's why everybody would have done anything for him and why all of us still feel this connection to him. We still feel like we're doing anything for him."

Jim Henson's influence continues to inspire his former colleagues to this day. "We're all trying, in our own ways, to do this kind of work and often with one another and if we can't do it together, we still try not only to do work that has similar values but produce them in the way that we all believe is a way you should be interacting with one another if you're in a creative endeavour. That's Jim."

EXPLORING NEW FRONTIERS

Larry's admiration for Jim's storytelling prowess and eye for talent is evident in his recollections of *The Storyteller*, a series that became part of *The Jim Henson Hour*, which Larry produced. "I loved *The Storyteller*. With regard to how it ended up on *The Jim Henson Hour*, they had produced the first five of them as I recall, they hadn't sold them anywhere yet, so that was going to be part of it and then they went on to do four more of them. I remember seeing them and I was bowled over by them. That's Duncan [Kenworthy], Jim and Anthony Minghella, and I think Steve Barron was the director. All I did on those was read the scripts and say, 'Yep.' I gave no notes, they were already produced and I just said, 'Let's put these in the show.' I think 'The Soldier and Death' is one of the best things ever on television. I had no involvement in it. I wish I had, but it was all those guys."

Larry's experience producing *The Jim Henson Hour* highlights the challenges of creating innovative, diverse content within the constraints of commercial television. Fresh off a demanding drama series in Paris and Montreal, Larry jumped at the chance to reunite with Jim on this new project.

The show's concept was ambitious and wide-ranging, aiming to capture the spirit of the classic *Walt Disney Presents* (1958–61). According to Larry it was a "hodgepodge of different kinds of things.

We were going to do what we called 'Muppet Variety', which had the classic characters in this multichannel universe control room. We were going to have *The Storyteller* and several other specials Duncan had produced in the UK which I'd given some script notes on. We did the 20th anniversary of *Sesame Street*, which Diana produced and I gave comments on the script, and then we did *Dog City, Song of the Cloud Forest, Lighthouse Island*... we did a huge amount of different kinds of things."

Even with the show's potential, Larry had concerns about its ability to find an audience in the fast-paced world of network television. "It must have been 1988, and I came to New York because Brandon Tartikoff ran NBC at that point and he was going to meet with Jim and I for lunch. Because there were so many different parts of it, he wanted Jim to be on camera. He felt that was the main thing that would give it unity. I remember saying to Brandon, 'Well, you know, this show is going to take time to build an audience. There are too many parts to it,' and he said, 'Yeah, we understand that.'

"But the truth is that doing something for NBC is different than doing something for HBO; it's different from doing something for the CBC. A US commercial broadcaster, a cable service and a public broadcaster all have different ways of thinking about what's successful and different levels of patience for that 'success' to be visible. I've always felt that Jim's best work happened in Toronto, London and New York, where he had the time to develop everything that he did. It took time to find itself and, incidentally, perhaps consequently, became successful commercially. But US commercial television is more driven by quick success, based on ratings."

The stark differences between the expectations of network television and the more nurturing environments of HBO or the CBC became clear when *The Jim Henson Hour* struggled to find its footing. "Just talking about the United States, we had three million viewers per episode for *Fraggle Rock* on HBO, and were a massive hit. I remember getting the ratings on the *Song of the Cloud Forest* episode of *The Jim Henson Hour* on NBC and we got 11-and-a-half or 12 million people and we were all upset because it's a failure. It's idiotic because then I said to myself, 'Well, look, 12 million people saw this, this is pretty amazing to me,' especially because the show was a heartwarming comedy about species extinction, but in that commercial world, particularly back then, it was about selling the commercials."

The series may have been short-lived, but Larry remained in awe of Jim's endless boundary-pushing creativity. "So much of what we did on *Fraggle* was so technically innovative and so much of what Jim did on *Labyrinth* and *Dark Crystal* was similarly ground-breaking. We were shooting the opening credit sequence for *The Jim Henson Hour* against blue screen in a way that would use digital elements. Nobody was doing that back then. Jim looked at me and said, 'Well, so what do you think?' and I said, 'I think it's great Jim, but I'm more worried about the next 20 minutes after this opening sequence, we still have some things we have to sort out there,' and then he said, 'Yes, but nobody's ever done this before.' So that's another key thing about him. He was always trying to break new ground."

Jim's insatiable curiosity and his willingness to collaborate with artists from diverse backgrounds were also evident in the development of *The Jim Henson Hour*. "In addition to writers, we had so many designers, he would just commission people. There was one of these big New Yorker cartoonists—it might have been William Stieg, but I might be misremembering—and one day we got this envelope from New York and Jim said, 'I just got this guy to work on these ideas, maybe we could do some of this for the show.' There was also a young puppet maker originally from Czecho-slovakia and she made these puppets that were cubist, they were like Picasso, and I just thought it was so interesting that they didn't exactly have characters... He was always trying other stuff, so there was lots of stuff that he would be doing that I wouldn't have been aware of.

"By the way, I use 'stuff' fairly consciously as it was one of Jim's favourite words. We even very briefly considered calling the show *Jim Henson's Wonderful World of Stuff*."

Even in the months before his death, Jim was exploring new frontiers, such as *Muppet*Vision 3D*, an attraction that opened after his passing, and an ambitious interactive movie project that would have allowed audiences to influence the story's direction in real time. "There was a script that Jeffrey Scott wrote. Jim was trying to do an interactive movie... We had a very rudimentary script, but the audience would have a device and they could decide where they wanted to go at certain points in the story and then somehow, based on what was happening in the audience at that point in the theatre, the projectors would be able to shift to whatever the right thing was.

"I don't think the technology was quite up to it at that point, it probably still isn't up to it, but he was trying to think about other ways of being interactive. If Jim had lived, there's so much he would have given us, and not just those of us who worked with him but the world, because he would be thinking about all these new technologies and how to use them for good and interesting purposes. It's a real tragedy."

A SENSE OF COMMUNITY

Larry's memories of Jim's proposed deal with Disney reveal the complex nature of the negotiations and the potential impact on Henson's legacy. According to Larry, Jim's longtime collaborator Jerry Juhl had shared his thoughts on the arrangement.

"Jerry and I had some conversations because we were a bit concerned about what it would mean. I think Jerry told me that the deal was going to be that Jim had to be involved for four years with Disney, but if he wanted to leave after that he had to leave everything there, including Kermit, Piggy, Rowlf and all these classic characters, including the ones that he performed. Jerry and I just sort of looked at each other and said, 'You know, he would hate it, but he was one person who could actually kind of do that and look towards the future, Jim might be able to do that.'

"Jim worked hard, he had tonnes of energy. I spoke to him on the Thursday before he died, and he was in good shape. What I understand is that he had to cancel a voice recording on the Monday, he didn't feel well and he just didn't get sick. He took care of himself, but he was just driven by work all the time. I remember there were times when he might be in Toronto for a couple of weeks. But on Friday night, he would fly to London and come back Monday morning to do something because he was prepping for *Labyrinth*. Not many people can do that and still function.

"Here's a really great Henson story. Jane Gootnick is a talented puppet maker, still making and wrangling puppets and still working for the Muppets out in LA. Wonderful, wonderful person. At Jim's memorial service, there was a separate reception for the people from out of town at the building on 69th Street, so I went to that after the big service at St. John of the Divine. When I had spoken to Jim on the Thursday before he died, one of the things we talked about was that they had just done *Greek Myths* with Anthony Minghella and he wanted to send me a copy of the tape of it, but then he died. When I came in, his assistant said, 'Oh, you know that tape we never sent out, it's sitting on Jim's desk and if you want to go pick it up, go pick it up.'

"So I went up, and the building had this gorgeous spiral staircase, and as you come up the staircase Jim's office was kind of off to the far left. But there's a little boardroom, just as you come off the stairs, where we'd have little design meetings, or script meetings, or whatever. So as I go past this office, who was in this office, but Michael Eisner, the Head of Disney and Jane Gootnick, and the line I hear from Jane is, 'No, no, no, you don't understand, our characters are nothing like your characters,' and I thought, 'Yep, that's it in a nutshell, the deep cultural differences just right there, not only in terms of how you create and develop and think of character, but also that a puppet maker would speak that directly to a CEO. You just don't believe that would ever happen at Disney. At least that's my interpretation.'"

Reflecting on Jim's legacy, Larry emphasises the profound impact he had on those who knew him and worked with him. "Jim's death was so awful on every possible level. Such a shock. I remember being called out of a meeting about it and it was like, 'What?' I couldn't wrap my head around it. We are fortunate to have what he gave us. And both concretely in terms of the work, but also kind of spiritually about what work was about and how to make it."

Larry also highlights the enduring bonds among Jim's collaborators and the sense of community he fostered. "You don't just work with Jim, it's this group of people... Jocelyn [Stevenson] is one of my closest friends in the world, and Jerry Juhl and I were very close until he died. I miss him every single day. Obviously there's no Muppets without Jim Henson, but I feel there's no Muppets without Jerry Juhl. Dave Goelz and I talk all the time, and Steve Whitmire and Karen Prell and many others.

"There's this kind of special world, even if you don't know some people in it. For example, when Jerry Nelson died, there was a memorial in New York and Louise Gold came over to be there and we didn't know each other but had heard of one another, and when we met there was this instant connection. That's because Jim just drew a certain kind of person to him, a lot of good people and creative people. People who like to laugh and eat.

"Working with the Muppets you laugh and eat a lot while you're working really hard and you are grateful for the rest of your life to be a part of this special group."

JOHN STEPHENSON

CREATIVE SUPERVISOR, JIM HENSON'S CREATURE SHOP (1979–2004)

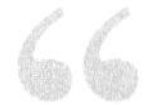 "He loved nothing more than seeing others succeed."

STARTING as a designer and craftsman on *The Dark Crystal*, John Stephenson would go on to become the Creative Supervisor of The Creature Shop, pioneering new technologies and techniques that revolutionised creature effects for film and television.

* * *

It was while doing an MA at London's Royal College of Art in 1979 that John Stephenson decided the film industry was where he wanted to be.

"I made several attempts to get jobs in art departments," he explains, before adding that after his degree show he received an invite to go to work in Los Angeles and travelled there with a friend and fellow RCA student and ended up living in Pasadena. "While there, friends living in New York told us about a film being made in London and after three days and nights on a Greyhound Bus I walked into what was then The Muppet Workshop in New York and within a matter of weeks, I was back in London working on *The Dark Crystal*."

One of John's first jobs involved working on *The Great Muppet Caper*. "You remember the bikes with all the Muppets riding around Hyde Park? The very first job I had in the film industry was helping make a couple of those bikes. But I was ostensibly working on *The Dark Crystal*, which was happening at the same time."

Development of *The Dark Crystal* took place while Jim Henson was busy with *The Muppet Show*, with John involved on the production for two years having been hired by Jim's right-hand man, producer Duncan Kenworthy. "Jim had done *The Muppet Show* on which everything was fabricated. The Muppets weren't sculpted—well, actually Miss Piggy's head was eventually sculpted —but *The Dark Crystal*, with Brian Froud's extraordinary design work, needed a different sort of methodology. Those were quite complex, organic-looking characters and they needed to be sculpted."

He recounts the blend of talents that came together for the film, many of whom travelled to the UK from New York. "In order to make the film, they had to tap into a whole different group of people who weren't already in the film industry. They had special effects guys, visual effects hadn't been invented in those days. They didn't need people who could do the delicate design work required for *The Dark Crystal*. So they hired a whole bundle of people who had never worked in the film industry before, a lot of them came over from New York. The film industry was sort of taken by storm by all these kinds of young art students who flooded into Elstree film studio and started making that film. There was a lot of invention, a lot of things that had never been done before, various forms of puppetry and manufacture as well."

John elaborates on the process. "I was a maker. I mainly worked on the Skeksis team headed up by the brilliant designer and sculptor, Lyle Conway. The whole business of sculpting things in clay, mould-ing, creating them in latex, then mechanising and making these puppets was very new. It was Jim's dream to create this extraordinary world this way."

THE CREATURE SHOP

While John left Henson briefly to work on films such as Hugh Hudson's *Greystoke: The Legend of Tarzan, Lord of the Apes* (1984) with the make-up effects pioneer, Rick Baker, he re-joined the Henson team for *Dreamchild* (1985) as an assistant cable-control puppeteer and wing maker for the Phoenix character. "We made all those characters like the Walrus and the Carpenter, they were absolutely beautiful.

"Technology was fairly limited in those days, so a lot was done with cables, lots and lots of cables. Although we had control over the movements, coordinating them was quite a challenge. On characters such as the Mad Hatter, there were probably six or seven people operating the head simultaneously—one person handling the eye blinks, another managing the corners of the mouth, another working the eyebrows and so on. You'd have six people all lined up with little mechanical controls, each contributing to the overall expression. It was quite a feat to synchronise everything and make it look meaningful."

A small Creature Workshop had been set up in Hampstead in 1979 for *The Dark Crystal*, but it was after production had ended on 1986's *Labyrinth* that a more permanent workshop facility was planned in Camden Town. It was at this time that Duncan Kenworthy approached John with a proposition. "He said, 'Jim and I have been talking, and we'd love you to take over this job of starting, really inventing a permanent facility, the Creature Shop.' I think I was called creative head or creative supervisor for about 20-odd years."

John revelled in the opportunities afforded to him and his fellow creatives from The Henson Company's injection of money and equipment. "We were well-financed, we had lots of resources, so we could invent stuff and work out how to do things. I could hire the right people and get almost any sort of equipment or anything I needed. It was a dream job and I was extraordinarily privileged. The people we hired over the years are now all over the film industry in all sorts of high places. It spawned an awful lot of creativity."

When asked if his role as creative supervisor involved assembling a team for each project and charting the course forward, John nods. "Pretty much. I had a tried and tested group of people that I worked with continually. I was there at the beginning, and we worked out exactly how we were going to do it all and put it all together. That was a great position to be in. None of this stuff existed; we weren't reinventing the wheel, the wheel had not been invented yet, which suited me perfectly. In a way, it all could have gone horribly wrong on several occasions, but somehow, we always managed to pull it off and get it done. As a result, we created something brand new and original, which was very satisfying. We were very much part of the filmmaking team. We worked alongside the designer and the director and everybody else, hopefully done as originally as possible."

RUNNING A MINI FILM STUDIO

One of John Stephenson's goals when he joined the Creature Shop was to streamline the process that involved multiple team members having to work on individual parts of a character's face. "We started developing a computer system to control all those actuators on the face, which allowed us to achieve more complex and realistic expressions. It was a pivotal advancement that enhanced our ability to bring these fantastical characters to life."

He describes the Creature Shop as "a mini film studio in Camden", explaining that they "had casting shops, wood workshops, metalworking shops, big sculpting studios, art studios, and graphic designers. Each project had its own producer, and we had a room full of producers managing their respective projects. It was full-on and running like a big machine, if a slightly eccentric one. The constant activity and collaboration made it an exhilarating place to work."

As well as using the technology available to them, it's clear that the Creature Shop was a hotbed of creativity, with new processes continually developed to meet the demands of filmmakers. "Everybody was innovating back then because there wasn't anything established. On *Greystoke,* I was part of the team that made the apes. We picked up a lot of techniques that we later integrated into the Creature Shop."

John's journey through these pioneering projects highlights the evolution of the Creature Shop's capabilities. "On *The Dark Crystal,* the characters were very sophisticated puppets, but later on, the Creature Shop moved beyond traditional puppetry. There wasn't anywhere else quite like it. It was ambitious, very young, very lively, and a bit unstructured. I'd hire anyone who was even slightly creative, whether they could draw, sculpt or make moulds. We had some pretty clever mechanical people and some real boffins from Oxford and Cambridge working on computer technology with us."

John is clear that the eclectic team at the Creature Shop was instrumental in driving its success. "I hired a guy from Imperial College named Dave Houseman, who worked with me for several years. He designed a lot of our software and computer technology. This blend of artistic talent and technical expertise made the Creature Shop a unique and groundbreaking place."

The volume of activity at the Creature Shop, particularly in the early years, is something John remembers well. "In those days, I felt like I was spinning on the spot. The progression, the creative ideas, and the sheer creativity were incredible. There was so much going on that we were all growing continuously. It's difficult if you're only working on a film once every two years, because your experience is limited. But at the Creature Shop, we could be working on three feature films, 10 commercials, and preparing for the next big feature film all at the same time. It was massive."

The fast-paced production schedule required everyone to work around the clock. "I kind of ran the place as if it was an art school. Everybody had a very specific task to do, but there was no sort of clocking-in or 9-to-5. You could go to the Creature Shop any time of the night and day and there'd be loads of people in there working, generally to quite loud rock music. You just had to get the work done. I used to spend days and nights there. It was a 24-hour place with activities happening all the time. Lots of different things were being made simultaneously."

THE STORYTELLER

John reflects on the work done for *The Storyteller*, the series that brought ancient folk tales and legends to life. "They were cleverly written by Anthony Minghella, but the big thing about those was Steve Barron. Steve was a young, very successful music video director. He had directed videos like Michael Jackson's *Billie Jean* [1983] and A-ha's *Take On Me* [1984] with its famous pencil-drawing animation. Jim brought in Steve to direct the pilot episode of *The Story-teller*, a move that set the tone for the series. "Using music video technology, Steve established a style that several other directors followed. He was essentially the showrunner."

The series featured directors like Paul Weiland, known for his work in commercials, and Charles Sturridge, famous for 1981's *Brideshead Revisited*, with each episode presenting unique challenges for the Creature Shop. "We'd collaborate with each director to figure out how to achieve the various effects. What you have to remember about *The Storyteller* is that there was no hiding.

"There were no post-production fixes, so everything had to work in front of the camera. Everything was operated from under the floor, or it was cable-controlled, or it was rodded, or sometimes it was put on a big polearm. The Storyteller's dog was a puppet, but pretty much everything else was done in other interesting ways. Jim was completely blown away because we were doing things he hadn't thought of before, using more rod puppets, cable puppets and things like that. It was pretty amazing when I think about it now, but it was just what we did at that particular point in time. It was very much Jim's thing."

JIM'S INFLUENCE

As might be expected, a creative meeting with Jim Henson didn't always take place in an office. "If you wanted to have a meeting, just kind of one-to-one, we'd go up and sit on top of Parliament Hill and look at London together. There's a bench there now with his name on it. We'd sit there and just talk about stuff. He would say things that were quite astounding because he could sit back and look at things from a distance. He was a great appreciator of the people who worked for him. He'd inject ideas into the mix and then sit back and see what happened. Having said that, he wasn't vague; he was very precise about how he needed things when he was filming. He was brilliant and, in many ways, ahead of his time.

"I can remember Jim saying, 'You know what, John, I think there's something we should be doing with computers. I'm not quite sure what it is, but I think we should do something.' He gave me the task of hiring someone who could work with us on this." This would soon lead to significant advancements at the Creature Shop. "Ultimately, we ended up making computerised control systems which ran all of the later projects. Dave Houseman came in twice a week to work with us."

John also remembers Jim's commitment to exploring digital technology. "I used to travel to New York quite a lot because I was also sometimes involved with a workshop making *Sesame Street* and various other things. I remember Jim having a meeting in New York with a group of people to work out the best way of using digital technology in our industry. It wasn't obvious which direction to take in those days, so we had a series of meetings to brainstorm."

According to John, Jim's innovative spirit was clear throughout his career. "If you look back at *The Muppet Show*, there had been puppet shows on TV forever, but most puppeteers, like Punch and Judy performers, couldn't see the product of what they were doing because they were hidden away. Jim came up with the idea of using monitors. He placed a camera on the puppet so the puppeteers could watch what they were doing on a TV monitor. The monitors were reversed, so they showed a proper image rather than a mirror image. This was a huge innovation and one reason why *The Muppet Show* was so much better than any other puppet show. The puppeteers could see exactly what the puppet was doing, which made a world of difference."

TURTLE POWER

Looking back at the busy time around 1989, John recalls various TV specials that would become part of *The Jim Henson Hour*. "We did *Lighthouse Island* and *Monster Maker*, the latter with Harry Dean Stanton, and that one was memorable. We built a huge creature in a deconsecrated church, which later became George Martin's AIR Studios. I was the designer on that. The creature was massive, with the head being the size of a small car and somebody sat inside the head. I think it was flywheels we were using in that. It was kind of old cable technology before we got into hydraulics."

Another character overseen by John was seen in 1990's *Living with Dinosaurs*. "It was written by Anthony Minghella and was about a boy with a toy dinosaur that in his eyes was real. The dinosaur was an Elvis Presley fan and would break out into Elvis songs. The little dinosaur, brilliantly puppeteered by Brian Henson, was amazing. It's one of the nicest things Minghella ever wrote, it's a bit of a mini-masterpiece."

John praises Juliet Stevenson's performance in the special, before mentioning some of the other actors who appeared in Henson productions. "Actors worked very differently with our sorts of productions. We had John Hurt in *The Storyteller* of course. We had Michael Gambon on *Greek Myths*. We created amazing pieces for

Daedalus and Icarus. Working with Michael Gambon on that was a pleasure. Having such talented actors around was amazing. Most of the time, they were interested in what we were doing and became part of the team. Harry Dean Stanton was fantastic."

John then moves on to Nic Roeg's 1990 film, *The Witches*. "What an experience that was! What we did to Angelica Huston on that production was outrageous, a make-up masterpiece designed by Steve Norrington. She had this massive nose that grew about a yard long and to put this thing in place it was a really big process. Hours of make up time. But she was an absolute sport."

One name that comes up a few times in our conversation is Brian Henson. "He wasn't a director or the head of the company yet. He did a lot of work on *Labyrinth*, including the character Hoggle." John explains that in the 1980s he was very much a puppeteer/performer, "a very, very good one", but unlike most of the other puppeteers he also got very involved with the build. "Later, he directed the second unit of *Teenage Mutant Ninja Turtles*. Brian was a great performer and puppeteer."

Teenage Mutant Ninja Turtles was the first live-action version of the animated TV series that had taken the world by storm. "We had actors in suits, but we didn't want them to look like actors in suits. The faces were done with cables running down the back of their heads into their turtle shells, which housed all the driver motors for facial features. We used a form of early motion capture, with puppeteers wearing rigs on their faces that translated their movements to the turtles' faces. It was a huge film, the biggest-grossing independent film of all time back then."

Turtles was the final Creature Shop production that Jim would see before he died. "I think there's a whole load of publicity shots that were taken of him with people in turtle suits. *The Sunday Times* did a colour supplement spread around that time as well. Remember, Jim was also running the Muppet empire and all sorts of other things, so there were probably other things going on."

Around this time, the Creature Shop was making the shift to

using CGI (Computer Generated Imagery) alongside the practical creatures. "We had as many people working on computer-generated elements as we did on physical effects. We aimed to get as much in front of the camera as possible and then use CGI to enhance it. This approach gives the final product a sense of realism that pure CGI often lacks. Some of the art forms and techniques we developed are no longer used because CGI has taken over. However, there's still a great value in having practical effects on set. They give a tangible presence that CGI can struggle to replicate."

LIFE AFTER JIM

John's recollections of the Creature Shop after Jim Henson's death reveal a company in transition. "It was a terrible shock. We were all so young. Creature Shop continued working for outside clients and I was still running that."

John reveals that it was during pre-production of 1993's *Jurassic Park* that the Creature Shop was invited to design some of the dinosaurs and bid for the creation of the physical/mechanical dinosaurs. "At one point it looked like we got the job and I came home celebrating, but they changed their mind because we were based in London. Because of that I thought, *This is ridiculous, we don't want that to happen again*, so we started a workshop in LA, run by David Barrington Holt, who used to work with me in London. Then Brian Henson and Charlie Rivkin took over the running of the company and moved everything to Los Angeles and bought the old Chaplin studios."

When asked about working with Jim Henson, John states that "he was remarkably egoless. He was very easy to work with, a great appreciator of other people's talents, and loved nothing more than seeing others succeed. He only ever reluctantly took the credit himself." It was only after Jim died and the Creature Shop was branded as "Jim Henson's Creature Shop" that his signature was added to the logo.

"Unsurprisingly, after he died, everything changed. It was a different atmosphere. Suddenly, I had to get used to schedules and budgets, which was a big shift from the creative freedom we had before. Despite these changes, we carried on. Neal Scanlan, who was instrumental in many projects, eventually started his own thing and ended up doing all the *Star Wars* creature effects."

The London Creature Shop continued for many years, working on films including *Babe* (1995), *The English Patient* (1996), *101 Dalmatians* (1996) and *Where the Wild Things Are* (2009). "We did a film called *Lost in Space* [1998] and built a robot that was a monster," says John. "It was all hydraulic, hugely powerful, and we controlled it through massive amounts of hydraulic power with special valves, which we computerised. We also did some work on the first *Harry Potter* film. I directed a film called *Five Children and It* [2004], which was in a similar genre to *Harry Potter* and it was a fraction of the cost but clashed with the beginnings of *Harry Potter*. By the time the second *Harry Potter* came out they'd set up their own workshops and took quite a lot of people from the Creature Shop."

John's time at the Creature Shop ended around 2004, but he still remembers Jim's enthusiasm for the workshop. "It was like Jim's absolute pet thing. He'd bounce back and forth from all over the world. He had a house in London opposite the Creature Shop, and the first thing he'd do when he got in from America was come straight to see what was going on. I used to show him all the various things we were doing, and he loved it. It was like his own very special, personal train set.

"The madness of it all is that they put me in charge of the Creature Shop. I came straight out of art school and worked as a maker and designer in the film industry, and then they put me in charge of this thing. Jim didn't micromanage. I was unbelievably privileged; I was running the Creature Shop and had enormous freedom to come up with ideas and try new things. I reported directly to him for years, up until the time he died. I got to know Jim incredibly well. He was a wonderful guy."

VICTOR PEMBERTON
WRITER/PRODUCER, FRAGGLE ROCK (UK)

"The Fraggles were a way of educating children without making them feel like they were being educated."

VICTOR PEMBERTON (1931–2017) wrote the first 24 UK lighthouse wraparounds for *Fraggle Rock* and later produced the remaining UK segments until 1990, working with actors Fulton Mackay, John Gordon Sinclair and Simon O'Brien.

* * *

Born in Islington, London, in 1931, Victor began his career in radio before transitioning to television, where he made his mark with several notable contributions, including writing the *Doctor Who* (1963–) story 'Fury from the Deep' (1968), which saw the introduction of the sonic screwdriver. He quickly established himself as a writer capable of blending imaginative concepts with relatable characters, a skill that would later serve him well in his collaboration with Jim Henson.

Speaking in 2007, Victor explained that it was while working in

Kuwait on an American TV series that he first met producer Duncan Kenworthy, but another few years until the latter began working alongside Jim Henson on numerous film and TV projects. It was during the development of *Fraggle Rock* that Duncan reconnected with Victor, explaining the idea of a new puppet show that would see its puppet sections filmed in Toronto while scenes in the "real world" would be filmed in different countries using local cast and crew.

Explained Victor, "He'd joined forces with Jim Henson and said to me one day, 'We're going to do a new show, based on material shot in Canada. Each country will do their own segments, can you come up with an idea for what we can do with the UK segments?' I said I'd have a go and I suggested various things, including setting it in a lighthouse. He said he'd put the idea to Jim and let me know. In the meantime, I had to go to Nigeria to do some TV work. I'd been busy teaching students and was knackered when one night I got a call out of the blue from Duncan who said, 'We're going ahead with it and I need a 20-page synopsis.' I asked for when and he said, 'Tomorrow morning!'"

Despite the tight deadline and the lack of internet in 1983, Victor managed to write the synopsis overnight and dictate it to Duncan's secretary over the phone. His idea of setting the UK segments in a lighthouse was well-received, and production began shortly after in England.

Victor described the creative process behind *Fraggle Rock*, likening it to a jigsaw puzzle, with each country's segments having to be distinct yet seamlessly fit into the overall narrative. "In France it was a chef in a kitchen, in Canada he was an inventor, in Germany it was a mad scientist or something, so we had to do something different and I thought that something very British was a lighthouse. I told them what I wanted the character to do, and what sort of inter-action there should be between him and Sprocket. I'd already seen the stuff that was shot in Canada and all our segments had to be slotted in, that's why I say it was a jigsaw puzzle. For the first series, I wrote all the UK segments and Duncan produced them. If you look at the credits you'll see there's the American side of the operation and the British. I shared credits with the US producer."

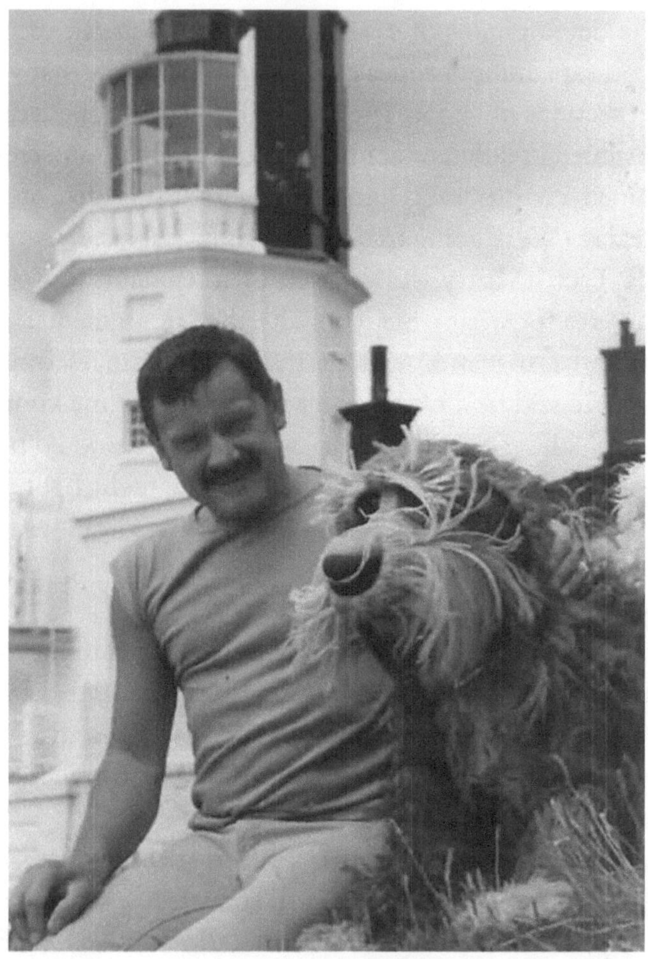

Victor Pemberton and Sprocket on location. Courtesy Victor Pemberton

When it came to writing for the UK version, Victor was well aware of the themes being touched on in the series, including prejudice, the environment and having your own identity, but he was never issued a "moral of the week" to work with. "I had to think of something. They had it in the US version. Never forget it was filmed in Toronto at the Canadian Broadcasting Corporation. Some things weren't quite as right for our viewers as they were for US viewers. *Fraggle Rock*, in a sense, is like *Sesame Street* because *Sesame Street* is a wonderful educational series without appearing to be educational and kids still love it around the world. I worked at the Children's Television Workshop and it's a great industry, and that's where the Muppets started.

"The Fraggles were a kind of a way of educating children without making them feel like they were being educated. One thing we never did, and neither I nor Jim would have allowed it, was to lecture. We never did that. We've moved on since those years and the issues are somewhat different, children are older in their thinking. We all know what's going on with teenagers. Sex was never mentioned unless in very, very oblique ways. I remember I did try to introduce it into one of the shows but we couldn't accommodate it as it just didn't seem right. We were pushing ahead of our time I think. Today you could do that."

Did he ever have a typical viewer in mind? "I wrote it for myself, but it was a children's tea time slot. Since then it's gathered momentum and appeals to adults. I was speaking to someone the other day here in Spain, she used to be a prison governor and I happened to mention I'd be doing this interview, and she asked what my involvement was and she nearly fainted because it was her favourite programme. She adored it and used to watch it in the prison! I didn't invent it but I suppose I was one of its dads!"

Would Victor have liked to have written for the Fraggles themselves? "I'd have liked to, but I was quite happy with what I was doing. I absolutely adored Sprocket and I loved the Doozers and the Gorgs. As I talk to you at the moment I have clockwork Doozers looking down at me from the shelf, making sure I tell the truth. I loved the Fraggle characters."

BUILDING THE WORLD

While the US *Fraggle Rock* starred Canadian actor Gerry Parkes as Doc, the UK version starred Scottish actor Fulton Mackay as the Captain, a lighthouse keeper. "I should mention that the UK side of things was a co-production with TVS. The head of children's TV at the time was Anna Home, and it was a kind of tripartite thing between Duncan, Anna and myself. I didn't cast Fulton, it was down to Anna and Duncan. I went along to meet him and I'd always admired him. I thought he was a terrific actor with a great personality. My initial response wasn't enthusiastic. I have to say I found him a little bombastic at that meeting. He'd brought along a tape recorder where he'd recorded his comments on how he saw his role, and it put our backs up a little, but we cast him."

One of the key creatives on the Canadian series was writer Jerry Juhl. "Jerry was a great guy, very talented and heavily involved with the Muppets. I can't claim to have had a close relationship with him, I didn't know him that well, but we always met at meetings and he came over from the States when we were in production. We took over an old cinema in Gillingham in Kent, and it was wonderful. The auditorium was cleared of seats, the stage was raised and extended."

After production ended on the first series, Victor was approached with an offer he couldn't refuse. "Duncan Kenworthy became head of international film production at Henson with Jim and they were concocting Muppet movies and all those sorts of things, so he was involved in finding new projects for Jim. He came to me to ask if I wanted to change hats for the next series and produce it. I was on it for seven years, on and off."

Production-wise, Victor explained that one episode would be filmed each day, and that he was on set "every minute of every day. I had to be there all the time as it was quite a technical production and I had to learn this side of it and the puppetry side of things. I'd watched Jim Henson and Frank Oz perform the Muppets at Elstree Studios and got the general flow of the thing."

Typically, Duncan Kenworthy would suggest the name of a director for the series, with Victor having input into the decision. "Jeremy Swan was suggested as the main director. He'd worked with Anna at the BBC and she suggested him. We liked to think of *Fraggle Rock* as not only a family for the viewers, but for us as well. We always felt like a family and tried not to let our artistic tantrums run away from us. Sometimes we got a bit cross, and sometimes one or two of the puppeteers behaved badly, but most of the time they were a lovely bunch and I'd never run any of them down. They were nearly all British and very experienced, and a lot of them had worked on *The Muppet Show*. We drank together, we ate together, we went out together and sometimes went to the movies together and so on. It was a wonderful experience."

Daily meetings and meticulous planning were crucial to the smooth running of the production, with a key consideration being how the Fraggle sections filmed in Toronto would match with the new scenes being shot in the UK. "It was like a mathematical plan. We'd start the day with a script read through every morning and everyone would throw in their problems and I had to oversee this. We ran the Fraggle sequences on VTR so we could relate to that and link the shots up. The director had to watch where everything joined up. The hole down into Fraggle Rock was the beginning and end point for the production. Sprocket would put his head through the hole and we'd cut to the overseas material. You can see what a nightmare it was, lining everything up mathematically.

"It didn't seem like a day's work. We loved getting into the studio and getting down to it. Every morning I'd walk into the auditorium, past wires and puppets, and suddenly I'd hear something—and of course, Sprocket never talked—would look around and Sprocket was speaking to me. The puppeteers would know when I was coming in and would be ready. I'd ask him if he had a good night, and the paw and tail would go up. This went on every morning. Then from another door, Gobo would appear and say "Good morning Victor!". All these Fraggles saying hello. It became normal after a while!"

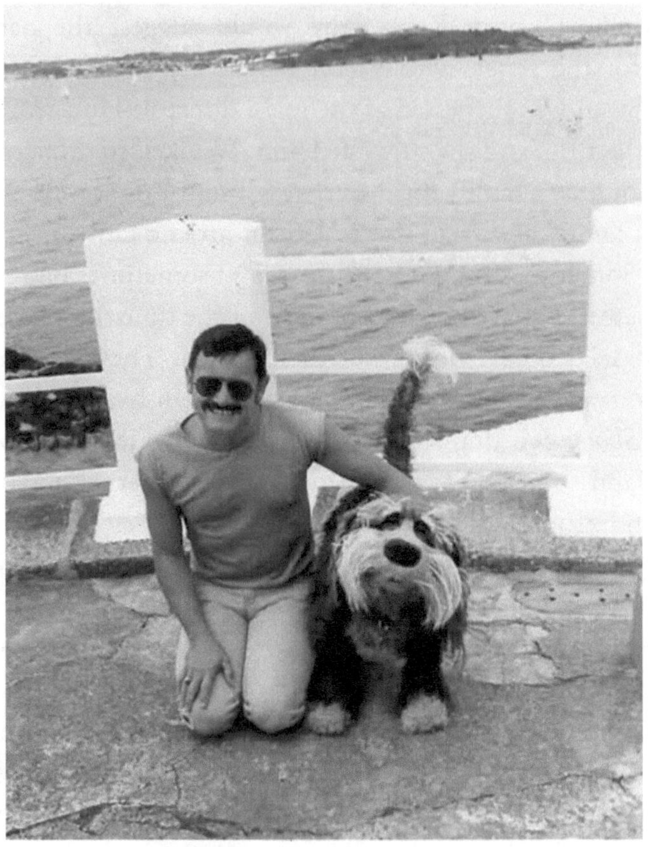

Sprocket and his producer. Courtesy Victor Pemberton

The situation wasn't always so straightforward with the show's sole human actor, Fulton Mackay. "On the whole it went fairly smoothly, but there were times when he was very difficult. A big problem was he was quite jealous of the dog, Sprocket, one of the great heroes of television. This isn't to run Fulton down—he got the show started for us and he was a great lighthouse keeper and he was very good—but when he had tantrums, they were very tiresome. When you work with Muppets, it's different from working with live actors, but you've got to treat them like real characters, not wooden or cloth things. At times he found that quite difficult, but basically he was splendid and was very popular with the viewers. By mutual agreement, we only took him on for two series."

While most of the UK segments were filmed in a studio, the production team did occasionally go on location to film the lighthouse exteriors. "We did a lot of location shooting down near St Mawes in Cornwall and had to do a recce by helicopter to find a location. Fulton stayed on location, as did his lovely wife, and we had good fun."

Fulton Mackay may have been Scottish, but Victor revealed the lighthouse was never intended to be located in Scotland. "Like everything with the Muppets, locations are quite neutral and we would have gone for Scottish, Welsh or Chinese, as long as the character was right and he could interact properly. He was Scottish and we were very happy he was Scottish because we cast Scottish again with John Gordon Sinclair."

After the departure of Fulton Mackay, Victor was faced with needing a new lighthouse keeper to keep Sprocket company for the series' fourth season. "I suggested we have someone younger next time as that might appeal to the kids, but little did we know many of the viewers were adults. I suggested him after seeing him in *Local Hero* [1983], and he was terrific, a good actor is Gordon. He was great fun to work with, we had a lot of laughs. He was very charming and the kids loved him. The only thing he wasn't so keen on was the publicity as he didn't want to advertise too much he was on a kid's show. He was great in the location stuff. His interaction with Sprocket was very funny because Sprocket was quite a handful."

After two seasons, John Gordon Sinclair's P.K. left the lighthouse in the capable hands of Simon O'Brien as B.J. "Duncan suggested Simon. I didn't know much about him, apart from the fact he'd played Damian on *Brookside* [1982–2003]. I have to say that immediately the chemistry was there. Why did I like Simon so much? Well, he was such a happy-go-lucky guy, and he was a true Liverpudlian, very funny, and he teased me mercilessly. We didn't interview him, but he was perfect. His rapport with

Sprocket was fascinating. The chemistry was absolutely right. You could believe he was his dog. Remember that so many families have dogs, part of the family, and he was important to whoever was in the lighthouse."

LEAVING THE LIGHTHOUSE BEHIND

When it came time to end the series after 96 episodes, Victor was sad to say goodbye to his Fraggle friends. "We hired Dover Castle for the farewell party. We held the party in the dungeons. Jim and Duncan were there, and the cast and crew had got together to put on a half-hour show to say thank you to me. There was a little stage and the curtains pulled back to reveal all of them impersonating me, every one of them, including Sprocket. They had every mannerism down to a tea. If I scratched my nose, they would do it. It was a very loving send-off, I was very happy and very joyous but also terribly sad. A few tears were shed that night."

On the subject of Jim Henson, Victor was effusive in his praise of the man. "I don't use the word lightly, but Jim Henson was a genius. His imagination was extraordinary. I'd been to Europe several times, to Prague, to talk to puppeteers, and they all revered him as a sort of god of the puppet world. That isn't to say he wasn't a very shrewd man, but artistically he was one of the great men of his generation."

What did Victor think is the legacy of the series? "Enjoy life and don't take it too seriously. No matter how hard times are, there's always light somewhere. The overall feeling is of joy. It was a joyous thing to do and to watch, helped enormously by those wonderful songs. They were so hummable. I don't know how they did it. Everyone used to wait for the opening song. They used to start swaying to the music as you saw the Fraggles. It's a very moral show. Kids learned how to do things and also things they shouldn't do and they learned respect."

Did he think 'Don't take life too seriously' was Jim's view? "Oh yes. Jim was a very moral man. I was with him in New York a week before he died. We went to an Italian restaurant and he ordered the entire lunch in his Kermit voice. He wasn't well and wouldn't see a doctor. It was very sad. He was a very loving man.

"Jim's legacy was to bring happiness to the world: when you watched *Fraggle Rock* you couldn't fail to have a smile on your face."

Postscript: *Despite the popularity of UK Fraggle Rock, in the years following its conclusion, it became apparent that many episodes had been junked or destroyed, either by TVS or one of its subsequent owners, leaving only 12 episodes of broadcast quality. Thankfully, Victor kept many of the series VHS master tapes in his home until his death, with the episodes later recovered by fans.*

DAVID GUMPEL
DIRECTOR AND PRODUCER

"Jim was this amazing, approachable person, who if you got his ear, he was interested in what you were doing."

STARTING in video production at the New York Henson offices, David Gumpel rose through the ranks to become a key director for the company, helping bridge the transition from Jim's era through to the 2000s while working across a wide range of productions.

* * *

Twelve-year-old David Gumpel couldn't believe his luck. An invitation to visit the set of *Sesame Street* from a neighbour who wrote for the show led to a trip to Manhattan's Reeves Teletape Studio, where David watched Jim Henson and Frank Oz perform Bert and Ernie. Little did young David know this encounter was just the prelude to a much bigger adventure.

Fast forward a decade to 1982 and David, now a 22-year-old running the video editing and equipment office at NYU, was about to experience another twist of serendipity. This time, it wasn't Oscar or Cookie Monster who would capture his attention.

"Jane Henson came and sat in my office because she was tired from going up the stairway and said, 'We're looking for some people to work at the Muppets.'" This chance encounter led to David's colleague Ritamarie Peruggi joining Henson Associates (HA!). "It wasn't long before Ritamarie invited me to work with her." David's ambitious nature quickly came to the fore. "I'm expansion-minded, so as soon as I got there, the trick was to find out what we could do in-house."

As the 1980s dawned, David found himself at the forefront of a video production revolution. The transition from clunky tape-based editing to sleek digital systems was underway, and David was determined to keep HA! ahead of the curve. "I started editing things because I told Jim we needed an edit system. We started editing all these little things for licensing and other projects." David's tech-savvy approach soon caught Jim's attention. "I kind of got Jim's ear really early because I was always bringing him tech to see. I remember bringing him the first portable Sony CD player, then he wanted one. So I'd always bring him tech stuff."

THE MUPPET MELTING POT

David describes the Henson headquarters in New York as something of a creative wonderland where imagination knew no bounds. This approach, rare in the cutthroat entertainment industry of the 1980s, fostered an environment where even the youngest team members could find themselves in impromptu brainstorming sessions with the boss. "Jim was this amazing, approachable person, who if you got his ear, he was interested in what you were doing. It was an amazing thing to have this bigger-than-life person, who if you said, 'I did this music video, do you want to see it?' would throw it in the machine in his office and he would look at it."

The Muppets operation, as David describes it, had a "distinct family atmosphere" that set it apart from larger, more corporate companies. "In New York, we had three people that ran the mailroom, it was like a sitcom. In the '80s, there was either a party every Friday afternoon or someone was doing something on a Friday afternoon that made us unable to work. That's the way all offices should be."

For David, the real magic often happened away from the studio, in the intimate setting of edit rooms. "Whereas now we just edit in a vacuum then send a tape out, he was there when we were doing something, you would hang out in the edit room for the likes of the *John Denver Rocky Mountain Holiday* [1983], working on a Muppet music video for the *Muppets Take Manhattan* and many more productions."

David's career took a leap forward when Diana Birkenfield, the New York Head of Production, tapped him to edit an HBO documentary marking the end of *Fraggle Rock*. "We got all the materials that [*Fraggle* producer] Larry Mirkin and everyone else had shot and I put something together as a rough." The resulting special, 1987's *Down at Fraggle Rock*, became a testament to the ingenuity of Henson's tight-knit team. Jim himself graced the screen in wraparound segments shot by David, while writer Bill Prady lent his talents to the voiceover. The special didn't just captivate audiences, it also snagged a Cable ACE Award for Best Children's Special, an International Emmy nomination and other accolades.

Riding this wave of success, David directed *Muppet Meeting Films*, short productions featuring Muppet characters navigating office life that injected humour into corporate gatherings across America. They proved the versatility of Jim's creations, proving that the Muppets could captivate audiences well beyond the realm of children's TV. "I have so few photos because I thought it was so cool that I was just there. I was doing the stuff, and I didn't think of myself as a fan. I thought of myself as one of the people doing the thing."

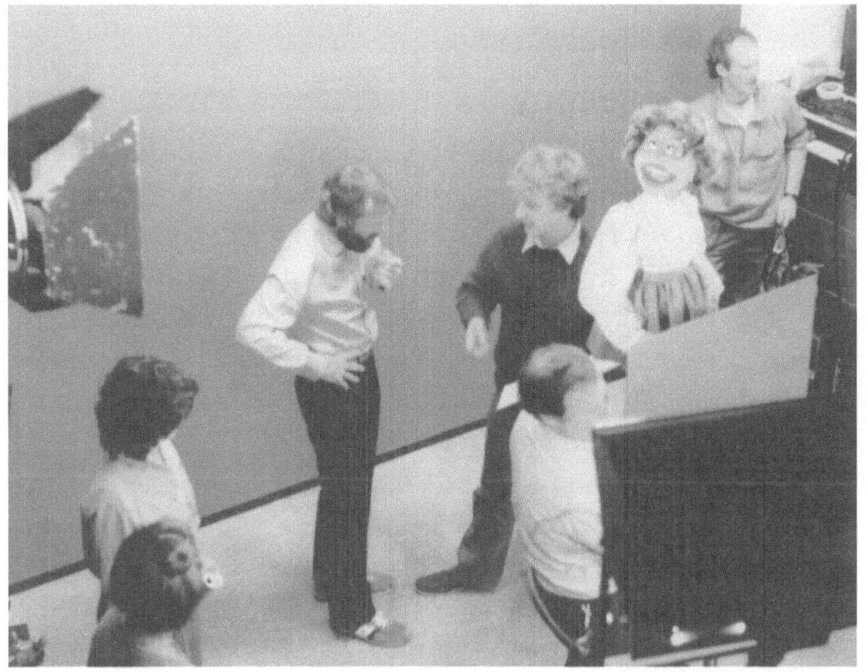

David shooting Muppet Meeting Films with Jim. Courtesy David Gumpel

David also mentions a rare opportunity to work with Frank Oz on a 1988 Lorimar home video. "The only time I got to work with Frank was while directing *Hey, You're as Funny as Fozzie Bear*. Frank turns to me and says, 'Are you directing this?', that thing that Frank would do, he would just bust everyone, that whole Muppet practical joke thing. The people who were really involved in the practical jokes were Steve [Whitmire] and Dave [Goelz], they did a lot of crazy stuff on *Fraggle Rock*."

Jim's approachability extended to spontaneous moments, as David discovered during an unplanned trip that likely occurred during the mid-1980s, a period of rapid expansion for Henson. "Once I got on a plane to go to an exhibit where I made the videos for a museum in Chicago with Jim. I didn't have permission to go, but Jim bumped me up to first class so we could talk. That was a great conversation about family, trusting the universe doing its job to take care of you and your family. It was a fantastic conversation that I'll never forget."

The Carriage House at 225 East 67th Street became David's professional home for 12 years. Acquired by Jim in 1984, this former photo studio transformed into a bustling creative video production facility under David's guidance. "I had a blast for 12 years setting up stuff, shooting TV series... we did the whole thing in this tiny building." The versatility of the space and the team was remarkable, hosting productions from NBC Saturday, pitch presentations for various shows, *The Song of the Cloud Forest* for The Jim Henson Company and *Singalong* videos for Disney.

But beyond the fun and camaraderie, it was Jim Henson's philosophy that left the deepest imprint on David. "The main thing that comes from Jim is the way you treat people and the way you do the work. If you treat it like something bigger than life that you're doing, because it's important to do good things in the world, that's what he passed on to me."

This ethos has stayed with David long after his time with the Muppets. Even now, when working on new projects, he finds himself channelling Jim's approach. "Your brain keeps saying, 'Don't forget that everyone on the set is important. Don't forget that however this comes out, there'll be these people that will have amazing changes in their life because they see this beautiful, emotionally connected piece that they'll remember all their lives.'"

David recounts his time as assistant director on the Emmy-winning *Dog City* episode of *The Jim Henson Hour*, which Jim himself directed while also performing. "He'd be working on this crazy show every night till 10 o'clock. Martin [Baker] was there pulling his hair out and Jim had the time to talk to me about what I wanted to do after that show. Jim would be puppeteering and I could keep everything going as an assistant director. We went into the puppet shop one day and he told the shop, 'David's helping me direct this.'" This nurturing quality is one David strives to emulate in his own career, though he admits "it's a hard act to follow. You can't be the quiet warrior mentor that Jim was.

"There's an amazing article someone wrote about Jim. It asks, did Jim get involved with puppets because he loved puppets and was one of these puppet freaks? Or was he a TV person? And he was a TV person. He was a great puppeteer, he mentored puppeteers, he did all that, but his main thing was to communicate through this box and the puppet. Frank is a puppeteer. Frank came out of the puppet world, the puppet nerd world. Jim came out of the TV nerd world. I always tell people that Jim happened to go into television and puppetry, but he probably could have done three or four hundred different amazing things."

This TV-first approach set Jim apart from his contemporaries, revolutionising puppetry for the small screen with innovative techniques like using monitors to watch performances. Jim's leadership style, as David describes it, was a blend of drive and respect. "He had this amazing charisma... his was this unique version of get things done, be sweet but respect everyone. I grew up in a house with artists and painters and then to meet somebody that would get things done on a commercial level was amazing, and nobody does things like that. When we're out pitching stuff it's now just so agenda-based with everything. It's tough."

It's the personal moments that David treasures most, such as Christmas parties with Richard Hunt and the puppeteers singing carols, or Jim asking for his opinion on logo designs. "Jim was picking out a logo for Jim Henson Productions. I walked into the room and he said, 'David, what do you think? Which ones?' Did I have good suggestions? I guess I did, but the fact that he would ask me... I don't know if he asked everyone, but he asked me and that was the miracle stuff where you felt included and then you were given a way to be in the world after you worked for him, a way of being. I still struggle with it because I have my own demons and happiness with the television and film world and sadness with the television and film world, but I still just keep making things."

A WILD RIDE OF IDEAS

Jim Henson's company was a place where innovation trumped traditional business strategies. While many entertainment companies were becoming slaves to market research and focus groups, Jim's projects always began with a spark of ingenuity, be it cutting-edge technology or an unconventional storytelling approach.

Says David, "I often tell people that Jim would start with what you might call a 'trick', though that's not quite the right word. It was more like a unique technique. He'd ask, 'What can we create using this approach?' Then Jerry [Juhl] or another writer would get involved." He illustrates this with the example of *Fraggle Rock*: "The initial concept was, 'How do we create an international show where these characters live underground but emerge in different countries?' That was the foundation. Then we built upon it, layering all the elements that eventually became *Fraggle Rock*, but you started with this idea." This made *Fraggle Rock* one of the first shows designed from its inception to be easily adaptable for international markets.

David notes Jim's uncanny ability to command respect and admiration. "Jim had this way of keeping people in awe of him. You couldn't manipulate him—it was as if he had some kind of supernatural shield. People would walk into his office with prepared speeches or agendas, but once they were face-to-face with Jim, they found themselves compelled to tell the truth. He had this remarkable ability to make people feel comfortable being their authentic selves around him."

David observes Jim wasn't interested in rehashing past successes like *The Muppet Show*. Instead, he was constantly driven to explore new territories. "I think *The Muppet Show* marked the end of the Muppets' vaudeville era. It was the culmination of all those techniques honed on late-night chat shows, Ed Sullivan, and those early commercials, people hitting each other over the head with a stick, coffee blowing up and all that. Jim wanted to make movies. We'd have these conversations about great things he wanted to make and one of the most exciting aspects of the Disney deal, from what I heard, was that they were going to give him the opportunity to make six films. I don't think he wanted to do *The Muppet Show* again. He wanted to delve into creature movies and then branch out further than that, from wherever that went to. He was always thinking forward, not sure what those techniques would be."

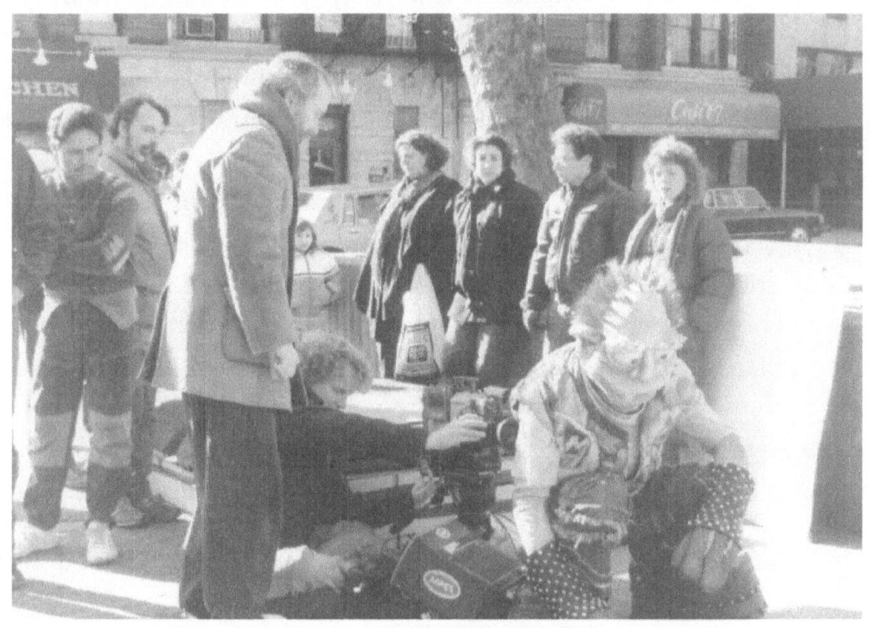

David shooting Crasher from the Jim Henson Hour's first presentation.
Courtesy David Gumpel

The Muppet television projects provided Jim with a platform to explore more personal, message-driven works. One such creation was *The Song of the Cloud Forest*, an environmentally themed segment of *The Jim Henson Hour*. This 1989 production saw Jim venturing into early virtual studio techniques, aligning with a growing trend in entertainment to address ecological issues as public environmental awareness surged.

David speaks fondly of the 10-minute *Inner Tube* pilot from 1987, a precursor to *The Jim Henson Hour*. "Jim gave me the fantastic credit of Visual Futurist. The only place I have seen that before was in *2001: A Space Odyssey* [1968]. The whole idea was to get inside the camera equipment and TV. It was pretty out there." This idea mirrored the zeitgeist of the era, echoing the tech-centric themes of films like *Tron* (1982) and TV series like *Max Headroom* (1987–88). "I think one reason it didn't quite hit the mark was because we didn't have someone who really got that kind of comedy. If we'd brought in a TV comedy pro instead of sticking to Muppet-style thinking, maybe that would've been the show's pilot. Instead, it came off a bit corny, like we had one foot still in vaudeville."

Jim was ahead of his time; in 1989, he was already involved in early forms of reality TV, prompting David to go to Los Angeles and film the pilot for a show titled *The Sink*. "He wanted to shoot a reality show with some comedians going somewhere in a van. So Dave Thomas's wife cast these comedians for Jim. Bernie Brillstein [Jim's manager] said to talk to her and three comedians were cast. So me and Jim get in the van and we're going to all these places with these guys and shooting it on two little eight-millimetre camcorders because he wanted this grand experiment and this amazing piece of equipment that would make television. Jim had that on his mind, again a technique that he wanted to try."

END OF AN ERA

David vividly remembers the events of May 1990. Jim, battling what seemed like a cold, maintained his demanding schedule. He left David at the LaserPacific post-production facility on Friday, flying between New York and London, before returning to the US and flying to North Carolina on Sunday and New York on Monday. As Jim's condition deteriorated, David arrived at Henson headquarters on East 69th Street on Wednesday, May 16th.

"I walked in the door and Bob Bromberg's there, the Head of Finance, and he said, 'Jim passed away during the night.' It was like losing the ideal father. Later Martin Baker showed up and said, 'Let's do the memorial service for TV.' I directed the six-camera shoot. We sent all the clips to CNN and other news outlets. We were busy the next day because we had all these different productions to get back to."

In the wake of Jim's death, the company united to honour his life and work. David collaborated with Bill Prady and Sara Lukinson on *The Muppets Celebrate Jim Henson*, a 1990 TV special featuring carefully curated clips. The special was part tribute, part therapy for the whole team. "Don Mischer came in to direct the show and set the tone for the whole show. I got an Emmy for editing the special that aired on CBS. Then we just moved on with doing other productions and we were busy from that day on. It didn't slow down at all even though our leader was gone. He had trained us well."

David directed the Starz movie, *Kermit's Swamp Years* (2002), *The Wubbulous World of Dr. Seuss* (1996–1998), *Telling Stories with Tomie* (2001), *Animal Jam* (2003), *Sid the Science Kid* (2008–2013), *Pajanimals* (2011–2013) and many other productions, before becoming Vice President of Production and Post Production while working at Henson's Hollywood lot. He left the company in 2004 and continued to do various productions for the Henson Company.

Looking back on his time with Jim Henson, David offers a nuanced perspective: "Every time I go there, I don't want to call him a saint, because he wasn't a saint. I don't want to call him a religious leader, because he wasn't that. Some people call him an old soul. He seemed like he was someone who had a grasp on what it's all about, what we're here for. He worked such long hours every day. He never got sick. He didn't know what it was like to be sick."

With the wisdom of hindsight, David muses: "I wish that I could look at him with my 66-year-old eyes and my 66-year-old experience and consciousness, and meet Jim right now and see how the starstruck 22-year-old saw, compared to the way I would see him now. That's one of the things I'd love to figure out.

"Jim believed in the dream that we could do these wonderful creative things and make a difference in the world."

ROB MILLS
PUPPETEER

"Jim nurtured a work ethic in everyone that saw us give our best in return for being invited to play."

ROB MILLS' entry to Jim Henson's world began with a suitcase full of props and a fraught audition which led to work alongside Fraggles, goblins and dinosaurs.

* * *

Toronto, 1982. As the city buzzed with the news of Jim Henson's arrival to shoot a new show, three young performers saw their chance to leap from street corners to TV.

Rob Mills, Trish Leaper and Gord Robertson, a trio of physical comedians, decided to take a shot at the big time. Armed with nothing but a suitcase full of props and a healthy dose of chutzpah, they set out to prove that their brand of what Rob calls "knockabout slapstick and cheap vaudeville larfs" could find a home among Henson's menagerie of lovable monsters.

For Rob, this moment was a far cry from his original career plans.

"I had a strong interest in stop-motion animation and special effects. I went to film school dreaming of becoming the next big-shot movie director." But somewhere along the way, Rob's path took an unexpected turn. He found himself drawn to the immediacy and energy of live theatre, diving headfirst into the world of mime, mask work and physical comedy.

With the entertainment section of the *Toronto Star* as their guide, the trio made a bold move. They dialled up the CBC, half-expecting to be laughed off the line. To their shock and delight, they were told auditions were happening the very next day. That night, Rob, Trish and Gord huddled around their "big fat suitcase", debating which bits of theatrical flotsam might catch the eye of Jim and his team.

"We were not, by any means, nor could we have been considered as 'legit' theatre folks," Rob recalls with a laugh. "We were the jesters, the clowns, the ones who'd do anything for a laugh." The next day, they found themselves in the middle of a cattle call audition that felt more like a circus than a job interview. At the helm was Richard Hunt, one of Jim's key collaborators and a force of nature in his own right. "Richard ran the operation like a well-oiled machine, but with all the subtlety of a Muppet explosion. He stuck his head out of a door and yelled at me: 'You! Get in here! Stand against the wall. Try to look intelligent.' FLASH! He takes a Polaroid, writes my name under the still undeveloped picture, clips it to my paltry excuse for a resume and tosses it on a pile of others on the table behind him."

Clutching his suitcase like a lifeline, Rob began his prepared pitch: "I'm with two other people out there, we're a team and..." But Richard, ever efficient, cut him off. "Yeah, yeah, yeah. Shut up. Do this. Now do this. Count to ten," he instructed, demonstrating a series of rapid-fire puppet movements. The audition was a blur of lip-sync exercises and hand contortions. Before Rob knew it, Richard was ushering him out with a curt "Okay. Get out. Who's next?" It was Trish's turn to face the gauntlet, armed with the same trusty suitcase. "She did and was right back out in the hallway as quickly as me."

Gord's audition, however, took an unexpected turn. "He disappears into the room holding out the same suitcase with a big grin and almost immediately the door flies open again and Richard sticks his head out (with a doughnut in his mouth) and yells: 'Is this guy with you?!'" When Rob and Trish confirmed, Gord vanished back into the room for a full 20 minutes, emerging with nothing more than a shrug.

Their unorthodox approach must have struck a chord. The trio received a callback, this time for body costume characters in a mysterious new project called *Fraggle Rock*. The pitch document, filled with Michael Frith's whimsical illustrations, hinted at the boundless creativity that had become Jim Henson's hallmark.

The callback day painted a stark contrast between himself, Trish and Gord and the established performers. "I'd been celebrating getting our call back rather heavily the night before," Rob admits, "and was hiding under my hat, with my feet propped up on that same damned suitcase, slouched on an old couch in one corner of the waiting area." He surveyed the room, taking in the competition: "The others who had been called in for this specific audition were known to us. A lot of them were luminaries in the Canadian mime scene. Names we respected and looked up to. And there they were, in their tights and leotards, strutting and stretching and looking like the dedicated dance and movement theatre professionals they were. I figured we didn't stand a chance but at least the coffee was free and good."

The audition process took an unexpected turn when Rob leafed through a set of character profiles. "I turned the page of the brochure thing and there was this illustration of these characters called The Gorgs. Three of them. One tall. Two short." In that moment, the gravity of the opportunity hit him. "I leaned sideways and showed the picture to Trish and Gord. I think we all held our breath then, I know I did. This wasn't a lark anymore. I wanted this."

Despite being surrounded by Canada's mime elite, Rob felt confident. Their unconventional style, honed on street corners and in dingy clubs, seemed to align perfectly with the Muppets' style. "I didn't want to jinx it by saying anything out loud but I was sure we had more than just a chance of getting hired."

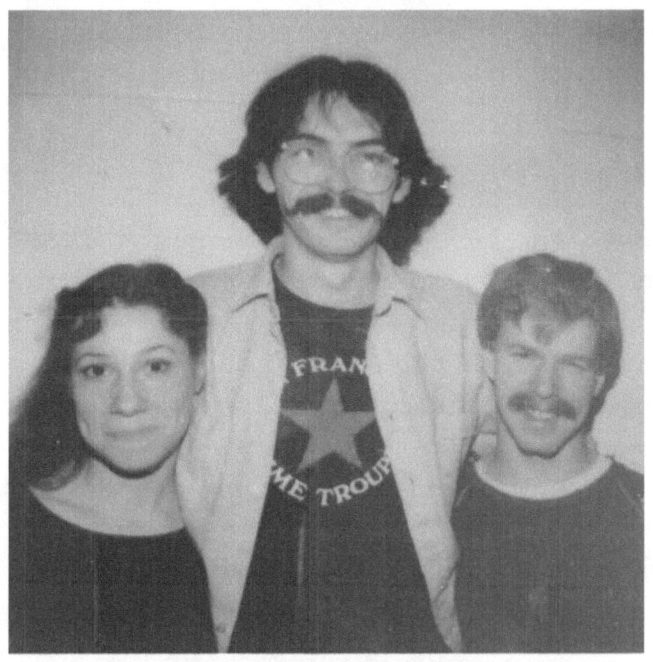

Trish Leaper, Rob Mills and Gord Robertson at their Fraggle Rock callback. Courtesy Rob Mills

Richard Hunt's enthusiasm during the audition only fuelled their hopes. Rob remembers, "I do recall Richard running around behind us as we did our goofy bits of business, grabbing props out of that suitcase for us and handing them to us, like a stagehand, but with a big grin on his face the whole time. He was definitely on our side." Hunt's support was a beacon of hope in the sea of leotards and perfect postures surrounding them.

Then came the waiting game. Weeks turned into months with no word from the Henson camp. The trio's big break came through a bizarrely roundabout channel, an encounter between a friend of a friend and Michael Frith and Kathy Mullen, *Fraggle Rock* conceptual designer and Muppet performer respectively, in Bermuda. "It turns out that our friends knew the people who they were so delighted to have cast as the Gorgs. Us! We had to call Henson in New York and ask if this was true or not because you guys haven't said squat. They said something like, 'Oh, yeah, sorry about that. I guess someone should have called.' It was true. We were working for the Muppets."

DOWN AT FRAGGLE ROCK

The Toronto set of *Fraggle Rock* was a hive of creative energy. "Everyone was so jazzed to be there working on this extraordinary show. I was just happy to not be a starving mime anymore. The studios were like magic with their fanciful sets and all the technical gear." For a group of street performers, it was like stepping into another world.

However, the transition from mimes to Gorgs wasn't without its challenges. The costumes, while impressive, presented significant technical hurdles, particularly when it came to visibility. "The original vision system for the costumes wasn't working out as planned. The heads contained radio-controlled servos and receivers to manipulate the eyes and mouths of the characters, we really couldn't see out of any obvious holes in the mouth and eyes."

Enter Faz Fazakas, a wizard in the world of special effects and a close collaborator of Jim Henson. Fazakas' first attempt at a solution was, to say the least, unconventional. Rob describes the setup: "The eyepiece was attached to an eyepatch of leather that hung off the interior helmet, sort of like a pirate. The other end with the lens was mounted up beside the right eye of the character and tucked amongst the fuzzy fur of the Gorgs."

The result was less than ideal. "We couldn't see anything. The helmets, no matter how tightly we strapped ourselves in, would shift on our heads and the eyepatch hanging from the helmet would shift with it, dragging the eyepiece away from our line of vision. There was no way for us to reach up inside the heads to adjust anything." This led to some unintentionally slapstick moments during filming. "For a couple of episodes, we couldn't see anything and did a lot of running into the sets at full gallop," Rob remembers.

Moulds of the performers' faces would be taken to produce half-masks that would help support the shifting helmet and maintain a snug fit against their eyes for the viewing piece. But Fazakas took it even further. "Faz came up with a very small—for the time, nowadays they look freakin' huge—black and white security camera mounted inside one of the eyes, looking out from the pupil, and a camcorder viewfinder hacked into the system and mounted on our face masks. We could see clearly now and could do all sorts of things."

The demanding schedule of *Fraggle Rock* did little to dampen Rob's enthusiasm. "It was hard work but I loved every minute of it." The production often pushed into the early hours of the morning, especially on technically challenging Gorg or Doozer days. "We'd be finishing at three or four in the morning and stumbling around punch-drunk from the long hours." Yet even in these exhausting moments, the spirit of the production shone through. "The whole shoot was a textbook case of how to run a production and even when things weren't working out as planned no one lost their shit, and there were always always always moments of hilarity."

For Rob, *Fraggle Rock* was more than just a job, it was an education. "I spent the first few weeks being completely in awe of where I was and what was happening around me, tripping over everything and asking every stupid question imaginable," he admits. But as he settled in, his curiosity only grew. "That place was like a university for me," he says, describing how he explored every facet of the production. From the bustling production offices to the intricate puppet shop, Rob absorbed knowledge from every corner of the set.

When not donning the costume of Junior Gorg, Rob immersed himself in other aspects of the show. "I'd be doing background characters or right hands and learning by observing the main cast exercise their chops for the different directors." Jim Henson's presence on set was particularly inspiring. "When Jim directed an episode I stayed in the studio and watched everything." This holistic approach to learning left an indelible mark on Rob. "I learned so much that would stand me well not just as a puppeteer but also as a writer, producer, designer and director. Much better, and more fun, than film school."

Rob seized every opportunity to learn from the talented cast and crew. "I'd be doing background characters or right hands and learning by observing the main cast exercise their chops for the different directors. When Jim directed an episode I stayed in the studio and watched everything. I learned so much that would stand me well not just as a puppeteer but also as a writer, producer, designer and director. Much better, and more fun, than film school."

The impact of his time on *Fraggle Rock* extends far beyond the show's run. Rob's dedication to the Muppet legacy is unwavering. When asked about participating in Muppet-related projects, his response is always enthusiastic: "I owe my entire alleged career to Henson so whenever they ask if I'm available the answer is always a solid and irrevocable 'Yes'."

CONTROLLED CHAOS IN GOBLIN CITY

Rob's journey with Jim Henson continued with 1986's *Labyrinth*, a film that pushed the boundaries of fantasy storytelling and practical effects. "I have so many *Labyrinth* stories. All of them give me a backache. Every new set I'd step into was just a mind-blowing experience."

The production's scale was unprecedented. "The Escher set was particularly extraordinary. Goblin City, if you shaded your eyes so as not to see the lighting grid in the studio, looked real; the streets extended off into forever and the attention to detail was gobsmacking."

Even the less glamorous aspects of the production showcased the Henson team's commitment to realism. Rob vividly describes the Bog of Stench set: "[Special effects artist] George Gibbs and his team had constructed the bog with pneumatic plants that would shudder and belch and fart, along with a trail of boulders that would rise out of the water on hydraulic lifts. After a few days of shooting on the set, the cellulose started to rot. When all those farting plants were quiet, the oil would cover everything and suppress the smell, but when the cameras were rolling and plants were belching, the oil was disturbed and the actual horrible rotten putrid disgusting odour of the bog billowed forth. We had to open the studio doors between takes to let in fresh air. It was terrible. But it looked good."

At the heart of this controlled chaos was Jim Henson himself, his enthusiasm infectious. "Jim was relentless in his pursuit of the work and thoroughly in his element on that shoot. At one point we were shooting on three different sound stages simultaneously and he would ride back and forth from one set to the other on a bicycle with a big grin on his face."

Even with the production's complexity, Jim's meticulous planning ensured that his vision could be realised. "Every scene and every set-up had its challenges, both in respect to storytelling and the technical aspects of the puppetry. There was, as is always the case with Henson, a lot of creative invention and innovation involved."

Rob's role as one of the performers for Ludo, a gentle giant in the film, presented its own challenges. Working alongside the character's designer and fellow performer Ron Mueck, Rob spent weeks in rehearsal, focusing on "the technical nature of the costume itself, finding the physical limitations and opportunities that the whole rig possessed." It was a process that exemplified the Henson approach: a blend of technical precision and creative expression, all in service of bringing fantastical characters to life.

The physical demands of bringing Ludo to life were formidable. During rehearsals, the toll became apparent when Ron Mueck threw out his back, a casualty of the restrictive hip harness and the sheer weight of the character's head and arms. However, as Rob points out, these challenges inadvertently shaped Ludo's distinctive presence: "The necessity of surviving the costume contributed to Ludo's gait and broader movements."

Rob's insights into the costume's mechanics proved invaluable, particularly during action sequences. "Knowing those physical limitations, where the mechanism of the costume construction will suddenly stop and provide resistance, helped me greatly when I did the fight scene with Didymus." It was a delicate dance of puppetry and physical performance, each movement carefully calibrated to the costume's constraints.

According to Rob, the battle in Goblin City "was just insane. Goblins, puppets, actors, chickens, Riding Goblins and big hulking Ludo charging through those narrow streets... Invariably I'd take a corner too quickly and not be able to maintain my balance and I'd just tip over, and more than once I ended up landing right on poor [actor] Warwick Davis. It was nuts."

Perhaps one of the most technically challenging scenes was the surreal "shaft of hands" sequence. It required a feat of coordination and endurance from the performers, crammed into a scaffolding tower to create a living wall of grasping hands. Rob commends the film's young star for her resilience: "Jennifer Connelly was a real trouper during all of that. She was fitted into a flying harness that was attached to an elevator rig that ran up and down the length of the shaft. As she descended, reaching out and grabbing at the hands around her, we would get whacked and clubbed by her flailing arms as we tried to grab at her. Her hair was always getting stuck to the foam latex hands and we'd end up holding small clumps of her tresses. Not an easy way to spend a day at work."

The scene where Ludo calls the rocks during the Goblin City battle stands out as a testament to Jim Henson's ambitious vision and the crew's dedication. Jim wanted to capture this complex sequence in a single take, presenting a challenge to the team. "This meant the camera crane would catch Sarah, Ludo and the others as they scramble to a house. The door is locked, so Ludo rips open the wall and they all go inside, and then the entire building shakes and sways from side to side as the camera rises to reach the rooftops over-looking the city. The roof flies off and Ludo stands up in the now open tower of the building and starts hollering for help from his boulder friends. Okay."

The logistics of this shot were daunting. "The tower was too narrow for any actual staircase that could allow anyone, let alone Ludo, to quickly scale to the roof. In addition, the building had been mounted on hydraulic jacks by George Gibbs and his effects team to provide the broad cartoon-like movements of the entire structure." This necessitated a creative solution: Ron Mueck would perform as Ludo on the ground, while Rob would be pre-positioned in the tower to emerge for the rooftop sequence.

The setup was as complex as the shot itself. Rob was fitted with a flying harness beneath the Ludo costume, then hoisted into the tower by the rigging crew. Dresser/wrangler Cas Willing was also squeezed into the cramped space to assist Rob between takes. "Space was tight up there so when we were rolling film, Cas had to crouch down on the floor of the tower behind Ludo so as not to be seen."

The physical toll of this arrangement quickly became apparent. As Rob was lifted in costume, there was an ominous crack from the fibreglass harness. "The additional weight of Ludo's legs and feet, usually supported by my legs, had stressed the hip harness so much it broke and split apart on my right side. When I was lowered into the tower with Cas, that additional weight was returned to my legs and the hip harness dutifully went back into its original position, closing the gap of the split, and catching a good fistful of my flesh and pinching it tight."

Each take brought new challenges: "Every time the building rocked the folks downstairs, Ron and the others would be jostled about but up in the tower the movement was bigger, tossing Cas and myself like dice in a cup. Cas was squeaking like a mouse with each bump of the building and I was swearing like a drunken sailor because the movement made the hip harness bite into me tighter and drag me around inside the costume. Very, very painful. I had a huge pinched purple welt the width of my hand down the side of my hip that hurt like blazes for weeks after. But we got the shot."

Working with David Bowie on *Labyrinth* left Rob with fond memories. "I had the pleasure of buying him a pint at the studio pub. There was one day when a large number of the cast were all traipsing out of the soundstage and off to the dressing rooms when the absurdity of the situation gave him a fit of the giggles. Everyone was still in full costume and makeup, including Bowie as Jareth, and he just looked around, surrounded by an entourage of little goblins, and he started skipping and singing 'The Lollipop Guild' from *The Wizard of Oz* [1939]. It was hilarious."

TURTLES AND DINOSAURS

Rob's journey with the Henson Company continued to evolve, leading him to work on a diverse range of projects. From the 1987 special *The Christmas Toy* to *The Jim Henson Hour* in 1989, Rob's versatility as a performer was put to good use.

In 1991, Brian Henson invited him to join the team for *Teenage Mutant Ninja Turtles II*, a project that pushed the boundaries of animatronic technology. "We spent some time in the UK at the Creature Shop testing and rehearsing with the computer-assisted animatronic rigs before heading off to North Carolina to shoot for several weeks. I enjoyed working with the animatronic rig and working with Leif Tilden who was inside the Donatello costume."

Rob's description of the puppeteer-costume dynamic offers insight into the collaborative nature of bringing these characters to life: "There's a simpatico that develops in doing that kind of work. That puppeteer/costume combination creates this 'third' entity that is the character itself and it's always amazing to watch it happen, especially when the heads come off and the two performers confer eagerly with words like: 'That was fucking awesome! You were right there!'"

His expertise with cutting-edge puppetry technology made Rob the perfect choice to step in on the TV series *Dinosaurs* when Steve Whitmire was called away to film *The Muppet Christmas Carol*. "They needed someone to take over the characters Robbie [the dinosaur son] and Mr. Richfield [the boss] and whatever other characters Steve would be doing. I had experience working with the computer-assisted animatronic rig they were using from my work on *Teenage Mutant Ninja Turtles II*."

The technology used in *Dinosaurs* was a testament to the Henson Company's commitment to pushing the boundaries of puppetry and animation. "It's a cool system and was the Creature Shop's own application, and was an extension of the work done during *The Jim Henson Hour* with Pacific Data Images, specifically with a character known as Digit, who was not a puppet but a CG animated character operated in real-time by a puppeteer. In the case of Digit, that was also Steve Whitmire."

Rob's enthusiasm for this technological evolution is evident: "I got to play around with that during the shooting of the Henson Hour and was equally jazzed to be working with the further iteration of that tech on *Ninja Turtles* then to be asked to play with a furtherance of that gear on *Dinosaurs* was a lot of fun." Rob's journey from traditional puppetry to these high-tech productions mirrors the company's own evolution, always seeking new ways to bring fantastical characters to life and push the boundaries of what was possible in visual storytelling.

An insatiable curiosity and desire to learn remained with Rob throughout his time with the Henson Company. His experience on *Dinosaurs* was no exception. "I got to soak in how they were running their show and I always loved learning more about that." This period was not without its challenges. Rob found himself balancing his work on *Dinosaurs* with a series back in Canada. "It was hard in some ways, but not because of the show itself; I was co-producing *The Big Comfy Couch* [1993–95] in Toronto and was constantly splitting my focus between the two projects, but it all worked out."

The *Dinosaurs* set left an indelible mark on Rob's memory, not just for its innovative technology, but for the warmth and camaraderie of the team. "There was always a game of chess going on behind the puppeteer's rigs." Summing up his experience, he states simply, "The people. Best part of it all."

When reflecting on Jim Henson himself, Rob's admiration is clear. "I think Jim was an icon to everybody. Of course, I was a fan of his work, but not as a devoted puppeteer, but more as a visual artist and storyteller. He didn't just inspire through artistry and craft; he nurtured a work ethic in everyone that saw us give our best in return for being invited to play. I owe my entire career to that man."

GORD ROBERTSON
PUPPETEER

> "Look at his designs. Look at his storytelling. That's why people call him a genius because he covered a lot of ground."

FROM ASPIRING mime to performing as a Gorg on *Fraggle Rock*, Gord Robertson became an integral part of multiple Henson productions, learning from masters like Jerry Nelson while developing his own puppetry skills.

* * *

In 1982, Toronto buzzed with excitement as Jim Henson's team held auditions for a new children's series, *Fraggle Rock*. Gord and fellow performers Rob Mills and Trish Leaper, who had invited him to join them after meeting at mime school, stumbled upon an opportunity that seemed tailor-made for them. "They were looking for two short people and a tall person who knew how to work inside bodysuits and so they hired us."

Landing a role on *Fraggle Rock* wasn't just a job; it was a passport to a whole new world of puppetry. For four years, Gord and his colleagues were immersed in a puppet boot camp led by the Muppet masters themselves. "They gave us a career," Gord reflects, his voice filled with gratitude. The Muppet team provided a comprehensive education in various puppetry techniques, including "hand and rod puppetry, where the hand goes up inside the head, and also in things like remote control puppetry, bodysuit work, in different kinds of rod puppet, and even a touch of marionette work. We got a really thorough education from the people who were the best in the business, especially at television puppetry."

The show's production schedule, leisurely by today's breakneck standards, allowed for a level of craftsmanship rarely seen in modern children's television. "Monday was for read-throughs, then Wednesday through Friday we'd shoot. Many 'kids' shows' now will do the same amount of work in half the time. Friday was often overtime. We could do lots because there were different layers to *Fraggle*. You had the Gorgs, I was inside one of the suits. You had the Fraggles, which were regular-sized puppets, and you had the Doozers, which were smaller. That's a lot of different elements, which many kids shows wouldn't have the budget, the resources, or the time for nowadays."

It wasn't until Gord started working on other shows that he realised just how unique his experience with the Muppets had been. "You could see that they didn't have the same experience shooting television, they didn't understand the relationship between puppets and a camera. I think Jim might have been the first to realise that if he could puppeteer using a monitor, then he could see what he's doing up here."

LEARNING FROM THE BEST

"The soul of the puppet is in the eyes," says Gord, quoting Jim Henson. This principle, aligning perfectly with Gord's background in mask work, became a cornerstone of his puppetry technique. "If you understand how to play a mask, then you understand that approach. And that was the best thing in the world to learn."

Reflecting on his *Fraggle Rock* journey, Gord laughs at his early attempts. "I remember on season three or four seeing something that I had done in season one and just going 'Oh my God, how did I not get fired the first year?' We had no control. We had no precision. We just didn't know what we were doing." The *Fraggle* experience, however, went beyond technical skills. It taught Gord professional etiquette and opened doors in the industry. "The Muppet name, once it was kind of in my credits, it gave me an automatic respectability."

Although not constantly present on set, Jim Henson's presence was always felt. "He was great because he would listen to anybody. He might not always take your suggestion, but he would listen. At the same time, he was terrifying. Because he was Jim Henson. I was terrified that if I made a mistake, I would be gone the next day."

But Jim's playful side also shines through in Gord's memories. He recounts a moment when Jim put him on the spot during a crowded scene: "I had to make an entrance, but the area we were in was so small that I couldn't get out of the shot and Jim just thought it was hilarious." Gord's voice fills with warmth as he describes Jim's teasing: "'We're about to roll, you better keep going.' He poked me and it was hilarious at my expense. He was kind of poking me, 'You've got to get a shot,' and I'm like, 'Where do I go?' And he said, 'We're about to roll, you better keep going.' It was serious, but that was his kind of bratty, I don't know if that's the right word, streak. He was really good fun."

When discussing the potential hierarchy among Muppet performers, Gord offers a newcomer's perspective. He recalls only one noticeable distinction: the allocation of dressing rooms. "I mean, the only difference was that the American puppeteers, the core Muppet troupe, had a small dressing room each and the Canadian puppeteers, who were in the main background puppeteers, had one room to themselves. That's about the only grading."

Gord shares an anecdote about veteran Muppet performer Jerry Nelson, who described how the core group had worked together for so long that they had "rubbed the sharp edges off of each other". This sentiment resonated with Gord, who found all the Muppet performers to be "really good people together and on their own".

Fraggle Rock's musical numbers presented a steep learning curve for Gord, a newcomer to puppetry and synchronised performances. He and his fellow background performers approached the choreography with dedication and a touch of anxiety. "That was homework every week for us if there were background Fraggles, working on that choreography and the absolute horror and angst if you screwed up. While everybody was going this way, you suddenly found yourself doing the opposite."

Gord's contributions to *Fraggle Rock* extended beyond his role as a Gorg. "When I wasn't in a Gorg they would bring me in to puppeteer, and that was great." These opportunities allowed him to refine his skills as a background performer. He reflects on a particular ability he developed: "One of the skills, I call it a skill, was in any shot you might have a second, because you're in the background, to try and get a little piece of business in or to get your choreography in. That was a really good skill to develop, it made us all more precise in what we were doing, more succinct in what we were doing."

Gord offers a perspective on Jim Henson inspired by a conversation with his friend and fellow *Fraggle Rock* puppeteer, John Pattison. "One day we were talking about Jim and he said, 'The thing is that Jim was a great comedian.' And I sort of went 'What?'" This observation prompted Gord to reevaluate his understanding of Henson's work. "I never really thought of him as a comedian, and it made me kind of look at Jim's stuff again, and John was right, he was a great comedian. I think that's why the word genius gets applied to him, because he was a great comedian, whether he gets credit for it or not."

Expanding on Jim's diverse talents, Gord paints a picture of a true Renaissance man in the world of puppetry and entertainment.

"He was arguably a great singer, a character singer because when you listen to his characters sing, they sound like that's what they would sound like. They don't suddenly break character and sound like opera singers or Broadway singers, they sound like those characters singing, which sounds obvious now, but I don't know if it was before."

Gord also highlights Jim's innovative approach to puppetry for the screen. "I don't know if he invented the way that puppeteers work in television and film now, but he was certainly at the forefront of it, the way they relate to cameras and monitors and all of that. Look at his designs. Look at his storytelling. That's why people call him a genius because he covered a lot of ground."

NEW OPPORTUNITIES

Following *Fraggle Rock*, Gord's journey with Henson productions continued through various specials and the *Sesame Street* film, *Follow that Bird* (1985). He touches on the challenges of performing in a Dodo bird costume. "I have pictures of me inside the suit covered in foam and fur, and everybody else is either shirtless or in shorts and tank tops. That's what I remember about that, sweating my little butt off and struggling to breathe."

Gord's experiences also include working with puppet builder Kermit Love, known for his contributions to *Sesame Street*. "Kermit gave me one of the best notes ever, 'You have no constancy.' And I went, 'You mean consistency?' And he went, 'No constancy, you never do the same thing twice.'" Gord explains the importance of this insight: "His point was that it's fine when you're on your own, but if there are other people around you, if you're in a suit and a guy is doing your eyes, he needs to know what you're doing. It was a good note."

Gord's career expanded beyond Henson productions, including work on the 1988 sci-fi comedy *Short Circuit 2*. He attributes this opportunity to Jim Henson's recommendation: "I think Jim was contacted because they were looking for puppeteers and he said, 'There are three people up in Canada you should talk to.' The reason he mentioned three is that the three Gorgs were myself, Trish Leaper and Rob Mills, the same two people that we had started the mime troupe. So, because they knew it was three people working on one character, and we had all worked together, that's one of the reasons that he suggested it. So that was another gift from the Muppets."

Reflecting on the enduring appeal of the Muppets, Gord touches on their inherent goodness: "I also think, especially in terms of the Muppets, that none of those characters have a mean bone in their body. One of the saddest things I find is when somebody who's a political or entertainment figure that I have respected has some scandal that tarnishes them. It's so disheartening because we all want to believe in something, in a certain purity."

Thanks to *The Jim Henson Hour*, Gord was offered new opportunities. "On a personal level that show was great because on *Fraggle* I was a Gorg and then I did background work, then I had maybe only two speaking parts, which was a big deal to get a speaking part if you're a background performer. Then on *The Jim Henson Hour*, I got a couple more, so that was astounding." He views the show as a reflection of Jim's innovative spirit: "Jim did something very different when he went from Muppets to *Fraggle* to *Labyrinth* to *Dark Crystal*, those were all different aspects of him trying to find different venues for puppets. Part of his restless imagination."

Despite his success with the Muppets, Gord remained in Canada, citing family ties and abundant work opportunities. He continued collaborating with the Muppets on Canadian-based productions such as *It's a Very Merry Muppet Christmas Movie* and *Muppets Wizard of Oz*. While acknowledging the role of Canadian content quotas in his hiring, Gord emphasises the importance of personal connections. "Part of that is personality as well. I teach at a college here just outside of Toronto, and one thing I say to my students is, 'Look, in any job situation, there are probably 20 people that can do your job, so what the employer looks at is, who do I want to spend six days a week, 12 hours a day with?'"

For Gord, working with the Muppets always feels like coming home. "I understand the aesthetic, I understand the comedy, I understand the way of working. They understand how to work in television and film so you don't you don't have to explain anything." He recounts a story from the filming of 2015's *Turkey Hollow*, where six puppeteers had to be buried in the ground for a shot, something that would raise concerns on most sets.

"For any other production, I would have a lot of questions. For the Muppets, I didn't have a single question, because I know they've got it covered. They understand safety. They understand about making it possible for the puppeteer to work and that means monitor, that means physical comfort." It's this deep understanding and appreciation of the craft that sets the Muppets apart in Gord's eyes. "They get it because they developed the whole craft."

Gord mentions his first experience working with Steve Whitmire as Kermit, likely during *It's a Very Merry Muppet Christmas Movie*. While acknowledging the difference from Jim Henson's portrayal, Gord has nothing but praise for his performance: "I remember he did a scene for somebody else on *Dog City*, it was a complicated dance sequence, and the performer asked Steve if he would do his character for this dance sequence. And Steve did it and could mimic the character so well, it was seamless."

Gord acknowledges that taking over a beloved character is no easy feat, as the original performer's essence is deeply ingrained. "All of those original characters who are being done beautifully by new people came from those original performers. There is an element that because I grew up with them, I'm fond of them, and that's no reflection on the performers who are doing a brilliant job and are doing their best to channel, in a psychic kind of way, those characters."

Gord recounts the emotional impact of Jim Henson's death, from the shock of receiving the news from Kevin Clash to a poignant moment at Jim's memorial when nearly a thousand butterflies rose from the audience during Harry Belafonte's performance. "That's what I remember about Jim's death. This crazy, beautiful moment. And great uncertainty about this company that I felt so beholden and loyal to, that so many people that I was close to worked for, that now didn't know what was going on."

When asked about the impact of Disney's acquisition of the Muppets, Gord diplomatically acknowledges that change is inevitable. "Are the Muppets the same without Jim? Of course not. That's a fact. So then you decide, and the fans decide, whether it's better or worse on the course that the company has gone. I worked with Jim, so of course I have an emotional attachment to the Muppets when he was around. So yeah, I'm gonna say, I liked the Muppets when Jim was there. Now, that's an emotional attachment that anybody can say, 'Well, I don't agree with you.' Have I seen decisions that were made that I don't think Jim would have made? Yes, of course. But I can't say with any certainty because he's not here."

Gord echoes the sentiment that it was the people who made the Henson Company what it was, not just Jim's brilliance. "I heard a story, which I think has been repeated many times, about how in the early script meetings for concept meetings for *Fraggle Rock*, that apparently Jim said something like, 'Let's make a show that will end all war.' People heard that and they laughed and then they realised he was serious. That theme of humanity and connection, that's an underlying theme for the Muppets.

"There's a goodness and a spirit of working together. I think that the most disappointing thing about what's happening in the States right now is the divisiveness that's being encouraged." Drawing parallels to his Buddhist meditation practice, he suggests: "If you want the world to be a kinder, gentler place, you have to practice. Whether that's taking a moment to put on a DVD [of *The Muppet Show*] and remind yourself that hey, here's an example of goodness, when you're in traffic, let that guy in, don't cut him off. He may not appreciate it, but actually, it works. It's all the little things, and that's all I'll say about that."

Reflecting on his career highlights, Gord fondly remembers working with ventriloquist Shari Lewis, best known for her sock puppet creation, Lamb Chop: "I loved working with her. I put her up there in the same category of fantastic experiences of working with the Muppets. She was a consummate professional, an old-time performer, and I especially loved the way that she talked about the craft of comedy because she came from an older tradition."

Gord expresses gratitude for his ongoing work in the industry, including recent forays into French-language television with TFO (Téléfrancais Ontario). "Another broadcaster that had attracted great people and such a pleasure to work with, especially because they're all francophones."

The conversation concludes with a touching personal anecdote that exemplifies Jim Henson's genuine interest in his team's creative endeavours outside of the Muppets. "At the time that I was working for the Fraggles, I'm going to say maybe in the second season, I had been making a lot of masks because I was still doing mask work and mime stuff. I had all these masks and I thought I should exhibit my masks. So I rented a gallery and put up the masks and made up a poster and sent it out, and kind of as a lark, I sent one to Jim.

"Well, he happened to be in town, and he came. And I thought, 'The dude has time to come see my mask exhibition?' It was amazing. So if I hadn't been loyal before, I certainly was then."

JEREMY SWAN
DIRECTOR

> "Anyone who shoves her hands up an animal, does a funny voice and gets paid for it has to be admired!"

JEREMY SWAN TOOK on the challenge of directing the UK segments of *Fraggle Rock*, working with both human actors and puppets to create seamless transitions between the international and domestic portions of the show.

* * *

It was after a stint as floor manager on ITV's *Coronation Street* (1960–) that Jeremy Swan's directing career in children's television began at the BBC with series such as the long-running *Rentaghost* (1976–84) and *Grandad* (1979–84) with Clive Dunn.

The early 1980s saw Jeremy invited to join TVS in Maidstone, part of the commercial ITV network serving the South and South-east of England, where his first assignment was to direct the UK scenes of *Fraggle Rock*. Although the main segments were filmed in Canada, the UK team focused on the studio links written by Victor Pemberton and starring Fulton Mackay and Sprocket the dog.

"Once the set was up it stayed there," says Jeremy. "We'd be there for about three or four weeks. The set was raised so that the puppeteers could operate below. Fulton was terrific, though occasionally had to be reminded he wasn't playing King Lear; he was feeding lines to a puppet tail-wagging dog!"

The series went on location around the UK to film the numerous Uncle Travelling Matt inserts. "The names were clever. As well as being one of the characters, a Gobo is a thing that's put in front of a light. All their names were technical to do with apparatus that's used in filming, like a travelling matte. It was very clever of Jim Henson to come up with those names. I did meet him up at Downshire Hill in Hampstead, that's where the Creature Shop offices were. He mainly worked in the Creature Shop in New York."

Jeremy went on to direct six episodes of another Henson production, 1994's *The Secret Life of Toys*, a series executive produced by Brian Henson, whom he describes as "a very nice guy, very charming, and very reminiscent of his late father. He was very respectful of anything that people had to offer by way of their talents, like the puppeteers. The puppeteers are the gods, they rule the roost and they're the ones who say, 'We want to do another take.' They would have their very good reasons, be it an eyeline or a rodding (that's what operates puppet hands or tails). You just say, 'Another take, stand by.'"

Filming for *The Secret Life of Toys* took Jeremy to Germany, with the shoot taking place in studios in Monheim, near Dusseldorf. Reflecting on the intricate process of working with Henson puppets, Jeremy explains, "The puppets haven't got any legs but there has to be a floor in evidence, otherwise the puppets looked as if they were floating in mid-air. So it's kind of one-foot square at the top of four thin steel pillars, all joined up. The square is removed for the puppet to 'stand' in and the puppeteer operated on typist chairs on the floor, looking at monitors that were strapped to their chests as they held the puppets up into the shot. If anybody had to do a long run or a big walk it took hours because you had to take out the floor, put in the floor behind them, all that sort of thing.

"The other thing with Henson puppets was the wonderful way they move their heads, there had to be tiny fans to give a bounce to the hair and these all had to be strategically placed. The stamina of the puppeteers was formidable. You try holding your right hand rigidly above your head and flapping your fingers against your thumb eight hours a day!"

Jeremy contrasts the painstaking work of puppet animation with the action-packed scenes his friend Andrew Morgan was filming for a police drama, Germany's answer to *The Bill* (1984–2010), in Cologne at the same time. "He said, 'We had a frightful day to day. We had to do this scene where we took over the main bridge going over the Rhine, and a motorboat came along and three prostitutes were thrown over the bridge, and police had to come and lifesavers had to get them out of the water and take them to the shore... Of course, we had cameras in helicopters as well as on the bridge.'

'Of course.'

'Well, that was my day, what was yours like?'

'It was a mouse running up and down a curtain. All day.'"

According to Jeremy, everyone involved in *The Secret Life of Toys* was sure there would be a second series. There wasn't. Disney were co-producers as well as the BBC, and then 1995's *Toy Story* was released. "The programme was broadcast on the Disney Channel in the States and it was very popular. I was nominated for an Emmy."

Jeremy's next job was slightly further afield. "Anna Home, the BBC's head of children's programmes, sent me to Australia to work on a series called *Round the Twist* [1990–2001]. Yes, another lighthouse. I was the associate producer on that and I was the script consultant for the BBC. It became wildly popular and my bank manager sings the signature tune. Then it was back to the UK and back to Oz to direct episodes and write scripts for *The Genie from Down Under* [1996], which was exactly what was written on the tin."

Back in the UK, Jeremy directed 1987's *Bad Boyes* and the *Uncle*

Jack (1990–93) series starring Paul Jones and Fenella Fielding. "I also directed the Saturday morning show *Going Live* [1987–93], which I called *Going Dead* because we had to start at 6.30am. Philip Schofield and Sarah Greene presented without a shred of exhaustion."

Jeremy reflects on his pride for having worked Henson productions and its impact on his career. "To say that you worked with Jim Henson's company was very impressive on a CV." Later, ITV asked him to direct episodes of *Sooty* (2011). "I was big in puppet TV. It was impressive for me to say I had directed the Henson puppets, as much as you can direct a puppet. Mind you, once you get into your head that all puppeteers are basically around the bend; anyone who shoves her hands up an animal, does a funny voice and gets paid for it has to be admired!"

s That You Maureen? My Life Making Children's TV & *Beyond* **by Jeremy Swan is published by Ten Acre Films.**

STEVE BARRON
DIRECTOR

"Jim was an amazing man full of ideas, full of great enthusiasm to innovate and to press things forward."

ALREADY KNOWN for music videos such as A-ha's *Take On Me*, Steve Barron brought his innovative visual style to *The Storyteller* and helped establish the darker, more sophisticated side of Henson productions.

* * *

In the 1980s, as MTV transformed the music landscape, Steve Barron was quietly reshaping the music video itself. His work didn't just accompany songs; it often became inseparable from them. The pencil-sketch animation of A-ha's *Take On Me* and the glowing sidewalk tiles in Michael Jackson's *Billie Jean* became as memorable as the tunes themselves.

Steve had a knack for creating visuals that lingered in viewers' minds long after the songs had ended, a talent that caught the attention of another visual innovator, Jim Henson, who was in the middle of production of *Labyrinth*. Henson soon invited Steve to direct two promotional videos for the film, *Underground* (1986) and *As the World Falls Down* (1986).

Says Steve, "I went in to meet with Bowie and chatted through the ideas, then met with Jim Henson who said, 'Look, I've directed the film, and I'll show you a cut of it, and if you want to use some of the creatures and characters from our Creature Shop, please go ahead. We can even leave the set up for a day or so for you to mess around with.' He left it very much open what to do and where to do it."

During the production of the music videos, Steve formed a friendly relationship with Jim, showing him some of his recent work, including the video for *Take on Me*, with its blend of pencil-sketch animation and live action. Steve's use of silhouettes, a technique he'd refined, particularly caught Jim's eye. "When I'd worked in post-production, I found that the best way to believe them and feel satisfied with them was through silhouettes, and doing them against white instead of green screen. I wanted to do a whole video that was about these silhouettes and the journey of characters and creatures."

Impressed by Steve's work, Jim approached him soon after to direct 'Hans My Hedgehog', the half-hour pilot for NBC's *The Storyteller*. The show would focus on early European folk tales, offering a darker take on fairy tales that predated the Grimms' versions, a stark contrast to the sanitised Disney adaptations that had dominated for decades.

Steve met with writer Anthony Minghella several times to discuss the format and direction of the show. "Jim had talked about what format the whole show could be, whether it was more of a storyteller in a room than it was about the actual images of the story. I said, 'We should do it on film, we could do it straight from negative and edit it digitally,' and he was fascinated by the new way of doing effects and online editing."

This conversation was taking place at a time when the film industry was on the cusp of a digital revolution. Traditional celluloid was still king, but new digital technologies were emerging, promising new creative possibilities and cost efficiencies.

"He let me go at it and we came up with something that looked quite abstract, quite out there. The silhouette technique was partly a cost-saving device, but mainly as a composite tool, to really make the composites work and also to keep the darkness and I'd seen some interesting animation and some silhouette drawings for the stories."

This approach aligned with a growing trend in visual storytelling that favoured mood and atmosphere over literal representation. Influenced in part by European art films and the resurgence of German Expressionist aesthetics in popular culture, this trend was evident in works like *Blade Runner* (1982) with its shadowy cityscapes, and Peter Gabriel's *Sledgehammer* (1986) music video, which used surreal imagery to create a mood-driven visual experience.

"Jim was amazing. He just said, 'Look, we'll get the creatures that Anthony's written and just shoot for seven or eight days,' that was for the pilot. And then it played in the States and they ordered eight more episodes of it."

CREATING THE STORYTELLER'S WORLD

The Creature Shop's expertise and dedication to character development quickly became apparent to Steve. At a time when practical effects were still dominant and CG was in its infancy, Henson's Creature Shop represented the pinnacle of puppet and animatronic technology. Their Camden Town studio was a hub of innovation, pushing the boundaries of what was possible in practical effects.

"They're all about character because Jim came from the world of character and that was his strength. They had so many great people working in the Creature Shop that I had no doubt when we went to do *The Storyteller* that it would be stunning," Steve says, confident in their ability to bring the stories to life assuming they had sufficient time to explore the numerous possibilities the project presented.

Despite the darker tone of some stories, *The Storyteller* was intended for a family audience. "It could have been very bright and colourful, and cartoony, and Disney and still with the same dialogue, but we went for dark. From my point of view, everything was about something that I was fascinated by and enjoyed, but I wasn't aiming it at a young audience. I was just aiming to do it as well as it could be for us to enjoy because I think that's the only thing you know. You've got to go with what you really enjoy."

Steve adds that John Hurt was an ideal fit for the role of the mysterious Storyteller. Hurt, known for his distinctive voice and powerful performances in films like 1980's *The Elephant Man* and *1984* (1984), brought gravitas to the role. "You couldn't have got a better voice, those tones are immediately evocative of beautiful storytelling," Steve says. "He was the number one choice for the Storyteller. On the first episode, we had quite an extended nose for him and it looked a little bit fake, so I remember on the following eight, which we just started five or six months later, we trimmed that down quite a bit. So he's telling more lies in the first episode."

Following the success of the pilot, Jim asked Steve to serve as a creative director for the series. "I went into the meetings with everyone and they showed me the scripts and we had a long meeting about the world of silhouettes and how the post-production would work. I brought in my editor who'd done most of my music videos. Everybody tries to keep that uniform look."

Regarding the experience of working with Jim, Steve explains that he "loved working with him, he was amazing, and we got quite close as friends, I saw him socially quite a bit. He was an amazing man full of ideas, full of great enthusiasm to innovate and to press things forward."

On the subject of a potential second season, Steve notes that *The Storyteller* was an expensive production for its time slot, with each episode being shot like a movie and the cost of the creatures being very high. "I think it was mainly a cost thing." While a second series was eventually produced under the title *The Storyteller: Greek Myths*, featuring Michael Gambon as the Storyteller instead of John Hurt, Steve wasn't involved in this iteration.

With rumours of a potential remake, Steve acknowledges the enduring appeal of *The Storyteller*, even if he doesn't expect to be involved in any new production. "I think it'll always have its place. It's got some naivety in there that's very hard to recreate."

FINDING THE TONE

Steve's collaboration with Jim Henson continued with *Teenage Mutant Ninja Turtles*, a project that came to him through writer Anthony Minghella. This adaptation came at a time when comic book properties were just beginning to be seen as viable sources for major film productions, predating the superhero movie boom of the 2000s.

Golden Harvest, a Hong Kong-based production company known for its martial arts films, had approached Minghella about adapting one of his plays into a movie set in the Far East. Although that project didn't materialise, the company was looking for Western properties to produce for both Eastern and Western audiences, reflecting the growing globalisation of the film industry.

"They said they'd got this thing with these turtles and they didn't quite know how to make it as a movie, and Anthony suggested I get involved in that. I got involved in developing the script and enjoyed what their world was and the back story."

Teenage Mutant Ninja Turtles, created by Kevin Eastman and Peter Laird, had already become a pop culture phenomenon through comics and an animated series. However, translating the concept to a live-action film presented various challenges and Steve and his team struggled to find distributors interested in the project. Undeterred, he reached out to Jim Henson, hoping to secure the Creature Shop's involvement in bringing the Turtles to life on screen. "I rang up Jim and I said, 'I've got this thing, it's a really mad comic book, but I think it'd be amazing if you do the creatures, or your Creature Shop could,' knowing that the ninja thing might be a problem with Jim."

Initially, Jim expressed concerns about the martial arts elements of the story. "He looked at it and he rang me up and said, 'Look, I'm worried about these nunchucks and these scythes and swords and it just kind of goes a little bit against what we've done at the Creature Shop, I'm not sure.'"

After a few days of discussion, Steve assured Jim that he would find the right balance in the film's tone. "I said, 'I'll find a tone that isn't stupid, but has got some magic to it.' In the end, he rang me up and said, 'Go on, let's go for it.'" The Creature Shop's involvement helped secure some distribution deals, but the team still struggled to find an American distributor until just before shooting began. Ultimately, the film defied expectations and became a massive success. "It went through the roof, which no one was expecting. It was a little low-budget thing. Half the budget went on creatures. We only had $7 million left to make it." This success—earning more than $200 million at the global box office—helped pave the way for more comic book adaptations and creature-heavy films in the 1990s.

The Creature Shop embraced the project, pushing the boundaries of their craft to create the Turtles' realistic movements and facial expressions. "They started using new technology, better radio control, all kinds of servers that would operate 17 facial expressions that were beyond what had ever been attempted before. These characters would then carry the packs that weighed 50 pounds on their backs. They were doing some super amazing, pioneering things which Jim got very excited about."

The film's release in 1990 coincided with the growing popularity of the *Teenage Mutant Ninja Turtles* cartoon series and toy line, demonstrating the power of cross-media synergy that would become increasingly common in the entertainment industry. "The cartoon came out first and got kids into it, although while we were shooting it had only been out for a few months and nobody had heard of it except kids who got up at about six in the morning. Then the toys appeared because the cartoon was paid for by a toy company. Kids started asking for the toys, but it was on a different level when the film came out. It went mainstream everywhere, it turned the franchise upside down.

Sadly, Jim Henson passed away shortly after the film's release, leaving a void in the industry he had helped shape. "I saw him in LA a few days before he passed and he had a bit of flu. He did get to see *Turtles* and enjoy the fact that it was a big hit."

Asked to sum up his experience with Jim Henson, Steve says, "You get to meet quite a lot of renowned and famous people in a career or where you work in film and TV, but there are very few, in fact, none like Jim because he was such a beautiful person. He had such a big heart that just poured into his work. He was lovely and generous, an amazing legend of a person."

MARK EADES

PRODUCER, MUPPET*VISION 3D

"I think he was creatively a lot like Disney and that he wanted to expand his creative horizons."

As PART of Disney's Theme Park Productions Group, Mark Eades worked closely with Jim on what would become his final directed project, *Muppet*Vision 3D*, while helping develop plans for a larger Muppet presence in Disney theme parks.

* * *

When Jim Henson began negotiations with Disney in the late 1980s to collaborate on new projects and potentially sell his company to the entertainment giant, producer Mark Eades found himself in the middle of the action from day one.

In 1989, Disney was undergoing organisational changes, while recent cinema releases included *The Great Mouse Detective* (1986) and *Who Framed Roger Rabbit* (1988). Mark became part of the newly formed Theme Park Productions Group, a move partly in response to the desires of Disney executives Frank Wells, Michael

Eisner and Jeffrey Katzenberg to work with "named talent" without risking the unionisation of WED Enterprises (later known as Walt Disney Imagineering). The fear of unionisation was a hot-button issue in Hollywood, with studios constantly seeking ways to maintain control over their productions.

Mark proposed a clever workaround: creating subsidiary companies that could be signatories to union agreements, allowing them to hire talent without involving the studio directly. This kind of creative problem-solving was typical of the era, as entertainment companies sought to navigate the complex world of labour relations in the industry.

It was during this time of corporate manoeuvring that Disney and Jim Henson began discussions about a potential acquisition and collaboration. "Michael Eisner and Jim Henson had been talking and suddenly one day there comes an announcement and we're told Jim Henson Productions had signed a deal to do stuff with Disney. They were also going to discuss buying the company and the first project was going to be a 3D film." This news sent ripples through both companies. For Disney, it was a chance to bring one of the most beloved and innovative creators in children's entertainment into their fold. For Henson, it offered the resources and reach of a major studio to expand his creative vision.

Mark found himself assigned to this new project from the outset, along with Kathy Rogers, a show producer from WED whom he had first met at Disneyland. The specifics of the project were still unknown, but it marked the beginning of an exciting partnership between two creative powerhouses in the entertainment industry.

The opportunity to collaborate with Jim Henson was a dream come true for Mark and the Imagineering team. Mark had already made a name for himself working on productions for Epcot that pushed the limits of film formats and technology. "My feet were in both technical and creative. Because they were weird films, I had to make sure that we knew what format it was going to be shot in and that the cameras were even working because there were maybe one or two of every one of those in the world."

NEW DIMENSIONS

"Jim and a couple of his creative people came and we had our first meeting, talked about what it would be," says Mark. "It would be 3D and he wanted to break the boundaries." This ambition reflected Jim's constant push for innovation, particularly in the late 1980s, when 3D technology was still a novelty in theme park attractions. Jim also brought in trusted collaborators like Muppet writer Jerry Juhl and a then up-and-coming Bill Prady to develop the 3D film, showcasing his knack for assembling talented teams.

In their initial meetings, Jim expressed his desire to showcase a newer Muppet character who had first been introduced in the 1986 TV special, *The Tale of the Bunny Picnic*. Says Mark, "Jim kept talking about how he had this new character, Bean Bunny, and he wanted to bring him forward. Remember theme parks work better when you have recognisable characters and Bean was not well known."

Mark also touches on Henson's interest in exploring CG animation, as well as his own team's role as "the special effects guys". This interest in CG was prescient, as the technology was on the cusp of revolutionising both film and theme park experiences. Mark recounts a particular evening when he showed Jim a projection device that could change the appearance of buildings, an impressive technology that sparked Jim's imagination. Mark suggested that this device could be used to not only break the fourth wall, a signature Muppets technique, but also to "blow it up", an idea that Jim embraced; quite literally blowing up the fourth wall would become a central element of the *Muppet*Vision 3D* experience.

Bill Prady began working on the storyline for the 3D film. While many of the elements that made it into the final product were present in his initial draft, the story primarily focused on Bean Bunny, with little involvement from the other Muppets. This approach was risky, particularly in the theme park industry of the late 1980s, where familiar characters were crucial for attracting visitors in an increasingly competitive market.

Upon reading the first draft, Mark found himself in a delicate situation. "I read that and I'm like, 'How do you tell this guy we can't do that?' but not say it that way?" Seeking guidance, he turned to his superiors, Tom Fitzgerald and Marty Sklar, who advised him to write a critique of the script, as one would expect from a professional reader.

In his feedback, Mark acknowledged the value of introducing a new character to give audiences an incentive to visit the attraction. However, he cautioned that centring the entire film around an unfamiliar character could prove challenging, particularly in a theme park setting where recognisable characters are key to drawing in visitors. The team took Mark's critique to heart, and the subsequent draft of the script more closely resembled the final product, incorporating a greater presence of the classic Muppet characters.

Mark also worked closely with Jim to maximise the 3D elements of the show, which were too light in the early plans. "I went over and spent about an hour with Jim and we talked about 3D and I expressed my concerns and talked about what's fun about 3D. I explained that because you can break the fourth wall, you can have a lot of fun with the 3D, you've got characters like Fozzie Bear who can go crazy and Gonzo can have some fun with it."

Following this meeting, the team, including Jim, travelled to Florida for a script readthrough. This trip to Walt Disney World, the home of the future attraction, was a crucial step in the development process, allowing the creators to envision how the show would fit into the park's landscape. The revised script, which had changed based on feedback from Disney executive Jeffrey Katzenberg, was much closer to the final product. Katzenberg, known for his hands-on approach to creative projects, had become increasingly involved in

Disney's theme park productions, seeing them as extensions of the company's film and television properties.

However, during the readthrough, Mark and others sensed that something still wasn't quite right. Mark's main concern centred around the opening of the film, which featured a blue curtain projected onto the physical red curtain of the building. "I'm thinking, *That's just not going to work very well.*" Despite bringing this issue up multiple times, it wasn't until the last readthrough, just a week before production began, that Jim finally agreed to change the curtain colour in the film to red. "He'd listen if you were passionate about it."

As the script continued to evolve, incorporating elements like the theatre being blown up, Jim also proposed the idea of including a live walk-around character. Although no one had ever done this in a Disney attraction before, Mark and his team accepted the challenge. Kathy Rogers, the show producer from WED, noted that operations staff might have concerns, but Mark encouraged her to handle that aspect of the project.

Mark also played a crucial role in specifying the sound system for the attraction, which featured an impressive 19 tracks to accommodate the various sound effects, such as the chef in the back and the travelling cannonball. When production finally began, he faced a personal challenge as he came down with the flu. However, due to the temperamental nature of the 3D cameras and his expertise in ensuring their functionality, a production executive insisted that Mark be present every day, assigning a PA to keep him well-supplied with fluids and aspirin.

As production on the film got underway, the first scene shot was the Miss Piggy bubbles number. Mark recalls the memorable take where Miss Piggy flipped over backwards, her rear end comically approaching the camera, which ultimately made it into the final cut. However, the temperamental 3D cameras posed ongoing challenges throughout the shoot.

One particularly crucial piece of equipment was the special glass that split the light between the cameras, requiring the crew to use more intense lighting. The team faced a potential crisis when, during the scene where the theatre blows up and bricks fly towards the camera, a brick shattered the glass on one of the three cameras. "We still had three days of shooting to go at that point," Mark remembers, highlighting the precarious situation.

To protect the remaining two cameras, the crew decided to place Plexiglass in front of them for the subsequent shots involving cannons and other potentially hazardous elements. The production managed to stay on schedule, even using the take with the broken glass by cutting the scene just before the impact.

The filming continued with various sequences shot on the back-lot, including the fire truck scene in the town square set and the patriotic finale, 'But Mostly America', which featured a black background. Because of the numerous puppets involved, some of the production crew members stepped in to assist with the puppeteering. During one memorable take, Steve Whitmire was operating a soldier character that got caught underneath a cannon or gun just as it fired, causing the puppet's head to blow off. Whitmire improvised a humorous death scene, falling out of the frame and eliciting laughter from the crew. Mark recounts Jim's amused yet firm response: "Cut, cut, cut. Very funny. Steve, don't do that again."

The production was a special experience for Mark, as it brought together all of the original Muppet performers for the last time. Witnessing skilled puppeteers, such as Frank Oz and Dave Goelz, collaborating on characters that required two hands and a head, was a fascinating sight. Mark still marvels at the coordination required for characters like the Swedish Chef, played by both Jim and Frank, each controlling one hand without knowing precisely what the other would do. Similarly, Bunsen Honeydew, a two-handed character portrayed by Dave, also performing Gonzo, showcased the intricate teamwork involved in bringing these beloved Muppets to life on screen.

After the three-week production wrapped, the film entered the editing phase, while negotiations between Disney and the Muppets continued. Mark, in his role as producer for Theme Park Productions, meticulously reviewed the contracts to ensure the necessary rights were secured. "They had done contracts with the production company and with all the performers that gave us the rights to *Muppet*Vision 3D*, supposedly, in case something went wrong on the overall deal. I read them all religiously, and I said, 'What we need in there is not in there.' Time goes by and the film gets edited with a temp mix and we look at it and it's not quite right, it was a good cut, but we had a feeling we were going to have to do some reshoots."

However, during this time, Mark received devastating news while on a family vacation: "I got the call to say Jim had died and I flew home. Now what do we do?"

Jim's death left the project in limbo. To salvage the film, Disney brought in Frank Oz and held meetings to determine the best course of action. The team decided to schedule two additional days of shooting to address areas that needed improvement, primarily involving scenes with Bean Bunny, Gonzo and other characters. "We actually added a little bit more of the Waldo character to kind of make the thing tie together a little better, and shot that and then did an edit."

Following the reshoots and a quick temp mix at Skywalker Sound, the film was completed without further involvement from the Muppet team. However, due to the unresolved rights issues, the attraction could not open.

"We could turn it over to operations, and nothing could happen because we couldn't open it because the rights were not established." He laments the loss of potential Muppet-themed additions to Disney-MGM Studios, including a ride-through and a restaurant. "The bathroom, which was going to have some running gags that we'd recorded with the characters, became a generic bathroom. We couldn't even do much on the outside initially."

Months later, Michael Eisner reached out to Brian Henson to discuss the project's future. "Michael got hold of Brian and said, 'We can't let this project die. Yes, there's a question of who owns rights, we own the film, we should open this as an ode to Jim.'" This meeting led to a deal that allowed the attraction to open and the pre-show video to be shot, albeit with limitations on expanding the Muppet presence beyond the existing building. "That was it. Couldn't put it anywhere else," Mark says.

A MISSING PIZZA THE PUZZLE

Despite the challenges faced during production and the untimely loss of Jim Henson, *Muppet*Vision 3D* opened to a positive reception at Disney-MGM Studios (now Disney's Hollywood Studios) on 16th May 1991. Years later, after Mark had left Disney in 1993, the company eventually acquired the Muppets, and *Muppet*Vision 3D* was added to Disney's California Adventure, though it closed in 2014. Says Mark, "Unfortunately, because Jim was gone, there wasn't a good creative lead for the Muppets characters themselves. The project turned out great."

Mark touches on some unrealised plans for a larger Muppet-themed area at Disney-MGM Studios. "We had a concept for a Muppet ride, I don't remember the storyline but there were going to be a bunch of little vignette scenes. It was a whimsical vehicle." The area would have included a pizzeria owned by Rizzo the Rat and a Miss Piggy fountain. "The restrooms were going to be themed to Muppets and have some crazy stuff in them. With the rats and Gonzo there was going to be a lot of dialogue going on that was very 'Muppet-y', though it might be more on the edge of good taste. It was going to be a Muppet land and of course, when that died we had to make it another fake front. The building for the ride didn't get built and the pizzeria died."

Mark suggests that had the Muppet ride been built, it would have drawn more people to the area and increased attendance at *Muppet*Vision 3D*. "When you keep people in the park they tend to spend more money on food and you can make more money. That's why the pizzeria would have been brilliant. You go on the ride, you would have gone to the attraction, there was going to be a refreshment car and a pizzeria and that would have been a moneymaker. From a business standpoint, that makes more sense."

Reflecting on his experience working with Jim Henson, Mark draws comparisons to Walt Disney. "I think he was creatively a lot like Disney and that he wanted to expand his creative horizons. Had he lived and done so we probably would have pushed the ride into new directions because he would have wanted to do things that we hadn't done."

Mark believes that Jim would have challenged the organisation to improve and innovate, much like Jeffrey Katzenberg did with certain Epcot attractions. "He would listen to passionate people, so some people who wouldn't be listened to as much could be heard. He would take what he heard and say, 'You know, why not?'

"I think creatively he could see beyond the obvious," says Mark, comparing Jim's journey from the world of puppetry to dimensional theme park experiences to Walt Disney's transition from animation to physical spaces. "I think the Muppet ride would have been brilliant and that there would have been some memorable songs written for it. Who knows what we would be humming besides 'Yo ho, yo ho' and 'It's a small world after all' now. He could bring all of those elements together and find good people to do it. If you look at the Muppets, it wasn't just Jim, there were a lot of different creative talents. The music was brilliant and his first film had some great songs in it. I think it just would have been a brilliant addition to the theme park world beyond *Muppet*Vision 3D*.

"I was very saddened when he died. If the deal could have been signed, we probably would have done it. I don't know that it would have been as good. But it's just kind of sad that none of it came about because of his death and the circumstances surrounding the business deal that stopped it in its tracks. Once the deal was made it was too late. Michael's interest went elsewhere."

Mark shares an idea he pitched for incorporating the Muppets into Disneyland, had the deal gone through. "One idea I had was to put [*Muppet Show* sketch] *Pigs in Space* into the *Flight to the Moon/Mission to Mars* building. We could have had the irreverence, we didn't have to do a lot other than fix some of the projectors. And if you think about *Pigs in Space,* that was tailor-made for that building. I pitched it and they loved it, but of course, we couldn't do anything."

In January 2025, Disney announced that the original Hollywood Studios version of *Muppet*Vision 3D* would close in summer 2025, though there are plans to retain some evidence of the characters as part of Rock 'n' Roller Coaster. After over 30 years of operation, Mark is philosophical about the attraction leaving the park: "As much as I will miss it, it's time for *Muppet*Vision 3D* to live in our memories."

BILL BARRETTA
PUPPETEER, PRODUCER, WRITER, DIRECTOR AND ACTOR

> "It's important to all of us to maintain the integrity of these characters, to stay true to them."

STARTING as Earl Sinclair's body performer on *Dinosaurs*, Bill Barretta would go on to become one of the main Muppet performers of the post-Jim Henson era, creating original characters like Pepe the King Prawn while taking on classic characters including Rowlf the Dog and Dr Teeth.

* * *

n the early 1970s, an envelope arrived at a Pennsylvania home, bearing a return address that would make any puppetry enthusiast's heart skip a beat: Muppets, Inc. Inside was a handwritten note from Jim Henson himself, along with detailed instructions on how to make puppets. The recipient wasn't Bill Barretta, who would later become a renowned Muppet performer, but his older brother Gene.

This correspondence was born out of the creative whirlwind that was the Barretta household. Family gatherings were never dull affairs;

they were impromptu variety shows, with Gene and older cousins orchestrating elaborate performances that captivated young Bill. Growing up, the great movie and TV stars of yesteryear—Charlie Chaplin, Laurel & Hardy and Jackie Gleason—fuelled Bill's imagination. These comedy legends ignited his early interest in show business, though he never imagined he would realise his own dreams of stardom through puppetry.

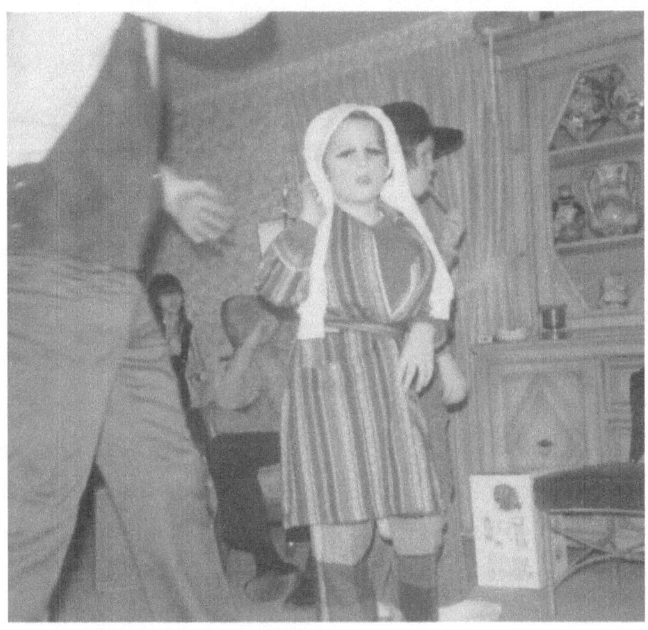

Bill starring as 'The Wife' in a home variety show. Courtesy Bill Barretta

Inspired by *Sesame Street*'s innovative approach, Gene took a leap of faith and wrote to Jim Henson, seeking advice on puppet-making. As Bill recalls, "Jim wrote back and sent instructions to him, which was bizarre. I was too young to realise how amazing and important that was."

Gene and their cousin Gary soon began creating their own puppets. The three of them would often cycle to the local foam and fabric store "where they had little googly eyes and fur and all kinds of foam and stuff. My brother and my older cousin, who were closer in age, created the characters and I was just helping them build their puppets." The budding puppeteers even put on shows at the school where their aunt taught deaf-mute children. "There was always confetti, and there was always some sort of puppet fight, and a lot of it was done to music. Years ago, they had those huge speakers and they would put the speakers facing the floor so the kids could feel the vibration of the beats of the music and follow along."

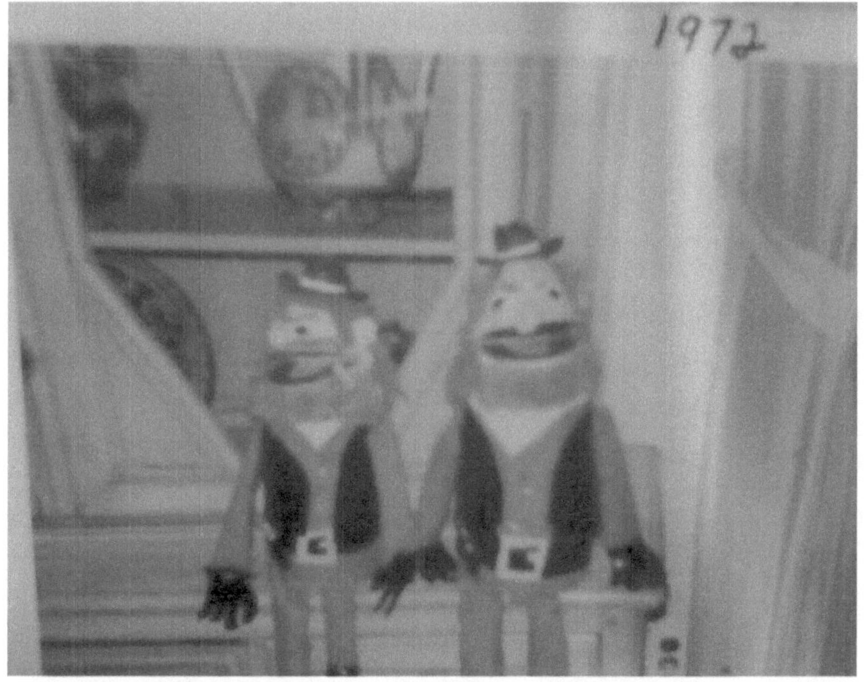

Gene Barretta and Cousin Gary's first Puppets (1972). Courtesy Bill Barretta

Although Bill's early experiences with puppetry sparked his creativity, he never thought of pursuing it as a career, deciding that acting and performing were more for him. Bill's mother continued to nurture his connection to puppets by bringing him one whenever she went on a trip. "I never made any connection to them, other than that they were fun to play with for a while, and then they'd go on my shelf."

Bill's passion for acting grew as Gene would cast him in their home movies. "My brother would always create some sort of storyline and make me jump out of a tree fort or jump off the roof of the house for the action sequences, so I was always in them, and he would direct them and create them. He even went into clay animation, and I would help him with that, so I was always assisting in these things."

By the early 1980s, *Sesame Street* had already cemented its place as a cultural phenomenon. The show's success led to the creation of Sesame Place in 1980, the first theme park of its kind dedicated to children's educational entertainment, embodying the imaginative spirit of Jim's work.

Bill was 17 when he landed a job at Sesame Place, mainly thanks to the park being near his hometown, and it was there that he met Brian Henson. "We met and became friends and hung out for the summer mostly and then kept in touch over the years. Little did I know what an important role in my life he would play." Bill was part of the Sesame Place operations team, moving around helping guests on and off the different rides and attractions, cleaning bathrooms and monitoring crowd safety.

"They had just installed these new animatronic characters; one was an automated Oscar in a trash can. The track would play, and Oscar would either do a song or he would say something, and people would stand around and watch it. I had to make sure nobody touched it. This was inside of the "Food Factory" restaurant, but there were enormous glass windows where you could see the entrance to the park. I was standing there guarding Oscar, and I saw Jim Henson coming through the front gate. Can't be him. But it was, and I just left my post, I could have cared less. I left, ran out there and said, 'Mr Henson, welcome to Sesame Place!' And he said, 'Thanks. Do you know where the new Oscar is?' I couldn't believe it. I took him there and just watched him watch the people enjoying it. He just kind of stood there, and he'd laugh a little."

At this time, Jim Henson was already a recognisable figure in the entertainment industry, not just for his work on *Sesame Street* but also for *The Muppet Show*. This period saw the Muppets transition from educational children's programming to a broader audience, combining puppetry with sophisticated humour and guest stars from various walks of life.

Bill was struck by Jim's humility and his desire to experience the park like any other guest, with no special treatment. "I never forgot that he didn't come through some special entrance. He didn't have some sort of VIP escort. He took it upon himself to just come in to experience it like everybody else. I think that's a huge lesson, for people of that stature to be that person, to be that humble and think *I'm no more special than these people.*"

JURASSIC LARKS

Bill and Brian Henson stayed in touch following their time at Sesame Place. In his late 20s, Bill moved to New York to study at the prestigious Neighborhood Playhouse, a school founded by Sanford Meisner and renowned for its Meisner acting technique based on the teachings of Constantin Stanislavski. "I actually got to study with Sandy! He was in his late 80s."

Jim Henson's death in 1990 reunited Bill and Brian. This devastating reason for their coming together and being invited to attend Jim's memorial solidified a deeper connection and friendship. Soon after, Bill moved to California to further his acting career while waiting tables and working as a carpenter's apprentice.

The early 1990s were a transitional period for The Jim Henson Company and especially for Jim's children, including Brian, who took on a more prominent role in continuing his father's legacy. Bill learned his friend had become the CEO of the company and was developing a new TV series called *Dinosaurs*, a collaboration between The Jim Henson Company and Disney.

This innovative show featured animatronic dinosaur characters performed by actors in elaborate suits. The use of animatronics was a hallmark of Jim's later work, building on the success of earlier projects like *The Dark Crystal* and *Labyrinth*, which pushed the boundaries of puppetry and special effects. "I said to Brian, 'When you do this show, if I can pull cables, or I can move a light, I'll do whatever, I just need to be closer to the business.'"

Brian surprised Bill while visiting him at his home in Los Angeles by suggesting he audition for one of the dinosaur characters. "He said, 'I don't know if you're going to be into this, but you'd be inside this big rubber suit.' They'd just done *Ninja Turtles*, so I was familiar with what he was talking about. He said, 'You know, there's this character, he's kind of like Jackie Gleason from *The Honeymooners* [1955-56] and I've seen you do that before, just messing around, why don't you come and do it?'"

Following a successful audition, Bill landed the role of family patriarch Earl Sinclair, which perfectly aligned with his Meisner acting training. "It was all about what Sandy taught us, interpreting dialogue through behaviour. So that's all I was going to be doing, gesturing and staying in sync with the other performer who was puppeteering the head and the mouth and all the facial expressions while also performing the dialogue."

Bill acknowledges the quirky nature of *Dinosaurs* and the challenges it posed for viewers and the network. "I think there was definitely a risk that they were taking; at the same time, I think *The Simpsons* [1989–] were very big. I think maybe that helped to have this kind of show that was a commentary on real topics." Despite its unconventional approach, *Dinosaurs* tackled serious issues of the time. "There were some really interesting topics that we covered; there was sexual harassment, there was one called 'A New Leaf' which was about weed, all kinds of stuff going on. So it wasn't just for kids, it was really for everybody."

During his time on *Dinosaurs*, Bill had the opportunity to learn from and work alongside experienced Muppet performers, including Dave Goelz, Steve Whitmire and Kevin Clash. "Occasionally, when I wasn't inside of Earl, which wasn't that often, I would assist, to kind of just start learning and watching these guys, watching what they do a little bit." This period was a critical learning phase for Bill, as he was surrounded by some of the most skilled puppeteers in the industry.

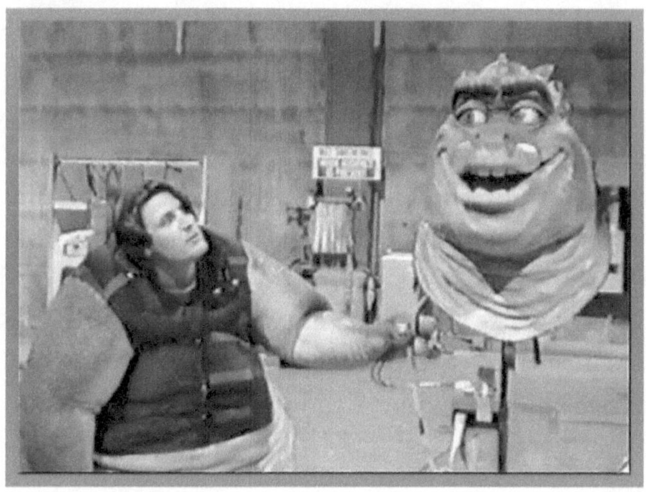

Bill in the Earl Sinclair body suit. Courtesy Bill Barretta

As new Muppet projects arose, Bill found himself increasingly involved with The Jim Henson Company. "As *Dinosaurs* finished, Brian invited me to come and work on a little music video that they were doing, and I did a little background character and assisted people. After that, there was a fairy tale-type home video thing *Muppet Classic Theater* [1994]. I did my first character for that, an Elvis Elf." The early 1990s saw a variety of Muppet productions that continued to expand the brand's reach, from direct-to-video specials to television appearances.

Bill credits his puppeteering experience on 1994's *The Animal Show*, where he portrayed approximately 26 different characters, helping him refine his skills and find a balance between character performance and technical proficiency. "I felt comfortable with characters, but technically I was terrible. When you start focusing on the technical stuff, you lose your characters, at least I did. The characters become weaker, because you can't do both. It takes quite a while to figure out how to maintain the character, maintain good quality technical stuff, watching what you're doing on the monitors, reading scripts while you're performing, interacting and reacting moment to moment off of other characters that are in the scene with you... you're doing this multi-tasking thing that takes quite a bit of time to get comfortable with."

The Animal Show was another innovative project from the Henson Company, known for blending live-action puppetry with environmental education. "Dave and Steve were the co-hosts on the show and that's truly who I learned so much from... they're the best! Jocelyn Stevenson and Jim Lewis were the writers. That was my first time working with the great [*Muppet Show* director] Peter Harris. I had heard so many stories about him. And he was just such a fun, larger-than-life character to be around. And he moved fast. You had to be prepared. There was no, 'Can we take a break?' He was just like [affects English accent] 'Let's go darling.' I think that really was my boot camp."

Bill's time in England for *The Animal Show* was not only professionally transformative but also personally significant. "I proposed to my wife Cristina during that time. Peter Harris is the one who told me I needed to do it. He set up a dinner for us at the famous Dorchester Hotel, which isn't actually where I ended up proposing, but he was kind of waiting to hear the news when we came back to work."

TREASURED MEMORIES

A major opportunity came Bill's way when production began on *Muppet Treasure Island* in 1995. The film marked a continuation of the Muppets' foray into feature-length adaptations of classic literature, following the success of *The Muppet Christmas Carol*. "Kirk Thatcher and Jerry Juhl wrote the screenplay and added this goat bad guy character [Clueless Morgan]. Brian was directing, and he asked me to come do the read-through, and that's my first character that had a full arc, that wasn't just a one-off kind of thing and actually was part of a story. I got to go to England and that was amazing, the best people to work with.

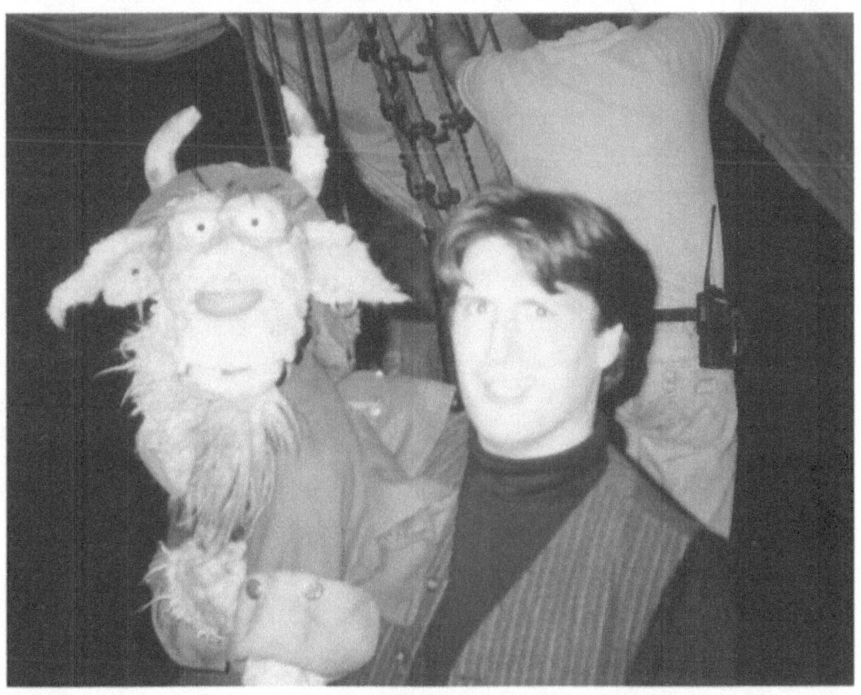

Bill performing Clueless Morgan on the set of Muppet Treasure Island.
Courtesy Bill Barretta

"The sets were incredible and there's some forced perspective stuff that had to be done because you're trying to balance humans and puppets, so you don't want the humans to look like giants and the puppets to look like insects. Val Strazovec's design was just absolutely brilliant. They built a ship that was on a gimbal that could rock and move. We all got seasick at different times, but it was so much fun."

It was towards the end of filming *Muppet Treasure Island* that it became clear a modern version of *The Muppet Show* was in the works. This led to a series of workshop sessions where Muppet performers experimented with various puppets to create new characters. These workshops were integral to the creative process, allowing performers to explore different personalities and interactions for potential inclusion in future projects.

"They brought in a big rack of puppets, some recognisable, some were background characters, and we'd just play around with them. We set up a camera. A couple of people would step up and grab a puppet and see what happened. It was maybe the second time I worked with Frank [Oz] and learned a lot just watching him, learned a lot about how to do both, how to do a great performance technically, and also to maintain the character. Frank would interview the characters off camera, he would ask you a few things and just play off of you."

It was during these sessions that Bill developed new characters, including Howard Tubman and Johnny Fiama. "Johnny was already a character to me because I was doing him as myself even before I got into *Dinosaurs*. That was a character that I was just playing around with and thought maybe I could develop something with him. He ended up being a Muppet with my partner, Brian. We always teamed up." The look of the Johnny Fiama puppet was a collaborative effort between Bill and designer Ed Eyth, based on pictures of Bill, his father and Robert De Niro from the film *Casino* (1995).

Similarly, the character of Pepe the King Prawn emerged from these workshops, with his voice and personality inspired by Bill's wife's aunt. "There was a wire figure that just had a little bit of fur around its body, you could see the wire mechanism and a couple of eyes. My wife's aunt was from Madrid, Spain, that's where I kind of picked up that character and the way she spoke, she always said 'Okay' at the end of her sentences, okay. Everything was a statement."

Discussions between members of the Muppet team helped decide what type of creature Pepe could be. "I was talking with Kirk Thatcher and I was describing my wife's aunt, a really fun lady, but a little bit selfish. So, while I was describing her I said, 'You know, she's a little bit shellfish' and I corrected myself. Then Kirk thought *Maybe he's like a lobster or a shrimp?* I said, 'Or a King Prawn because they're bigger! He's got a big attitude!'"

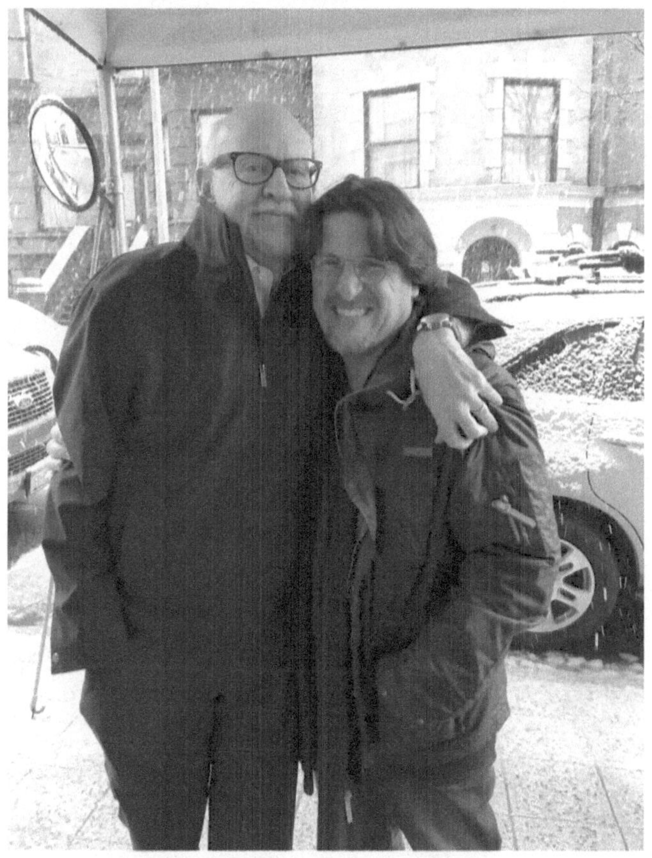

Frank Oz and Bill Barretta meet during filming Muppet Guys Talking. Courtesy Bill Barretta

Johnny, Pepe and Howard from that workshop joined Kermit, Piggy and Fozzie for what would become 1996's *Muppets Tonight*.

This show marked a return to the variety-show format that made *The Muppet Show* a hit in the late 1970s and early 1980s.

Like its predecessor, *Muppets Tonight* welcomed a new celebrity guest to the studio each week, including The Artist Formerly Known As Prince, Sandra Bullock, John Goodman, Garth Brooks, Martin Short and Paula Abdul to name a few. This approach continued the Muppet tradition of blending puppetry with popular culture, attracting a diverse audience and maintaining the Muppets' relevance in the rapidly changing entertainment landscape of the 1990s.

"When we found out Prince was coming to do the show, we were told that you don't speak to him directly, not to make a lot of eye contact with him. I remember he had a white parka coat, and they brought him onto the stage and put him in a little director's chair. He's just sitting there all by himself. He had a couple of his handlers around him, but he was by himself. I thought, *This is no fun for him, forget this no eye contact stuff*. I went up and I said hello. He was sweet, kind, soft-spoken and easy to talk to, but very subdued. Then they called him on to do what he had to do, and he pulled you in like a magnet. This guy was phenomenal, he just drew you in, such power. The expectation that was set up was that he was going to be very hard to connect with and it was completely the opposite."

Commenting that producer Martin Baker secured an "unbelievable" number of big names for the show, Bill mentions an incident with the then incumbent James Bond, Pierce Brosnan. "I guess he was a circus performer at some point, and he would breathe fire, and so at the end of the episode he does the fire thing. But whatever liquid they gave him was thicker than he was used to. When he blew out, it came back and he literally burned his lips, but he kept going. The only take we have is the actual ending that got aired. His lips were burnt, but he was a real sport about it. He was very funny. Sandra Bullock was amazing, so young and fun and wanted to just play and be silly. She just wanted to hang out with the puppet guys and have fun."

Bill singles out Tony Bennett as a personal favourite guest, describing the experience of working with the legendary singer as "a dream come true. Just being in the same space with Tony Bennett, it blew me away. It took him a bit of time to make a connection to the Muppets. Different people connect differently to them. Some don't even have to think about it, they're playing off of that character. They're not looking down below to see what's going on down there, they're not distracted, they just connect. Michelle Pfeiffer just instantly connected... amazing. Tony Bennett, who is also an artist, was more interested in the shapes and colours and how they were made, so it took longer to get him to connect to the characters, especially Johnny Fiama.

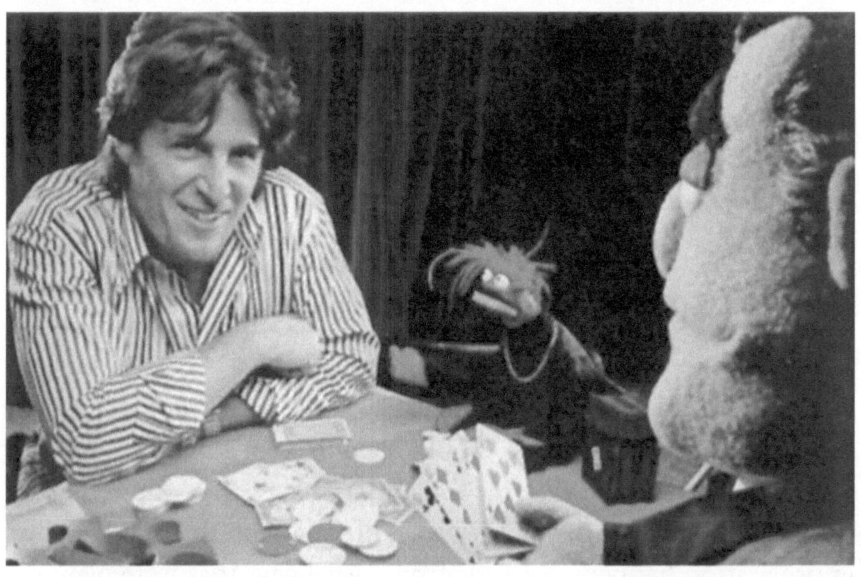

Bill, Pepe and Johnny Fiama settle down for a card game. Courtesy Bill Barretta

"The way that I finally got him to do it was in between takes, Johnny just said, 'Tony, you know, what's wrong with the bread in California?' And he said, 'No, what is it?' and he actually spoke to Johnny and I thought, 'Oh, I think I got him.' I said again with Johnny, 'It's the water. You don't get good water out here, like back east.' He goes, 'Yeah, that's right, and you know what else...' and he started telling me why. Then we started talking about our favourite pastas. So, he needed that personal connection first and then from there on, he was comfortable, and I disappeared... beautiful."

Like its 1970s predecessor, the creators aimed *Muppets Tonight* at a family audience, but that didn't stop some adult jokes from making their way into the scripts. Including writers and producers from *SCTV* (Second City Television, 1976–84), a Canadian sketch comedy show known for its edgy humour, brought a unique comedic perspective to *Muppets Tonight* that appealed to both children and adults.

"I think the writers were really clever, you had a showrunner who was an *SCTV* guy, Dick Blasucci, and Paul Flaherty was also from *SCTV*, you had Kirk, who's insane and the veteran Muppets writer, Jim Lewis, as well as additional seasoned comedy writers. Just a great writing room of people who weren't writing for kids, they were writing for themselves, trying to make themselves laugh and, in turn, bringing that to us and us trying to make ourselves laugh with the material.

"I don't know if there was a conscious effort to try and do anything other than just think of ridiculous crazy things to put the Muppets in and then I guess somebody at the time, probably Brian, decided and guided what we should try, and see if it works. Pepe was a character that could say some things that maybe the Muppets don't normally get away with. So, they were playing with that, plus a lot of improvisation happens. So aside from visual gags that were planned, we would just improvise things and things would happen."

Bill highlights the collaborative nature of the Muppet performers, noting how they tend to form comedic partnerships, such as Jim Henson and Frank Oz, Jerry Nelson and Richard Hunt and Dave Goelz and Steve Whitmire.

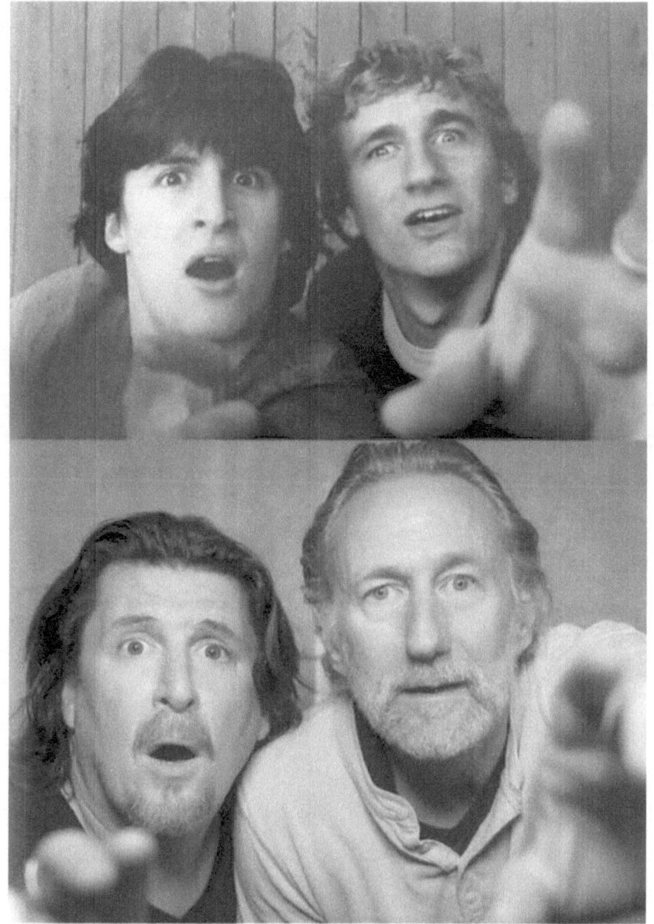

Bill and Brian Henson pose aged 17 and three decades later...
Courtesy Bill Barretta

He also touches on his own partnership with Brian Henson, which led to the creation of Dr Phil Van Neuter and memorable pairings like Johnny and Sal or Pepe and Seymour. "We had a lot of fun doing Dr Phil; he was a great character. I love the Christmas party where he gets so drunk and sloppy, it's just awful."

Muppets Tonight lasted just two seasons, ending in 1998 after 22 episodes. The late 1990s saw a television landscape heavily influenced by successful sitcoms like *Friends* (1994–2004), *Seinfeld* (1989–98) and *Frasier* (1993–2004). The dominance of this genre made it challenging for a variety show like *Muppets Tonight* to find its place. "It's all about their lineup for the different evenings and what type of shows are being aired that night. There wasn't really a variety style format happening and it seemed out of place for most people. So, format-wise, I think it just didn't fit in, even though I thought they were great shows, with great guests and great storylines. It was a sitcom-driven time, I think."

Following the end of *Muppets Tonight*, work began on 1999's *Muppets from Space*, the sixth theatrical film to feature the Muppets. It marked a shift from the literary adaptations of the previous two films to an original story focusing on Gonzo's origins.

Bill is quick to state that the performers "had a lot of fun" on the production. "A lot of stuff didn't make it into the movie. I think my favourite thing about *Muppets from Space* was working with Jeffrey [Tambor], we just got along really well. I worked with him one time before, in *Dr. Doolittle* [1998]. He was the veterinarian, and I was playing the puppet version of the dog. That's where we first met and kind of clicked. I pushed for him to be in *Muppets from Space*, I whispered it in everybody's ear, and he came and did it. We just had so much fun. Like I said, there's a lot of stuff that didn't make it, I think because our rhythm together was a little more... I don't want to say on the slow side, but we took our time a little bit with our moments between Bobo and him and it kind of didn't fit the pace of the movie. So, when the time came to edit it, they had to try and pick up the pace of it."

The film was notable for introducing Pepe into the Muppet movie canon, a character who had quickly become a fan favourite since his debut on *Muppets Tonight*. "They stuck him in there quite a bit. He was being his mischievous self, building a Jacuzzi for selfish reasons and all that stuff. I didn't have to remember a lot of dialogue; I could just be more reactionary. That's really my favourite thing to do. I prefer not to drive scenes, I prefer to just be in them, listen and then kind of throw little things in occasionally."

Although he has fond memories of *Muppet from Space*, Bill

acknowledges it wasn't a highly profitable film, which may have contributed to the decline of Muppet productions in subsequent years. "That was 1999, before Henson sold the Muppets, and that was the financial decline, and it was becoming difficult to get Muppet movies, or Muppets in general, produced."

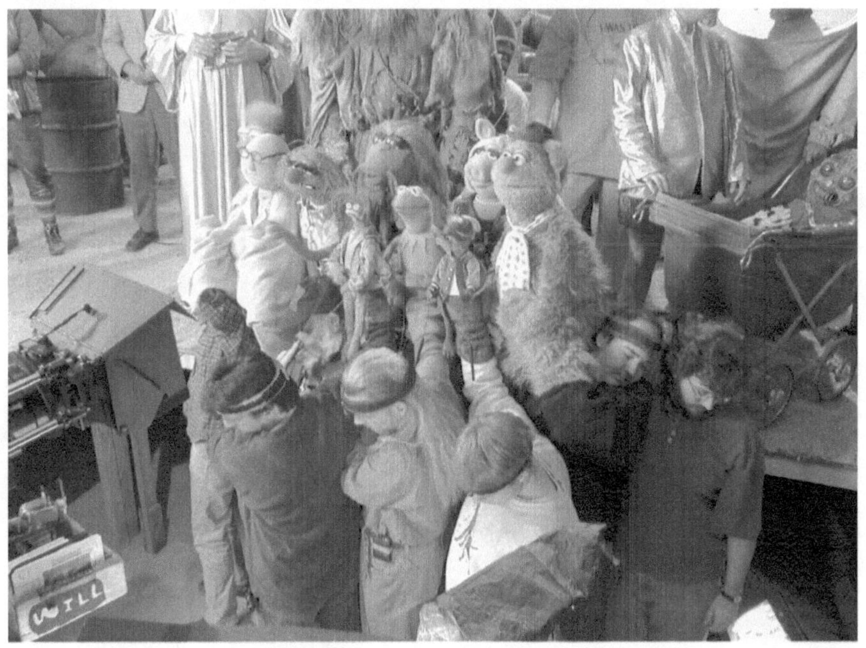

Filming the spaceship landing in Muppets from Space. Courtesy Bill Barretta

The late 1990s saw significant changes for The Jim Henson Company, culminating in the sale of the Muppets to German company EM.TV & Merchandising AG in 2000. The franchise then shifted focus to television movies like *It's a Very Merry Muppet Christmas Movie* and 2005's *The Muppets' Wizard of Oz*, with Bill having a fondness for the former. "It had the *It's a Wonderful Life* tribute twist; Kermit finds out what it's like if he had never been born. I had a lot of fun with Joan Cusack, her and Pepe. I liked that movie; I thought Kirk did a great job directing that."

A NEW ERA

Regarding post-Jim Henson Muppet projects, Bill emphasises the crucial role played by long-time Muppet producer Debbie McClellan, who transitioned to Disney from The Jim Henson Company when the Muppets were acquired by them in 2004. This marked a significant shift in the stewardship of the Muppet franchise, aiming to revitalise and integrate the beloved characters into a new era of entertainment.

"Debbie was the Muppet representation coming from Henson for Disney and I knew that she understood what we should be trying to do and what we should be trying to create. It was really about going through her to the people that were her bosses at the time and asking, 'How do we create things? Is this something we can do? Is there a budget for it? Let's keep them going.' She fought every day to try to make great things and find the balance and find the right people. Without her, I think the Muppets probably would have gone away quite a while ago."

The conversation shifts to 2011's *The Muppets*, which marked a big screen reboot of the franchise under the stewardship of Jason Segel. This film was crucial in reintroducing the Muppets to a new generation and reigniting interest among long-time fans. While Bill enjoyed the film, he expresses some reservations about the portrayal of the Muppets as has-beens who had faded from the public consciousness.

"It was really designed to feature Jason and the new character, Walter, to help get the Muppets out there more, which I guess they needed at the time. It was a challenge. People have great intentions, and they're big fans of the Muppets, and they want what's best for them, but they don't quite know how to achieve it all without the help of people who have been doing it for years. Just logistically, it's a huge challenge. You try to explain that to people, the director of photography and the director himself, but there's no way anybody can understand it until they're actually going through it and doing it.

"With the Muppets, because it's so specific how you need to shoot them and try to create great compositions and great shots, you need to take into consideration how do we achieve this out in the real world? Where are the performers? Where are all the monitors? Where are the wires? How does this happen? Having a director and a DP [director of photography] that have some familiarity with that, or some experience, is really important and really helpful to keep things moving along."

The 2011 film was both a critical and commercial success and featured the introduction of Walter, a new Muppet character who embodied the enthusiasm and fandom surrounding the Muppets, serving as a bridge between the classic Muppets and new audiences. Bill notes that he encouraged Peter Linz, the performer behind Walter, to draw from his own personality in bringing the character to life. "I just kept saying, 'Just be yourself, because that's who this is.' He did an amazing job."

Bill also recognises the difficulties in integrating Walter into the established Muppet ensemble. "Since then, we've tried to put him in certain things but it's hard because the character was set up as a fan, which is great. But he also had personality traits that were similar to Kermit in a way. What's the dynamic between him and Kermit? What's the dynamic between him and other characters? That's stuff you need to think about when you're creating a new character like that, how do they fit in, so you can keep them going. You don't want to just do a one off and he's gone."

In contrast, Bill notes that the production of 2014's *Muppets Most Wanted* was a more rewarding experience, as the same team had already gone through the learning curve on the previous film. "That was a different thing, because now you had the same people who had been down this road and it was much more enjoyable for everybody, because we all knew how to get there. I just wish there was some sort of magical guide or chip that you could implant so that everybody's on the same page from day one. It just becomes a better situation. The understanding of how to play certain visual jokes is better because you understand how you need to shoot something, it all ties into this logistical approach that's so unusual for most people."

The short-lived 2015 television series *The Muppets* presented the characters in a more adult, mockumentary-style setting, an idea that had surfaced as early as 2007 when former Muppet writer Bill Prady approached Disney with the idea. "I had my production company and Bill Prady had gone to talk to Debbie and the people that were kind of overseeing the Muppets at that time. They put us together." The pair bonded over the idea of bringing the Muppets back into the real world and exploring a more documentary-style approach inspired by series such as *The Office* [2005–13]. They even produced a pilot presentation, which Bill directed and Prady wrote, though it failed to gain traction.

Fast forward eight years, and Bill once again pitched the idea, this time with Prady on board as a consulting producer when he was riding high as the co-creator of *The Big Bang Theory* (2007–19). As his involvement increased, the show began to deviate from Bill's original vision, with a greater emphasis on the office setting and Miss Piggy hosting a talk show.

"It became more about being in an office environment behind a talk show, which isn't really what I was thinking. I was thinking they were bringing back *The Muppet Show* but with this docu-style behind the scenes. That's what the original presentation we created was about, getting them out into the real world more and finding out more about them and their backstories behind *The Muppet Show*. We could always go to *The Muppet Show* for a fun skit or music, which I think people would have loved much more than a Piggy talk show, and also having celeb guests out in the real world with them in their everyday lives. It just didn't take that direction."

Despite the show ultimately not aligning with his initial vision, Bill recognises the talent involved, praising director Randall Einhorn, known for his work on *The Office* and *Parks and Recreation* (2009–15), and highlighting some of the positive elements that emerged, such as the exploration of new character backstories for the Electric

Mayhem band members. Behind-the-scenes tensions and creative disagreements that arose during the production led to changes in the creative team, with Bob Kushell being replaced as showrunner by Kristin Newman, who brought a different approach to the show.

Ultimately, the series lasted just 16 episodes, a disappointment for Bill and the rest of the performers. The show aimed to modernise the Muppets by exploring their personal lives and relationships in a contemporary setting, but it struggled to find a consistent tone and audience, reflecting the ongoing challenge of balancing innovation with the beloved traditions of the Muppet franchise.

"It's so important to all of us to maintain the integrity of these characters, to stay true to them. The people who've taken on characters for Jim, Jerry, Richard or Frank, we're all very aware of how important it is to stay true to them."

Maintaining the integrity of the Muppet characters has always been a cornerstone of the franchise, especially in the years following Jim Henson's death. The performers who inherited these roles had to balance honouring the original characteristics while also adapting to new contexts and audiences. "Those are usually where the battles happen, because we're open to new things. I'll try anything, give me something new that I didn't expect. But if it's not working, then you need to find a way to make it work, and unfortunately, you don't always have the time to do that. So, you feel compromised to a certain degree, because you can't just lay down the law, you can't say, 'That character wouldn't do that.' You can say, 'Is there another way we can approach this?' Sometimes it works and sometimes it doesn't.

"Our biggest struggles are usually due to the lack of involvement in the creative process from the Muppet performers and other people who have a deep understanding and experience with them, like veteran writers, producers and the artists from the Muppet Work-shop. These people are the ones who are also protecting what we all love and what Jim created, and that's really the most important thing to me."

Bill also praises Frank Oz as a great ambassador for the Muppets, noting his willingness to speak out in support of the performers and the characters. "Look, Frank is the Muppets. Maybe I'll get in trouble for saying that. Obviously, Jim Henson is the Muppets. But Jim and Frank were the root of what made this all explode, and then the other amazing performers who are part of that as well. Frank can say these things. He's all about protecting the characters and the integrity of the characters. He knows if you're looking to do something interesting or new with them, come talk to us a little bit, see where that might take you first. It's all about collaborating."

Frank, whose collaboration with Jim Henson set the standard for Muppet performances, has been vocal about the need to preserve the depth and complexity of the Muppet characters. He's also criticised the Muppets for becoming too saccharine, a view Bill can sympathise with. "It's people who are fans and have great intentions but have never worked with the Muppets and who rely too heavily on stereotypes. They know that Piggy is a bossy diva. They know that Kermit is supposed to be the benevolent leader who says 'Hi-Ho!' But there's so much more to them. And the relationships, it's not as black and white as people would think."

On the subject of the puppeteers, Bill is often approached by young performers seeking guidance or opportunities to work with the Muppets. "I try to point them in the right direction. The hard part is that there are a lot of puppeteers that have been with us for many years, and you have established relationships with those people. There's a puppeteer who I know that I always want to work with as the Swedish Chef's hands. There's a certain puppeteer who I might know would be great to assist, because their sensibilities to that specific character or their skills are very good, and they know my timing. It's the same for the other puppeteers, I know who they like working with. You're trying to find people that fit in and that have a similar sense of humour. But you also have people who aren't exactly a good fit, but they're perfect for a character because that character shouldn't fit in. I'm always open to new people, it's just hard to find the project to bring them all in on."

Following the short-lived *The Muppets* TV series, an attempt was made to bring the Muppet characters for the streaming age in 2020's *Muppets Now*, a short-form series of sketches subsequently edited into segments between 22 and 26 minutes long. "I thought this was a really fun idea to try and achieve. The simple format of a series of *Muppet Show*-like sketches. The pace was fun, the guests were great, and it was simply just about entertaining and making people laugh in short pieces. I'm not really sure why we ended up not doing anymore. It could have been the ratings on Disney+, but I wish we would have had another shot at it to perfect what we tried to do the first time around."

In 2021, Disney+ announced that the Muppets would star in a Halloween special set in the famous Haunted Mansion ride. The 2022 Emmy Award-winning *Muppets Haunted Mansion* saw the likes of Will Arnett and Ed Asner join the gang as Gonzo and Pepe spent a night in the mansion. Says Bill, "This would be the first production under the new 'Muppets Studio' team, a department that now lives under Walt Disney Imagineering, Disney Parks and Entertainment. David Lightbody and Leigh Slaughter have done an amazing job being extremely collaborative with the Muppet performers and writers who have long been in the trenches before representing The Muppets for many, many years. Because of their influence and connection to Disney Parks, the opportunity to combine the Muppets with a park's attraction like The Haunted Mansion, an idea that had been kicked around many times over the years, it was because of this collaborative leadership that we were able to finally achieve it."

The Electric Mayhem Band also took centre stage for 2023's Emmy Award-winning *The Muppets Mayhem*, an update on an idea suggested by Bill a number of years earlier. Bill's 2006 pitch to executives was called *The Muppets American Roadshow*, which would have followed the Muppets as they took their show on the road. "Then we did a gig at the 'Outside Lands Music Festival' with just the Electric Mayhem and people loved it. They estimated 30,000 people came to the open field to witness the band live on stage. Crazy! We had phenomenal reviews and it was just a lot of fun to do. I thought, 'What if we just took the band out on the road, and did a series about them travelling to these festivals?'"

Jump to five years later, 2021, where Bill pitched his Mayhem Band on Tour series idea to the new team at the new Muppets Studio. "I have to thank Leigh Slaughter for having the foresight in bringing myself together with Adam Goldberg and Jeff Yorkes, who also happened to have a Mayhem series idea at the same time… Fate… We really hit it off. Adam and Jeff's talents were hugely integral in making such a wonderful series. Couldn't have done it without them. But it was our friends at the Muppets Studio who were such a driving influence, allowing us to maintain the integrity and supportive control of the Muppet characters as we did."

Bill adds that the Muppet performers were also given the same respect and support to collaborate with the writing team, the workshop and on set. "These are all the cornerstone reasons why the show turned out so beautifully. I don't think there is anyone out there that has watched it that would say it wasn't a good show. In fact, without tooting our own horns, I would say, they would say, it's a great show. The care and comedy and attention to detail, along with the integrity and tone of the characters was right on the mark. I'm extremely proud of that series and certainly wish we could have done more.

"Unfortunately, without going into many details that I believe was the reason we didn't get a second season… I must say, such is life. Perhaps there'll be another opportunity to continue this journey with this insane band down the road. My hope is that we'll get to do another series or special where we take them out on the road on tour, as I originally had conceived back in 2016. I think that would be a blast."

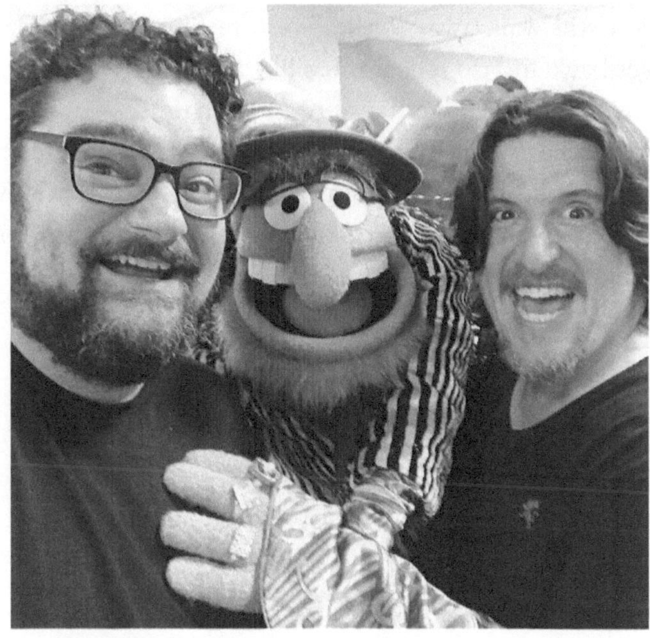

Bobby Moynihan, Dr Teeth and Bill at The Muppets Take the O2. Courtesy Bill Barretta

Bill reflects on his favourite aspect of working with the Muppets: the camaraderie and sense of family among the performers, Muppet workshop and crew. "I guess the best thing about doing what I do is getting to see the people that I work with coming back together. You go away and you have your lives. People are doing all kinds of things, and then you come back together, and it just feels like you were together yesterday. We just have so much fun and we have a lot of respect for each other. And I'm not only referring to the performers, but that's the workshop and our crews that we get to play with... everyone who's involved. It's like a family coming together again."

This sense of camaraderie has been a defining characteristic of the Muppet troupe since its inception. "I think that's something that Jim taught everyone by example, and that has been passed along by those who were with him, that the work is important, but the experience together is the most important thing. You walk away having enjoyed what you've done, even though it was very hard or difficult or frustrating, you still walk away with a good feeling and know that you want to get back and do it again. It's like a joy drug. That's what I've learned through the people that were around him.

"I can't believe that I perform some of Jim's characters. Who would ever think they'd be doing something like that? And I'm honoured that I've been allowed to be a part of it for so long now. Thanks Gene, thanks Jim and thank you Brian. I wouldn't be here without you."

EDITOR'S NOTE

Thank you for reading *Rainbow Connections*.

If you've enjoyed this book and would like to see further volumes, please consider sharing your review or thoughts on your preferred online book platform or social media. Even a few words or a photo can make a huge difference.

If you want to read more about the worlds of Jim Henson and the people that shaped it, I can recommend Brian Jay Jones' *Jim Henson: The Biography*, Karen Falk's *Jim Henson's Imagination Illustrated: The Jim Henson Journal* and Christopher Finch's *Jim Henson: The Works* for starters.

Also make sure you subscribe to *Tough Pigs'* newsletter and to the many Henson/Muppet podcasts, including *Muppeturgy*, *Below the Frame*, *Kermitment* and *Movin' Right Along*.

You can sign up to my newsletter at jonathanmelville. substack.com for updates and extra content.

Feel free to contact me direct for speaking opportunities or to buy copies of the book in bulk: linktr.ee/jonathanmelville

ABOUT THE EDITOR

Jonathan Melville is an author, development researcher and freelance arts journalist based in Edinburgh. His work delves into the creation and legacy of classic films and TV series, offering comprehensive behind-the-scenes insights from the creatives involved.

Seeking Perfection: The Unofficial Guide to Tremors examines the horror-comedy franchise through interviews with 50 cast and crew, including Kevin Bacon and executive producer Gale Anne Hurd.

A Kind of Magic: Making the Original Highlander looks at the 1986 classic and featured new interviews with Christopher Lambert and Clancy Brown, Queen's Brian May and Roger Taylor and many more.

Local Hero: Making a Scottish Classic, provides an in-depth look at the making of the 1983 film, with contributions from Bill Forsyth, Peter Riegert, Denis Lawson and more.

Hamish Macbeth: The Making of a BBCtv Classic, covers the genesis of the hit BBC One comedy drama *Hamish Macbeth*, with input from the cast and crew.

Jonathan is currently working on a new book covering action TV series of the 70s/80s/90s.

ACKNOWLEDGMENTS

Thanks to everyone who took the time to discuss their work and memories of Jim Henson for this book.

Many thanks to Paul Manchester for sharing Tony Charmoli's memories of working with the Muppets.

Thanks to Gordon Barr and Stephen Pasqua for their feedback on the manuscript, and to Garrett Gilchrist for helping out at a crucial moment.

Finally, thanks to Ben Morris for the book's cover. Find him at benmorrisillustration.com